WHAT A FOOL BELIEVES

WHAT A FOOL BELIEVES

A MEMOIR

MICHAEL McDONALD

WITH PAUL REISER

DEYST.

An Imprint of WILLIAM MORROW

DEYST.

 For information, address HarperCollins Publishers, 195 Broadway, New York, NY 10007.

HarperCollins books may be purchased for educational, business, or sales promotional use. For information, please email the Special Markets Department at SPsales@harpercollins.com.

FIRST EDITION

Designed by Jennifer Chung

Insert photograph credits are as follows:
1, 2, 3, 4: courtesy of the Michael McDonald family; 5, 6: Steve Scorfina (on behalf of Vito Scorfina); 7: Gerald J. Schulte (on behalf of Emil Schulte); 8: Greg Edick; 9: George Johnson; 10, 11, 14: Blytham Limited (permission granted by John Baruck); 12, 13, 20, 24, 41: courtesy of Michael McDonald; 15: Michael Putland / Getty; 16: Gijsbert Hanekroot / Redferns / Getty; 17, 18: Michael Ochs Archives / Getty; 19, 21, 22, 28, 44: © Dan Fong; 23: Robert Landau / Corbis via Getty Images; 25: © Annie Leibovitz / Trunk Archive—the *Rolling Stone* logo is a registered trademark of the Penske Media Corporation and is used under license; 26: Larry Butler; 27: © 1979 Lynn Goldsmith; 29: Jim Pierson; 30: George Rose / Getty; 31: Jim Shea; 32, 34: Henry Diltz; 33: courtesy of Capitol Records, LLC, under license from Universal Music Enterprises; 35: Sam Emerson—the GRAMMY Award logo is a registered trademark of the Recording Academy® and is used under license with Promo Partners; 36: Chris Haston / NBCU Photo Bank / Getty; 37: Ron Galella, Ltd. / Ron Gallela Collection / Getty; 38, 42: © David Pack; 39: Diane Bondareff for WhyHunger; 40: Dana Edelson / NBCU Photo Bank / Getty; 43: Jeff Kravitz / Film Magic / Getty; 45: Jim Trocchio; 46: Lyndon Jackson

Library of Congress Cataloging-in-Publication Data has been applied for.

ISBN 978-0-06-335756-3

24 25 26 27 28 LBC 5 4 3 2 1

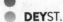

For my wife, Amy, my son, Dylan, and my daughter, Scarlett, who will always be the best part of my life story

CONTENTS

PREFACE

VAN NUYS, LA COUNTY JAIL
1971

I'm getting fingerprinted and processed—for the second time *this week*. Maybe my third or fourth interaction with LA County's finest that year. I'd lost track. Earlier that week it was for driving home drunk from some dive where I was playing keyboards in a country and western band to an audience of two—possibly three—remarkably indifferent barflies. This time I was pulled in after falling asleep in a booth at Du-par's pancake house following a forty-eight-hour marathon party-for-two with a female friend, walking the tightrope between a cocaine binge and copious amounts of Jack Daniel's. I had stopped at Du-par's to try to drink enough coffee to sober up somewhat before getting back behind the wheel. I'm nineteen and already feeling past my prime, any career aspirations appearing more like an ever-receding mirage.

Standing in the harsh fluorescent lighting of the Van Nuys precinct, I'm steps away from the cell I'll be occupying as soon as I finish this tortuously slow admission process. I had been a guest here frequently enough as of late that the admitting officer felt comfortable asking me what I planned to do about my obvious problem. As usual, that all-too-familiar feeling of righteous indignation welled up inside of me as I thought, "Who the fuck are you? You don't know me, or any problem of mine, for that matter!"

While he was doing all the talking, my eyes zeroed in on the closest thing to salvation on this otherwise bleak morning: through the steel bars, I noticed a vacant cot bolted to one of the drab beige cinder block walls of the holding cell. My single greatest hope in that moment was grabbing that cot before anyone else did. I just wanted a horizontal space to sleep it off and briefly escape the noise in my head. I wasn't concerned with making any phone calls, as there was no one left to call. Certainly, no one who wanted to hear from me again under these circumstances. My life, in that moment, had come down to one small prayer: "God, please let me make it to that cot." Nothing more.

Mercifully, my prayer was answered, and, assuming the fetal position on my little metal refuge, I did manage to grab a few hours of much-needed shut-eye, when I was suddenly rudely awakened by a loud disturbance. As I sat up in the bunk, I could just make out through the now standing-room-only crowded cell three or four dudes, yelling, cursing, and throwing aimless, drunken punches at each other.

I remember thinking, "Jesus, these assholes need to get their shit together!"

Yes, miraculously, in that moment, the fact was somehow lost on me that I was occupying the same cell with them.

Still, somewhere way down deep, I might have been wondering how I got here.

CHAPTER 1

LOVE IS A MANY-SPLENDORED THING

I started my life in North St. Louis, where my father worked as a streetcar driver for the St. Louis Public Service Company city transit, and in the summer of 1956, when I was all of four years old, he took me to work with him one day.

Now, if you've ever been to St. Louis in the summer, you know that a breeze in mid-August would be noteworthy in and of itself. But there was one moment—and one breeze—that I remember right now as vividly as the day it happened.

We were the only two people on that Number 40 crosstown streetcar that afternoon, and with the whole cabin to myself, I picked a seat about halfway back, my dad up front at the helm. In his impressive driver's uniform and cap, I figured he must be one of the most important men in the whole city—like a general in the army or something.

For my dad, though, this trip was bittersweet. Times were changing, and these electric streetcars were being phased out. In fact, the car we were riding had just completed her last full day in service and was now officially decommissioned. So my dad arranged to have me join him on this sentimental journey, as the car traveled back across town to the maintenance yard one final time, where, sadly, it would be stripped down and left to rust in some back-lot graveyard.

The streetcar, a PCC Streamliner, was like a giant art deco toaster: beautiful on the outside, hotter than hell on the inside. I recall my dad turning back to me, smiling, as he instructed me to pinch the two small levers at the top of the window and pull down to open it for some fresh air. It didn't help that much.

"Wait till we get rolling," he assured me. "The breeze will feel really good."

And sure enough, as the car's electric motor started to hum and whine, we picked up speed, and the resulting breeze that came through that window was like a message from God that all was right with the world.

I can still hear the summer trees rustle as we sped close by them and see the late-afternoon sunlight flickering through their leaves. Most of the trip was along the tracks that ran behind the old neighborhoods downtown, and I was intrigued by the rare view into the backyards and lives of all these people whom I'd never met and probably never would. Then the thrill of being slightly startled when suddenly we broke out into the busier, more chaotic downtown intersections. It's all still right there in my mind's eye.

Though I was too young to appreciate the range of emotions he must've felt that day, the idea that my dad wanted me to share this experience with him, in hindsight, makes the memory grow even more precious for me.

—

I THINK IT'S FAIR TO SAY THAT MY DAD WAS LARGELY RESPONSIBLE FOR MY CHOICE OF career. Well . . . to be more accurate, if my mother had trusted my father more, I might never have become a musician.

See, there was always a lot of cat-and-mouse maneuvering going on between my mom and dad, due in no small part, I'm sure, to my old man's restless nature. He was the guy with one foot always out the door. So on any given night, he would be on his way out to one of his favorite saloons, places that generally had one of his favorite piano players on hand and the invitation always there for him to come and sing. It all seemed innocent enough.

Still, with a certain percentage of the usual patronage being my dad's many female admirers, my mother, Mary Jane, clever woman that she was, would suggest that since he hadn't seen me all day while at work, he should let me tag along. In truth, I was the designated spoiler. Having me in tow would, at least in theory, limit the amount of trouble he might otherwise get into. And, of course, since I was all of five or six, he'd have to get me back home at a decent hour. So, like clockwork, we'd bounce into the house most nights no later than midnight, one in the morning at the very latest.

In spite of his occasional lapse of parental judgment regarding curfew, my dad would always be a larger-than-life hero to me. I aspired to carry myself the way he did, seemingly so sure of himself, ever steady and confident. However, that was not me; I never spent a day feeling sure of myself—in anything. And furthermore, I was convinced I was the only one who felt that way.

My father had enlisted in the Marines during World War II, and by the time he was nineteen, he was off in the Pacific theater fighting in the hellish campaign that included Iwo Jima, Tarawa, and Peleliu. And while he chose mostly never to talk about the war, it was clear the experience had left its mark. His constant anxiety (before the phrase "post-traumatic stress" became popular) manifested itself most notably in his insatiable need to keep moving. Postwar hell for my father was being stuck within the confines of four walls. Forward momentum, in some form or another, seemed to relieve his stress.

He and his brothers grew up on the streets of downtown St. Louis during the Depression. The oldest, Michael, was a long-haul trucker and early local Teamsters organizer, and the other three all worked for the city in different capacities: Ed was a cop, Frank worked for Public Housing, and my dad—Robert, "Mac" to his friends—was a streetcar operator, the perfect job to keep him in constant motion.

Which also meant that he knew every cop, transit worker, and city hall employee in St. Louis. I never met anyone who didn't love the guy, and why not? He was a tall, handsome, and engaging young Irishman with wavy black hair, a wicked sense of humor, and a beautiful tenor voice, which made him a fixture at many a policeman's funeral, city hall function, and Hibernian event. He once kicked off a Democratic rally in support of then presidential hopeful Senator John F. Kennedy, singing "It's a Great Day for the Irish." We were all so proud as we watched the young Massachusetts senator spring from his chair to shake my dad's hand before he took the podium to deliver his campaign speech to the massive crowd assembled at Northland Shopping Center.

My dad's reputation as a singer throughout the greater metropolitan area was such that he was welcomed warmly in any place he chose to patronize, usually greeted with a hearty "Hey, Mac, sing us a song!" I don't know that he ever really considered attempting a career of it for himself, though I do know he was proud of having sung with Bob Crosby and the Bobcats at a couple of USO events while in the service.

I've often wondered just how much of a dream that might have been for him. But I think he also knew what a long shot it was. To his way of thinking, show business was a pursuit with terrible odds, usually leading to nothing but faded hopes and disappointment. And though it might hold a certain promise, it was reserved for a very few. In any event, now, postwar, with a wife and baby and more to come, working for the newly formed Bi-State Transit Authority seemed a much more practical way to go. It was a solid job with a salary on which a man could raise a family in the 1950s.

—

IN MY IRISH CATHOLIC UPBRINGING, THERE WERE TWO SUREFIRE VOCATIONS THAT would keep one in good standing: you could become a priest or a nun, or—swinging wildly in the other direction—you could go out and become a famous entertainer, "famous" being the operative word, because short of that you'd just become another black sheep in the family.

My father's parents were Irish immigrants. His father—my grandfather Edward McDonald—the son of a Thoroughbred trainer in Tullamore, came over as a young man and joined the US Army, serving in a cavalry regiment, probably in hopes of a fast track to American citizenship. After he was discharged, he returned several times to Ireland to woo my grandmother Mariah, finally convincing her to marry him and move to the States, settling in north central St. Louis. But in the bargain, determined to bear her children in her heart's real home, among family in Tullamore, my grandmother insisted that whenever it was called for—which seemed to be almost annually—she, along with my grandfather and their ever-growing brood, would make the crossing back to Ireland to deliver the next arrival. At some point, however, that got to be too expensive, and so, while my aunt Mary and uncles Mike, Frank, and "Chub" (Edward) were "Americans" born in Ireland, my father and his younger sister, Rita, were born back in St. Louis.

When my dad was about seven, during the depths of the Great Depression, my grandfather died, and so my grandmother, a widow raising six kids on her own in tenement housing, took work as a prison matron (guard) in a women's prison, an experience that no doubt further hardened the demeanor and resolve of an already tough and determined young woman. Consequently Nana Mac, as we called her, was not exactly the traditional genteel and affectionate grandmother. She was no Mother Machree. To be honest, as a little kid I was scared to death of her. Even in her later years, when she was ailing and wheelchair-bound, she didn't soften that much. Which is not to say she didn't love us—it was just in her own, not overly sentimental way. Come to think of it, I don't recall her ever calling me by my actual name; I was usually referred to as either "this one" or "that one." (I remember thinking it preferable to be "that one," as it presumed you were out of striking distance.)

My grandmother's kitchen table was where the grown-ups spent an inordinate amount of time smoking Camel nonfilters (with very little ventilation) and drinking extremely strong black tea while scouring the obituaries. As far as I could figure, if there was even the slightest connection or shred of lineage between the deceased and anyone they might have remotely ever heard of, they were going to that wake.

My family loved attending wakes and funerals, but not necessarily weekly Mass or even church services in general, mind you. Sunday mornings, to my parents, were for sleeping in; they would kick us kids out to go to church—which, of course, we always skipped, and with the dollar they gave us for the collection basket, we headed instead for milkshakes at North Hills Dairy. But if it was a wake or a funeral, they were there. And usually straight to the saloon afterward.

In all the years I knew them, I never saw my parents once take a drink. For my dad's part, the story he stuck to was that alcohol made him break out in a rash. But in truth, I believe he had enjoyed drinking as a younger man but stopped when he came home from the war, a bit shattered, and realized alcohol just wasn't helping things. He was what we call a "white knuckler"; he could quit at the drop of a hat, through sheer discipline and willpower. For him, it was more about the camaraderie he found in those social gatherings and in the taverns, being "out among 'em." These were rituals that all served, I believe, to connect him to the life he remembered before the war, offering him something familiar and comforting.

My mother's family, the Hanleys, were long-settled, second-generation Irish American, not so prone to the habits and rituals of the "auld sod," a bit more emotionally demonstrative. Family lore has it that her father, my grandfather Frank Hanley, was so over the moon upon my arrival, the first boy of that generation born into the Hanley family, that he came to visit me in the hospital every day against strict doctors' orders, due to his failing heart. He would take the bus—in the coldest days of February—to visit his daughter and new grandson, holding me in his arms as long as the nurses would allow, remarking to anyone within earshot, "Isn't he just perfect?"

He died seven days after I was born. Like ships passing in the night on this physical plane, I was just arriving as he was leaving this world. Of course, I have no way of knowing how much of the story is factually accurate, but just having heard it told repeatedly over the years by my mother and my grandmother Genevieve, the very idea of it has filled me with a warm feeling that to this day informs my understanding of family and paternal love.

—

ANYWAY, BACK TO ME AND MY FATHER. ON THOSE OCCASIONS WHEN HE GOT SADDLED with dragging me along to his favorite nightspots and was inevitably beckoned to get up there and sing a few songs, we had our routine worked out: he would order his Pepsi-Cola and bring me my Shirley Temple—because what else are you gonna serve a five-year-old? (The bartender was at least kind enough to refer to it as a Roy Rogers.) Then I would make myself comfortable on the windowsill behind the piano, happily sucking down my grenadine and club soda through a straw, my eyes usually fixed on the piano player's hands. My favorite of them all was Ida Burns. She was a sweet, beautiful woman of, shall we say, ample stature. I would sit there mesmerized, watching her hands, like two small hams, glide effortlessly across the keys, creating a magical, harmonic universe that my dad would then step up to the microphone and join with his soaring, transcendent tenor voice. He could sure sing, all right, but he could also deliver a song with that nuance that made you believe every word of the lyrics. Even as a kid I had to fight back tears almost every time I heard him sing "Danny Boy." You could tell he was Ida's favorite guest vocalist; when others volunteered to sing, she'd tell them in no uncertain terms, "Go sit your ass down and wait till Bob's finished!"

Well, after seeing my dad go up there and bring down the house time after time, it seems one night I was stricken with a bout of extreme self-confidence. I put down my Roy Rogers, so the story goes, and walked over to the piano and tugged at Ida's sleeve to let it be known that I wanted to sing a song. Keep in mind: I'm five. In a saloon. After a quick glance over her glasses at my father, Ida smiled and asked, "What would ya like to sing, honey?"

When I told her the song I had in mind, she reared back with an astonished expression that gave way to a grin from ear to ear. My dad brought the mic back around next to Ida, adjusted the height down for me, and, as I stood alongside her, she played a short intro ending with a single can't-miss-it starting note and nodded, whereupon I proceeded to deliver my emphatic interpretation of "Love Is a Many-Splendored Thing," a song I'd memorized after listening countless times to Mario Lanza's version on a 78 rpm recording on my Aunt Mame's old Victrola. Now, all three and a half feet of me was belting it out with the full bravado of an opera star—an opera star with questionable pitch and not the slightest concept of what the lyrics were actually saying.

Of course, at the end of the song everyone in the place burst into uproarious laughter and applauded—and that was it. I was forever smitten. I had apparently found my calling. And from that night on, I'd sing with my dad all over town.

CHAPTER 2

MY PARENTS, RAY CHARLES, AND DR. BILSKEY

Not long after that, Nana Mac bequeathed to me my grandfather's beautiful old tenor banjo, so I learned to play some chords from a Mel Bay instructional book and started to back up my dad, along with Ida, on some great old ragtime/Dixieland tunes—"(Up a) Lazy River," "Do You Know What It Means to Miss New Orleans?," "The Saint Louis Blues," "One of These Days," "Bill Bailey, Won't You Please . . . Come Home?," etc.—which we played everywhere from city hall events to Hibernian dinners and, of course, in all my dad's favorite haunts around north county. This was the basis of our relationship from then on. The music he loved, I loved, and we shared that common thread throughout our lives.

By the time I was in fourth, fifth grade, my horizons started to expand a little. While I don't imagine I was particularly gifted on that banjo, my dad must've seen enough of a spark of promise, because next thing you know, he decided I should take piano lessons. So it was decided that one night a week, after dinner, my dad would drop me off for my lesson, which, conveniently enough, gave him another weeknight out without having to drag me along the whole time. The real victim in this nefarious plot might have been my poor teacher, Tom Hanlon, another piano-player friend of my dad's, a wonderful guy who would be tasked with more than he bargained for.

He lived downtown in a garage apartment where I would constantly be distracted by the sounds of other kids playing outside in the alley, while I was trapped in a sweltering little room with the infamous St. Louis humidity—all the while struggling through elementary piano pieces to that annoying clicking of the metronome.

Then came the dark and cold winter months, which made the experience even more depressing. By then I had developed the questionable habit of memorizing the music by ear, clearly lacking the attention span required to expand my sight-reading ability, and the whole endeavor started to seem increasingly futile.

However, Tom was not only kind but also wonderfully patient and resourceful. When my dad would invariably be hours late to pick me up, Tom, who had boxes of every kind of flash card known to man, would try to keep me engaged with drills on musical symbols and note values, the state capitals, and multiplication tables. By the time my dad came to get me, I was usually asleep on the couch, only to be awakened by the sound of his voice and his struggling efforts to get my coat on me while I was still half asleep. Then, on the long, freezing walk down the alley to the car, he would brief me on how we would explain to my mom why we were so late.

"Okay, now, listen. When your mother asks, you just say, 'We got to talking.' All right? After your lesson, time got away from us—'You know how Tom likes to talk . . .' But I was here the whole time, okay? You know . . . We don't want your mom getting all upset."

I remember thinking, "Yeah, good luck with that."

My mother was already suspicious about my dad's sudden interest in my piano lessons. After all, we didn't even have a piano. So when my father heard that his friend Buddy Walsh knew someone who was trying to get rid of an old upright, my dad offered the guy ten dollars, and the next thing you know, he and "Uncle" Buddy are carrying this upright grand piano across the front yard. No professional piano movers, mind you, no dolly . . . Just Dad and Uncle Buddy carrying this huge, solid oak behemoth up the stoop and into the house. (What a guy won't do to get himself a night out!) The whole maneuver was surely not made any easier by me keeping pace alongside, banging out "Battle Hymn of the Republic" with two fingers, my father sweating profusely and straining under the load while swatting at me intermittently with one hand, yelling, "Get the hell outta the way!"

Somehow, they managed to make it through the living room, into the kitchen, halfway out the back door, then down the narrow stairs into the basement. And that piano called to me. My first thought upon waking every morning and coming home from school was getting myself to that piano. I spent an awful lot of time down there, especially in the summer, when the basement seemed to be the only place to escape the heat. I would go downstairs and sit at the piano for hours, usually in my underwear, playing longer than I ever did as an adult, teaching myself songs I heard on the radio by Dionne Warwick, Ray Charles, Chuck Berry, Etta James, etc. And of course, not satisfied leaving well enough alone, at some point I discovered that putting tacks into the felt hammers gave it an extra juicy, slinky sound—perfect for playing ragtime.

I even endeavored early on to write some original songs. I wrote one with my father called "My Heart Just Won't Let You Go." It was a lyric he came up with at work, and he came home all excited: "Hey, Mike, see if you can put some music to this!" There was one line he was especially proud of: "If it was UP to me, I'd bring you DOWN, DOWN, DOWN, go out and do the town." Oh, he was proud of that line. "See what I did there, Mike? A little play on words!" So I came up with a melody that more or less followed the lyric up, up, up . . . then down, down, down. We were pretty convinced we had a bona fide hit on our hands.

—

OUR WHOLE FAMILY APPRECIATED GOOD MUSIC. MY SISTERS—KATHY IS TWO YEARS older than me, Maureen four years behind me—my aunts and uncles, we all revered those great songs, songwriters, and the performers who made them magical: Nat King Cole, Frank Sinatra, Ella Fitzgerald, Tony Bennett . . . Anyone who could wrap their vocal cords around a good song in that special way was held in high regard in the McDonald home.

My Aunt Ann Catherine's big console stereo was the first I'd ever heard, and her record collection included Ray Charles's *Modern Sounds in Country and Western Music.* I would lie on the floor of her apartment, close my eyes, and listen to that album on repeat for hours on end. There was something undeniable in his melodic interpretation, vocal performances that you just knew were purely inspired in the moment and likely to never be repeated exactly the same way again, the way he mined the hidden poignancy of the lyrics. I couldn't have explained it at the time. I just knew after hearing Ray Charles, I would never be the same.

My Aunt Bitsy taught Kathy and me some of her favorite Brenda Lee and Patsy Cline songs. She used to take my sister to the St. Louis Municipal Opera Theatre to see all the Broadway musicals as they came through town and then would buy her the soundtrack albums to commemorate the occasion. And it was from those records that I learned to love the songs of Rodgers and Hart, Rodgers and Hammerstein, Leonard Bernstein, and Stephen Sondheim.

While all this wonderful familial exchange was going on and this musical bond was blossoming between my father and me, the fraying of my parents' marriage continued. Maybe things were different before my sisters and I were around, but as far as any of us kids could recall, it had always seemed a tenuous relationship at best. Love had surely existed there at one time; we heard tell of it in the stories and reminiscences of their friends—how my dad first spotted her as the pretty young passenger on his streetcar route, how he wooed her by ringing the streetcar bell every time he passed the office building where she worked. But over time, their fights were ongoing, and my sisters and I just learned as a matter of course, and of survival, to ride the waves of drama.

They would usually start around dinnertime, the fights. And they could be about almost anything. There were money problems, for sure; my father constantly bristled at my mom's "splurging"—though the occasional wall hanging or kitchen appliance she might have bought with her earnings from working at the S&H Green Stamp store were not exactly examples of extravagance. I think, for my father, those battles were just convenient excuses for his deeper discontent.

And, as always, there were his indiscretions. I can only assume there were other women, though I never really knew where my dad went back then—and strangely, to this day, I've never asked anyone.

But really the fights could have been about anything. There was this constant, overwhelming burden they just couldn't seem to drop. A tension that would inevitably end up with my dad, in the middle of one of their heated exchanges, frantically throwing his clothes into a bedsheet spread out on the floor, while I desperately begged him not to go.

I never knew what plans he had in mind every time he bolted out that door. But when I was younger, having no idea if he was coming back at all was terrifying for me. My time with my dad was so brief and sporadic to begin with; it was always incumbent on me to keep up with him. But I was willing to do it because that's where I found that guy I admired so much, who I wanted to be like. It's as though I felt the need to claim my identity as his son. So, as a child—four, five, six years old—watching my father leave, each time not sure if he was ever coming back, would be traumatic. It would hardly have been worse if I had seen him drop dead on the floor in front of me. It was that brutal, only more repetitive. And though for years it seemed he'd always return, along with that came the anxiety of wondering how long before it all blew up again.

—

EVERY TIME HE WENT AWAY, I'D BE LEFT WITH MY MOTHER AND SISTERS AND A MONSOON of emotions that I was hardly prepared to deal with. I would just sit there on the front stoop for days. My mother confided in me years later: "I would really worry about you. You were just . . . kinda catatonic. I didn't quite know what to do for you. You missed him so much." And I absolutely did miss him terribly, but even that was beyond my ability to process with any clarity.

One of my earliest, more vivid memories is of my mother taking me down to a bus terminal to pick up my dad. I remember being held in my mother's arms, so I'm guessing I couldn't have been more than three. My father had been gone for days? Weeks? Months? Whatever it was, I had apparently been missing him so terribly that she took me with her to pick him up at the bus depot that night.

As we entered the terminal—I can still picture it: my dad walking toward us and setting down his bag, reaching for me, arms outstretched . . . And me, overwhelmed and confused, turning away from him and burying my face in my mom's shoulder, clinging to her as my father tried to take me. Somehow, for all my sadness at having missed him so much, my reaction was to reject his affection and my own desperate need for it. I remember, even then, feeling bewildered by my response. I also remember feeling his disappointment. And I remember hearing my mom gently tell my father, "He hasn't seen you in a while. Give him a minute."

I'm struck by my mother's sensitivity and generosity at that moment, especially considering that every time he left, it was she who was stuck with the collateral damage that was our family. But for years to come, it would be my mom that I blamed for his leaving. After all, it was always after she blew up at him that he would bolt. As I saw it then, she just wouldn't "let it go." She kept pushing and pushing, and it would just escalate till he left. And I would yell at her: "Why did you do that?! Why did you chase him off again?" To my young mind, his leaving was always her fault, and in those moments, I hated her for it.

Sadly, that attitude colored my relationships with women for the longest time going forward. For years, I carried a general disregard, almost a subconscious resentment, toward women. As if they were the enemy and needed to be kept at arm's length, that if you let them get too close or trusted them too much, they'd eat your lunch and consume your life. That was the relational motif put forth by most of the men in my immediate family. You'd think a guy who grew up surrounded and nurtured by so many strong, loving women—a single mother, two dedicated grandmothers, my sisters, and a multitude of loving aunts—would've known better.

I probably knew even then that my unflattering image of women was faulty and the fear irrational. But that doesn't make it any less operative. It's like: you may know olives aren't really eyeballs, but because you thought that when you were little, it can be a long time before you can look a jar of olives in the face.

Of course, in hindsight, I understand it differently. My mother was just trying to get some respect, to get my father to put in the hard work required to have a marriage. Also, if I'm being honest, as a little boy, it was easier to blame my mom than to face my real and deeper fear: that maybe I was also somewhat responsible for my dad's leaving, that possibly I was a disappointment for him as a son, and that maybe he thought there was something out there better than us, better than me. A son who would live up to his expectations more. I mean, I knew how much I loved my dad. I knew I could never leave *him*! At that young age, I couldn't fathom how you could just walk away from someone you loved that much.

So whatever words were tossed my way as he walked out the door—"Listen, don't worry, boy. I'll call ya later," "It's okay," or the old thumbs-up, which I would learn to always look for in the years to come—they were of little comfort and invariably delivered chaotically, on the fly, because my mom was either on her way home or already home, chasing him down the driveway with a few final choice words. We never once sat down as a family, like in the movies, to discuss what was wrong with this picture.

—

ADDING A TOUCH OF FUEL TO THE FIRE, MY MOM, LIKE MILLIONS OF YOUNG HOUSEWIVES in the '50s, had grown very fond of the "mother's little helper" pills that Big Pharma was only too happy to supply. Promising to make life's tedium more manageable—even enjoyable!—the drug industry offered everything from appetite suppressants to mood elevators to energy enhancers, or, in my mom's case, Dr. Bilskey's diet pills, which pretty much covered all of the above. She'd usually run out of them around Wednesday night, begin to crash somewhat on Thursday, and spend Friday desperately leaving messages at my dad's work: "Tell him not to forget to go by Bilskey's!"

Having dutifully swung by Dr. Bilskey's, my dad would come home at the end of the day to find my mother standing in the driveway, arms folded, waiting for him to fork over the prescription before he could even get out of the car. Just after dinner, the first pill would already be kicking in, and my mom was off and running; she'd start with the two days' worth of dishes piled up in the sink and then, in a whirlwind of manic energy, tackle every corner of the house, all the while muttering to herself under her breath. We all did our best to stay out of her way during these domestic frenzies, and my dad would often retreat to his refuge: the relative calm of some crowded tavern. But even that didn't always guarantee his safety.

One morning, after having left in a huff the night before, my father waltzed into the house (a particularly brazen move) just in time to shave and change clothes for work. I was getting ready for school at the same sink in our family bathroom, and while it was unusual for him to still be home when I left for school, I chose not to ask questions. I sensed that his offer to give me a ride to school was less about sparing me the walk and more to do with concern for his personal safety; he just didn't want to be left alone with my mother, who was on a tear in the other room.

In the mirror, he quietly made some offhanded joke to me about her ranting. Unfortunately, she heard it and obviously didn't find it all that amusing. The next thing I recall is her bursting through the bathroom door, grabbing his wrist (the one holding the razor), and struggling to push it in the general direction of his jugular vein as he was forcibly arched backward over the sink—at which point I wasted no time bolting down the hallway, toothbrush in hand, mouth full of foaming toothpaste. Too afraid to look back, I ran to the kitchen, spitting the toothpaste into the sink, and into my room, where I got myself dressed in record time. It seemed a better idea to get to school by myself—especially having just witnessed, along with a couple of the neighbors, my dad backing out of the driveway while my mother proceeded to shatter as many of the car windows as she could with an unplugged iron before he gassed it down the street.

So I headed off, on foot, to Saints John and James parochial elementary school.

CHAPTER 3

GOD, GIRLS, AND GUITARS

The whole purpose of Catholic school, as far as we were told, was to instill a healthy fear of God and set us on the path to a life of service to the Catholic Cause. And remarkably, in my case, it almost worked.

In fifth grade, my best friend Danny and I were actually toying with the idea of becoming missionary priests. It seemed like such an adventure. The nuns, quick to recruit, would entice us with colorful publications printed by the archdiocese with comic-book-style graphics—a machete-wielding Father Tom Dooley leading the orphans to safety through the jungle, saving them from the communists! It was better than Sgt. Rock! Like a Catholic Captain America!

On top of that, the nuns lavished upon the two of us all the coveted and prestigious perks a couple of promising seminary prospects could hope for—privileges sure to get you out of class early and often: eraser cleaning, patrol boy duty, not to mention potentially shooting to the top of the list for the more lucrative wedding and funeral gigs, where an altar boy could potentially get slipped a card with a crisp five-dollar bill inside. (I never quite made that list.)

It was right about this time, and largely the result of these awesome opportunities, that I came face-to-face with my seeming host of limitations and propensity for making poor choices. I proceeded to fail miserably at each and every one of these endeavors: I caused a three-car pileup on my first day as a patrol boy, got kicked out as an altar boy during Forty Hours' Devotion—which, despite the daunting moniker, required literally nothing more than a short shift of kneeling and staring straight ahead. And while it's not easy to fail at eraser cleaning, I somehow managed that as well. It may have been the result of some overzealous eraser clapping on my part, but who knew that thick clouds of chalk dust could actually travel on an updraft and into an open window . . . where the Mother Superior was leaning out, choking frantically, desperately signaling for me to stop. That was fifth grade.

Then, come sixth grade, I discovered girls.

Well, one girl in particular: Diane, my first true love. She was the cause of my ultimate fall from grace with the good sisters, and they were very keen to express their disapproval. Where I might have been forgiven for earlier infractions, this was the proverbial straw. I was instantly blacklisted for the crime of my new discovery and seemingly overnight went from privileged status to marked man.

However, there were also more than a few wonderfully encouraging faculty members. Unquestionably, the coolest was Mr. Bosey, the school band director and instructor. A talented trumpet player and vibraphonist, he used to work nights playing the jazz clubs downtown on Delmar Boulevard and in Gaslight Square, and his group later recorded a couple of live albums at the local Playboy Club (which I'm guessing was not widely known among the nuns at the time). But he was a great teacher and had a real capacity for encouraging young talent. He even convinced me to try the trombone, despite the fact I had specifically requested to play the snare drum. Having seen the percussion section crush it on "The Little Drummer Boy" in the Christmas pageant, I really coveted that spot. Unfortunately, so did every other kid in my class. So, with all the drum chairs filled, it was suggested I take a seat in the brass section.

I was sent home with a shiny new trombone and advanced pretty quickly, or so Mr. Bosey had me believe. I got as far as sight-reading some music written for trombone—infinitely easier to read than piano music. But what I remember most fondly is the smell of the thing. I loved the scent of the stainless steel mouthpiece and the slide oil, as well as seeing the light reflecting off the bell. I even romanticized working the spit valve with a certain swagger like I had seen older guys do. To this day, should the occasion ever arise to hold a trombone, those are the sensations that come back to me in a kind of nostalgic rush.

During this new adventure as a horn player, two school band colleagues, Tim Fizell and Bob Bortz, and I formed a Dixieland combo, the Mound City Three. We knew exactly one song, "When the Saints Go Marching In," and with Tim on clarinet and me on trombone, we basically abused the melody in unison while Bob tapped out a military march rudiment on snare drum. We made the kind of music only a mother could love; Tim's mom, Margie, would sit at the top of the basement stairs and applaud for us, bless her heart.

—

BUT ALAS, NO SOONER HAD MY SELF-ESTEEM BEGUN TO RISE WITH MY NEWLY DISCOVered aptitude as a horn player than my trombone got repossessed. Apparently, my folks had missed a few payments. So when the repo guy from Wellston Music Store appeared at our door, I went to my room, packed up my horn, and handed it over. My parents felt bad, and I felt bad for them having to watch this whole sad debacle, and I'm sure the repo guy didn't feel too good either about having to yank away some kid's musical instrument.

Still, it might have been a blessing in disguise, because in the following months, I turned my focus back to piano, just as some other musical instruments made their way into my world. In addition to the aforementioned banjo, I was given a one-of-a-kind homemade electric guitar—a loan from a friend of my dad's whose son built the thing in high school shop class. But as he was presently in the army on a tour of duty somewhere on the border of North and South Korea, his mother thought I might be able to put it to use in his absence.

And it was with that homemade guitar that, at the age of twelve, inspired by the British Invasion groups everyone was emulating, I started my first band: Mike and the Majestics. (Not sure how or why I got top billing, but . . .) We had Bob Bortz (now the proud owner of a complete set of drums), our buddy Pat Molloy on "bass" (in actuality a regular guitar on which he played only the lowest four strings in the thickest gauge he could find, with the treble rolled all the way off), and me on the Shop Class Special guitar. The neck was like a tree trunk, but it was well made electronically and . . . it played.

There was another kid down the block, Steve Scorfina, who was reported to be a pretty decent guitar player. Steve was two years older than me, and with his skintight jeans, white socks, black shoes, and shirttail-out ensemble, along with a Sal Mineo pompadour hairstyle, I figured him to be a "hoodlum" type and frankly kind of intimidating.

Anyway, he somehow had gotten my number and called to invite me to listen to some records—"and maybe bring your banjo." There was some vague hope that maybe this guy could show me some actual guitar chords. So with that I headed down Highmont Drive to Steve Scorfina's house.

If I'm being honest, most everything good that's happened in my life and career—virtually none of it was of my design. If I had anything to do with any of it, it was that when doors opened, I trusted some vague instinct to say yes before overthinking the situation, or I recognized soon enough that a door slamming shut in my face might just have been another one of those blessings in disguise. Like most of us, progress for me has been incremental, a crooked path between best and worst instincts, virtue and character defect. My best-laid plans, it seems, have had little to do with how my life has actually played out.

Case in point: meeting Steve. When I got to his house that first day, his mother told me he'd be out shortly, whereupon I heard the telltale *flush* and out of the bathroom came Steve—wearing his electric guitar around his neck. My first thought was "Man, this guy is serious!" He gave me a casual nod—"How's it going?"—while nonchalantly riffing on some Ventures tune. We've been friends ever since.

Our fledgling little rock band had, up to that point, been outfitted, indirectly, courtesy of the US Army. In addition to my Shop Class Special guitar, Bob Bortz's older brother, Jerry, before being shipped off to some small Southeast Asian country none of us had ever heard of, had given Bob permission for us to use his beautiful Epiphone guitar and amp. Our sound wasn't exactly state of the art; we were running both guitars and a small tape recorder mic through the amp's two channels and its beleaguered twelve-inch speaker with the help of a cheap (and faulty) Y adapter. But now, with Steve and his gear coming on board, we were about to take it up to a whole new level.

Then, some good news / bad news. The good news: the guy whose guitar I was using returned home from Korea in one piece. The bad news: he wanted his guitar back. But then that Christmas, much to my surprise, my grandmother Genevieve managed to buy me a beautiful black-and-white six-string Silvertone electric guitar—with "amp in the case." I know it wasn't easy for her to afford such an extravagance; at seventy-five dollars, she was able to do it only by using the layaway plan at work. But she could never know how much it meant to me. Between that guitar and the banjo Nana Mac gave me, both my grandmothers contributed significantly to my pursuing music. And I still have both of those instruments to this day.

—

WHILE MY MUSICAL WORLD WAS EVOLVING NICELY, THINGS AT HOME WERE HEADING VERY much in the opposite direction. The tension between my mother and father was finally becoming too much to ignore. Even to the casual observer, the outward signs of our family's demise grew more and more evident: the screen door, on its side, permanently propped against the front of the house, the dying shrubs in the front yard, the gutters in constant disrepair, and, for that matter, the whole back porch falling away from the house. To be sure, home repairs were never my father's strong suit, nor skills he ever bothered to pass along to me.

It seems their marriage just wasn't destined to make it to the finish line. I was about thirteen when it ended, and by that point, I had grown pretty numb to the dramatic flare-ups.

I remember my dad's final exit. I had come home to hear someone moving and slamming drawers down the hall—unusual activity for that time of day at our house. I wondered if we were being robbed. But I walked into my parents' room to find my dad frantically tossing his clothes into a bedsheet one last time; he'd come home early, I guess, to make a clean exit before my mom came home from work.

He searched for some words of wisdom while he packed. "You know, boy, sometimes people will just suck the blood right out of ya if you keep letting them. Sometimes you just gotta cut your losses, do what's best for yourself. Because eventually, that's what's best for everyone. Make the hard choices. I'm sorry, boy, but it's better this way."

To which my only response was a tepid muttering: "Yeah, no, sure . . . Gotta do what you think is right."

It didn't even feel like a big deal anymore.

"I'll call you, boy, okay?"

"Yeah . . . yeah, Dad . . . sure."

And that was it. The last time he left the house. They were divorced within the year, and what I felt more than anything was relief, because it was painfully obvious that what they had wasn't working anymore—for anyone.

After the divorce, my father was still around, still in my life, though not as much, and that was, frankly, much easier. He and my mother were better friends divorced than I'd ever known them to be while married. Once they were no longer the day-to-day source of each other's frustrations, their compatibility and the sense of humor they shared—all the things that were good about their relationship—seemed to return with time.

I recall my parents' closest friends rooting for them. I believe they still recognized something inherently good between them. And I think even as kids, in the middle of it all, we did too.

—

MEANWHILE, THERE WAS NO SHORTAGE OF SELF-INDUCED WRECKAGE WITH MY OWN love story. Having met Diane in the sixth grade, I never doubted that my love for her was real, even at that tender age. In a very short time, we developed an emotional dependence on each other that became more than a couple of fourteen-year-olds could handle—as did, ultimately, the consequences.

We were in the eighth grade when we discovered Diane was pregnant. And with that, what might have been a beautiful beginning had we been a bit older turned out to be, instead, a sad and remorseful ending, as it was decided by our parents that we'd give up the baby for adoption. This was the '60s, and for two very Catholic families, abortion was not even considered.

I've spent a lot of years wondering: What if I had decided to take responsibility and man up, marry Diane, and be a father? That was, after all, what Diane and I first assumed was the logical and only way forward—though I don't think anyone else involved, taking their measure of me at the time, would have seen the makings of a very responsible adult. I was a clueless eighth grader who, on the day I went to face her parents to discuss the situation, actually pedaled over to her house on my sister's bicycle—hardly the image to inspire the confidence of your potential in-laws.

I'm pretty sure the consensus concerning me was that I had done enough damage and should stay the hell away from her. I also think the fear was that if we saw each other during the pregnancy, together we might have had second thoughts about giving the baby up.

In truth, Diane already had second thoughts, but we were both too young and too overwhelmed to have a voice in the matter. The overall collective shame of the situation rendered us mute in the discussion. So in their best judgment, her parents made the choice to send Diane away to deliver the baby in anonymity.

It was hard to quantify the feelings of guilt and shame for what I had caused. Though I'm not proud to say this, I chose instead to disassociate, while her life was obliterated at fourteen. She was snatched from the midst of her childhood, from school and her friends, who were left to only speculate as to where she'd gone. A helpless infant was sent away out into the world without a trace, and we could only hope our baby would be in the care of someone much more capable of providing a child with the things that make for a stable life.

I had no idea how to process this all; I only knew I had to stop the downward spiral of morbid reflection on the what-ifs, if just for my sanity. I felt I could never reconcile the immense wreckage I'd caused, so I started a pattern of behavior that I would go on to fine-tune with time. Disappearing became my MO, distancing myself from whatever it was that might require accountability. It seemed like the only option for someone like me, with few or none of the attributes it would take to be a responsible adult.

I think when you are a prisoner of your perceived limitations, you fail to honestly and adequately come to terms with your past. That denial, in time, becomes a compounding element that can result in a lifetime of erratic behavior, all of it a struggle to hide from your fear of not being enough, and the guilt of past actions only seems to prove it. Life becomes a futile attempt to take your darkest secrets to the grave, and until they're honestly dealt with, no matter what other good things come your way, this struggle becomes an ever-widening hole that, I came to learn, no amount of drugs and alcohol will ever fill.

At the time, of course, I couldn't see any of that. I just knew that my life up to this point was a nonstop pageant of chaos. I needed a focus, something positive and productive to give my life some shape, some purpose.

And music, as always, was my salvation.

CHAPTER 4

THANK YOU, BUT THAT WON'T BE NECESSARY

Mike and the Majestics started like most bands—close to home. We'd rehearse in our drummer's basement after school, playing the only three songs we knew: "Boys," "Rock and Roll Music," and "Money"—which all sounded uncannily similar when we played them. These of course were originally American R&B songs that only came to us by way of the Beatles.

At this point in my "career," I was just trying to imitate the singers I heard on the recordings. My buddy Pat Molloy and I handled the vocals, and while I like to think I could decently carry a tune back then, it's safe to say that whatever vocal qualities one might associate with my singing today, they for sure hadn't developed yet. At twelve, I may have been aiming for Little Richard but probably clocked in closer to Alfalfa. I can only imagine what a relief it was for our drummer's poor mother when we finally pulled the plug at dinnertime and went our separate ways.

We eventually expanded our song list, adding more Beatles, plus a healthy dose of the Kinks, Rolling Stones, Dave Clark Five, Zombies, and Animals—basically what every other kid our age and demographic was listening to on mainstream AM radio. Although I'd listened to hours of Ray Charles and Nat King Cole as a younger kid and held their recordings as sacrosanct, still it was generally their more popular crossover material; I had yet to discover the more passionate, grittier tracks ignobly labeled "race music," played only on Black-owned and -operated radio stations. As history has come to note, our introduction to many of those very songs was on albums by white British Invasion bands, like the Stones' cover of the Valentinos' "It's All Over Now" and Irma Thomas's "Time Is on My Side," the Animals' reworking of Nina Simone's "Don't Let Me Be Misunderstood," and the Moody Blues' version of Bessie Banks's "Go Now."

—

OUR TOWN OF FERGUSON, MISSOURI, IN THE '50S WAS A MOSTLY WHITE SUBURBAN enclave, a blue-collar, working-class town with most everybody, it seemed, working on the factory lines at McDonnell Douglas or Fisher Auto Body. In more recent times, of course, Ferguson has become infamous for its incidents of racial tension, but back then it was fairly typical of the largely unspoken kind of segregation that existed even in the northern states.

In fact, while I didn't learn this till my more worldly seven-year-old sister Kathy explained it to me, the reason we even moved to Ferguson in the first place was that my grandmother Genevieve, alarmed that my sister and I had befriended some Black kids in the alley behind our house—the first Black family to have moved into our area of North St. Louis—hastily sold her house and whisked us all out of there.

Those kids were, in fact, the first friends I ever had. Before meeting them, for the first four years of my life, my memory is of being bored shitless; my only "entertainment" was either being dragged along on errands with my mother or sitting at a small picnic table in our yard watching my sister cut out paper doll clothes and coloring them with crayons. These new kids—especially the older brother, all of maybe ten—were so welcoming, inviting us into their games, teaching us the rules, instructing me along the way. I remember that older brother as being sort of a male role model for me: his patience, encouragement, and kind leadership were so striking. But as vivid as my memory of that kid still is, for the life of me I cannot recall the color of his skin; that particular detail apparently didn't hold enough significance for me at the time so as to even register in my mind's eye. I'm guessing it was, as it should ever be, quite simply unimportant.

So many white families were fleeing to the suburbs to avoid integration of their neighborhoods, but guess what? Black families lived in the suburbs too, albeit in seemingly more compartmentalized existences. Like in Kinloch, an unincorporated hamlet "across the tracks" from Ferguson, where Black families were forced to live with an oppressive status quo, institutionally maintained by the police departments, school boards, banks, churches, etc. But most white people exercised a collective denial that seemed to fly in the face of the indisputable impact the Black community has had on American culture—music more than anything.

Ultimately, the beauty of art can transcend all barriers, and, as I discovered, it has its own way of finding you.

One beautiful summer night, I was standing in our doorway on Highmont Drive, eating a baloney sandwich (the official McDonald family instrument of self-soothing), when Kathy and her friends came speeding up the street in Larry Cotner's old souped-up '52 Plymouth, jumped the curb, and came to a sliding stop on our lawn. The doors flung open and blasting out of the car's stereo eight-track speakers came Edwin Starr's "Stop Her on Sight (S.O.S.)."

As they piled out and danced enthusiastically across the grass, I stood there eating my sandwich, expressionless, but pulled into the moment in another way: my ear was drawn to the infectious piano part—a simple, syncopated rhythmic hook. I remember having something like an epiphany: "Shit—I'd much prefer to play that stuff!" The musical and rhythmic sophistication spoke to me. It was something beyond the more simplistic, folkish reinvention of American soul music we were digging by the British bands.

My sister Kathy was also our band's first manager. She even had actual business cards made up. Clearly, we were headed straight to the top!

We had all the bases covered. We'd learned fifteen songs by now and even had a professional wardrobe of sorts: we made our own dickies. For anyone not familiar with this particular highly questionable item of clothing, a dickie was a fake turtleneck, with just enough material visible under an open collar to give people the impression—for whatever reason—that you were wearing a *real* turtleneck sweater underneath. Operating on the cheap as usual, we cut out T-shaped pieces of cotton cloth and safety-pinned them under our shirt collars. However, by the end of the first set we were so sweaty, the things were just wet, lifeless, and unrecognizable rags hanging around our necks, the safety pins by now plainly visible in the front. It was not a great look. But the thrill of taking the stage as a band for the first time? Unparalleled.

Our first gig was playing for a PTA women's group at the Episcopal church on Elizabeth Street. We'd gotten through a few songs when the pastor came onstage and said, "Boys, that was wonderful! Thank you so much."

I chimed in, "And we have a whole other set for you!"

To which he responded, "No, no, that won't be necessary," as he handed us an envelope containing our full fee of nine dollars—basically paying us to stop.

—

WE ULTIMATELY GRADUATED TO PLAYING BASEMENT PARTIES, MOST MEMORABLY THE ones organized by my neighbor's college fraternity, who, having been kicked off campus, would then move the action to the basement of whoever's parents weren't home that weekend. It was at these *soirees* where, in addition to learning all the filthy lyrics to "Louie Louie," "Long Tall Texan," and "Hot Pastrami," we also got to witness some rather eye-opening sexual rites of passage that were sure to amaze any twelve- or thirteen-year-old. And as if that wasn't reward enough, at the end of the night, they'd pass the hat, and one night we left with sixty bucks—a veritable bonanza for four tweens! Definitely a "God, I love show business!" moment.

Fearing exactly such influences at our tender age, my mother persuaded my dad to step in and take over as our manager. And for a while he got us some more upscale gigs: the Bi-State Transit and Kiwanis Club picnics, as well as civic events like the city hall Christmas show—events at which one was much less likely to see college kids fucking under the buffet table.

—

STILL, I DON'T THINK MY DAD'S MANAGERIAL DUTIES WERE EVER GONNA CRAMP HIS social life. The pattern was: my father would drop us off at a gig and split, we'd play as long as the audience could stand listening to our unseasoned ensemble, and then we'd pack it up and sit out front with our gear . . . waiting, while my bandmates took turns asking me, "Hey, when's your old man gonna get here?"

The likely last straw for the guys was a farmers' association dinner at Benld Coliseum, when, in the middle of our set, a fistfight broke out among the five hundred farmers gathered. As the sound of chairs and tables being thrown and overturned made its way toward us through the haze of dense cigarette smoke, we ducked out of there for our own safety, while Illinois state troopers were called in to clear the hall. As my buddies and I waited outside on the steps with what was left of our gear and my father once again MIA, this time it was an impatient security guard who felt compelled to ask, "So when *is* your dad coming?"

As much as we all loved my dad, when Steve Scorfina's dad offered his services as manager, the other guys were unanimously in favor of the move. As for me, I was torn. On one hand, I felt obliged to stand up for my dad's investment of time, but in reality, I just feared the change might hurt his feelings. On the other hand, these guys were my best friends. They were like my brothers. Plus, I had to admit that my dad's genuine interest in the band was more a figment of my imagination than fact, and as it turned out, he wasn't exactly reluctant to turn over the reins.

So in stepped Vito Scorfina, and his influence definitely raised the bar for the group. "Mike and the Majestics" became simply "The Majestics"—fair enough—and we really matured as a band. We acquired some better gear, a real PA (including more microphones so we didn't have to gang up on one), eventually adding keyboardist John Weitekamp and his brand-spankin'-new, fancy red Farfisa organ, and started playing some motel pool parties (very cool). We even got some much-improved business cards—"mother-of-pearl" with embossed lettering. I mean, c'mon!

I stayed on with the band until, for reasons I'm not sure any of us remember, I drifted off on a different musical trajectory. As I look back now, I start to see that in most of my relationships, even then, I always had the nagging thought that there might be something better just over that hill, and if there was, I was likely to go after it.

—

ONE SATURDAY AFTERNOON I WENT TO HEAR MY FRIEND JOE MANNINO'S BAND PLAY IN the food court at the local E. J. Korvette department store. One of the band members' mom worked there, so they had a solid "in" to land what was a pretty slick gig at the time.

Two things impressed me about Joe's band that day: their three-piece horn section and the guy fronting the band, Chuck Sabatino. I knew Chuck from Ferguson Junior High—a great guy with a heart of gold. But I'd never heard him sing. Man, what a voice! I was definitely impressed. It was the first time I heard a white guy sing with that much soul.

After their set, I went over to tell the guys how great they sounded and how cool I thought their song list was. When I mentioned that I wasn't all that familiar with a lot of those tunes, Chuck made a point of inviting me down to the record department—most large department stores had them in those days. They didn't have those fancy listening booths like in the Big City stores. This one just had a small, mono hi-fi turntable out in the open, and you could pull out any record to sample before deciding to purchase.

Chuck pulled out a small pile of his favorites and proceeded to educate me. Again, I knew the stuff my parents played by Etta James ("A Sunday Kind of Love"), Nancy Wilson ("How Glad I Am"), Ray Charles, and Nat King Cole—mostly their lushly orchestrated ballads. But these deeper cuts—"Something's Got a Hold on Me," "Tell Mama," "Tell the Truth," "Drown in My Own Tears" . . . Wow!

And I certainly was familiar with the Temptations, who at that moment had a No. 1 single with "My Girl." But then Chuck played another 45, a track called "Since I Lost My Baby," which still remains one of my all-time favorite recordings. It was one of the very first songs I covered forty years later on my first album (of three) diving into that bottomless catalog of great Motown hits.

We had a veritable listening party in the record department that day. The Temps, Smokey Robinson, Stevie Wonder, the Supremes, Martha and the Vandellas, as well as artists on other labels, like Little Anthony and the Imperials. "Goin' Out of My Head"? "Hurt So Bad"? I defy anyone to name a better-written song than those two right there. For Chuck and myself, that day was the start of a lifelong friendship, but we couldn't have known then how soon our destinies would again intertwine.

—

IT TURNS OUT THAT WE BOTH SHOWED UP TO AUDITION FOR THE FAIRLY RENOWNED NORTH St. Louis band Jerry Jay and the Sheratons, who were looking to fill a male lead vocal spot. Awkward as it could've been, I really got to know Chuck a little better that day, as he could not have been more gracious. And oddly enough, they wound up hiring us both.

Chuck and I were teamed with a young female singer named Jodi Brumagin, and together we worked as a vocal trio to front the band. We would form a triangle center stage, and whoever was singing lead was up front, the other two back a few feet on either side, singing backgrounds. If the song called for a male-female duet, Chuck and I would take turns pairing with Jodi, and other times it was Chuck and me downstage with our Righteous Brothers and Sam & Dave repertoire, "rockin' the house"—at least in our own minds. (All these years later, I've grown so accustomed to playing keyboard while singing that now I feel a little insecure singing without one. I have no idea what to do with my hands. But at fifteen, fronting a band as a lead singer and not knowing any better, the hands were somehow never an issue.)

Though the guys in the band were all eighteen, nineteen, twenty, I was thankfully never made to feel like a kid. Yeah, it was a great perk getting to hang out with some of the older girls the band attracted, and the crowds we drew were much bigger than the pool/basement parties that I was familiar with. But more than anything, the fact that these guys thought I had something to offer was terrifically encouraging—and a temporary panacea for my nagging insecurities.

—

WITH THREE VOCALISTS, A FOUR-MAN RHYTHM SECTION, AND A SIX-PIECE HORN SECTION, Jerry Jay and the Sheratons were a soulful powerhouse revue, a force to be reckoned with.* Our songbook consisted mostly of classic and contemporary R&B hits. And to heighten the entertainment value, as

* Full lineup was: Bob Eagle (guitar), Jerry Jay Schulte (bass), Joe Mondello (drums), Wayne Erting (organ)—they were the rhythm section—and horn players Jack Story (alto and tenor sax), Claude Kaufman (tenor sax), Bill Ehelebe (tenor sax), George Johnson (baritone sax), Ludwig "Ludi" Heinrichs (trombone), Lou Otten (trumpet), and Dan Bitza (trumpet), who rotated according to personal schedules and were rarely all there at the same time.

we'd hit the vamp-out on tunes like Bobby Bland's "Turn On Your Love Light" or Ike and Tina's version of "Tell the Truth," we had one single strobe light (courtesy of Jerry Jay's father, Emil Schulte, an electrical engineer at McDonnell Douglas) that, upon killing all other light sources, would add a hectic illumination to the slick choreography: horn and rhythm section players sliding forward and back, swinging their horns and guitars wildly over each other's heads—no easy feat for the bari sax player. The strobe's frenetic effect definitely looked great, but it also made for more than a few collisions and busted lips—and, if I'm not mistaken, a near fistfight or two.

It was hard to find bookings for a band the size of the Sheratons. We played our share of debutante balls, high school proms, local events like grand openings of supermarkets and car dealerships, and a few nightclubs in the greater St. Louis metro area. On occasion, to meet union requirements, I would be enlisted to take a seat as a trombone player. (I was able to fake my way through most of those nights, usually just hitting the strategic notes and then silently moving the slide up and down for visual effect.)

It wasn't all glitz and glamour, though. During the summer months, we played a semiregular Thursday night gig at a VFW hall in Blanchette Park, an old wooden structure with no air-conditioning that, even with all the windows open, on some nights was so oppressively hot, the audience wouldn't come inside. They stood outside and listened to us through the open windows. We were literally the only people in the building, and with our fancy choreography, we were drenched in sweat before the end of the first song. It was like being the house band in Hell.

—

A BAND THE SIZE OF THE SHERATONS REALLY NEEDED A REGULAR GIG TO STAY IN business, so when we were chosen to be the house band at the new

Castaway Club, it seemed like a natural fit . . . And since it was air-conditioned, kind of a win-win.

The Castaway became a popular—and eventually legendary—hotspot in north St. Louis County. The club and its owners, Gary and Lenita Koen, provided us young local musicians a much-appreciated venue and platform to develop our talents, and, for the patrons and bands alike, enough memories to last a lifetime. It was located below street level, and when the joint got crowded, the cinder block walls would actually sweat and pool up on the dance floor, causing people to slip and fall. From the stage, we'd notice heads suddenly disappear in the crowd, and when enough people fell, they would simply stop the show and send everybody out to the parking lot while a crew came in to mop the floors. (But that was only when *enough* people fell. In this pre-lawsuit era, the first half dozen or so to go down were apparently not a big concern.)

At the Castaway, we'd nightly share the stage with other prominent bands from the area: the Klassmen (featuring vocalist Gayle McCormick of "Baby It's You" fame); Head East; the Aardvarks; a great all-female band called the Sweet Young Things; the Acid Sette (with front-man blues singer Jan Marks and brothers Joe and Bill Marshall); and the Public Service blues band, who changed their name to Hour Glass and eventually became the Allman Brothers.

Also in rotation were my old pals from the Majestics, now known as the Good Feelin', who, under Vito's steady hand and with new lead vocalist / front man Steve Burns, had risen to become one of the most popular bands in St. Louis.

—

I LEARNED SO MUCH FROM MY TIME WITH THE SHERATONS. IT WAS AN INVALUABLE experience in becoming a more professional musician, from stage presence, song sequence, and live arrangements . . . to just listening closely to the drums and bass for the "pocket" and especially following visual cues—all of which really came in handy when playing behind guest artists.

That was one of the perks of being the house band: we regularly got to back up some great, nationally known artists like Bobby Vee, Bobby Vinton, Bobby Sherman, and a few people *not* named Bobby, as well as legendary blues artists like Muddy Waters, B. B. King, Albert King, and Howlin' Wolf. These iconic artists regularly toured Europe to sold-out audiences, but back home they would often play a pickup gig at the Castaway when passing through town. Forgoing the usual overhead of carrying their own musicians, they'd perform with local pickup or house bands.

I have to admit, having been more focused up till then on pop R&B, I was not terribly familiar with these more traditional blues artists. But I realized, once again, that so many of the songs I already loved—by the Rolling Stones, the Yardbirds, the Animals, and Cream—were actually written by these guys. My education continued.

We also took the Castaway stage with St. Louis's own musical ambassador to the world, rock and roll legend Chuck Berry. By this time in his career, Chuck had traveled the world many times over—sometimes with legendary pianist Johnnie Johnson and other musicians, but oftentimes solo, playing with pickup bands like us. For the night we were to back him up at the Castaway, he sent ahead a set list, mostly songs we were already very familiar with, and we spent that afternoon rehearsing the songs ourselves.

Come the night of the show, the place was packed, and the band was pumped and as ready as we could possibly be. Chuck showed up minutes before downbeat (as apparently was his custom), and we watched him glide down the stairs of the club, guitar in hand—no case, no cord—where Gary the owner was already waiting with a wad of cash. Chuck, a man of some physical stature, looked out over the house, doing some rough calculations in his head, and leaned over and whispered in Gary's ear as Gary peeled off bill after bill, Chuck making a point to recount it himself for good measure. A seasoned veteran, Chuck was no stranger to the golden rule: Get your back end up front—and count it.

The show went great, even with the initial panic right off the bat when we discovered Chuck's guitar was tuned about a quarter step down from the rest of us. Nonetheless, he rocked the house, as usual. The crowd of teens, who were at best only toddlers during Chuck's initial radio success, sang along and knew every word of every song.

And along the way, we learned the second golden rule, of which Chuck Berry was an avid practitioner: If you fire the backup band before the show is over, technically you don't have to pay them. So one by one, over the course of the evening, each of us was summarily released for reasons we'll never know, until finally Chuck was left onstage with just the drummer, at which point he closed with the rousing audience sing-along "My Ding-a-Ling."

The guy was not a walk in the park. However, it's hard to put into words the feeling of taking the stage with a living, breathing legendary icon of American music history. In fact, we may have been part of rock and roll history that night ourselves.

In addition to the set list of his well-known hits, Chuck had also sent down an acetate test pressing of the latest tune he'd recorded. It wasn't even out yet! We were told he was particularly excited to be trying this brand-new song out on his hometown crowd that night.

For years, I didn't think much about that, nor did I remember the title of the song, but I always recalled being impressed with the lyric reference to "safety belts," as they had just become mandatory the year before.

Now, truth be told, having dined out on this story for years, it was only recently pointed out to me that his hit song "No Particular Place to Go"—with the line "Can you imagine the way I felt? / I couldn't unfasten her safety belt"—was in fact released a couple years before that night at the Castaway. And though we had never heard the song before, it's more than possible he may have played it with someone else before us.

But hey, it's my story, and I'm sticking to it: I was there for that seminal moment in history, playing a brand-new, destined-to-become-iconic Chuck Berry song—*with* Chuck Berry—the first time it was ever played to a live audience! Anywhere! . . . Well, possibly.

CHAPTER 5

NEW THREADS AND NEW YORK CITY

Joe Pokorney was the Sheratons' manager, and every one of us in the band will always be grateful to him for his conviction and dedication, having instilled in all of us the value of working as a group toward a common goal. Having said that, Joe was not without a few notable personality traits. He was extremely self-assured and definitely opinionated. If you ever had the misfortune of disagreeing with him, he would be quick to inform you that you were just misguided and "psychologically impacted"—a phrase I'm pretty sure he made up, as he was the only person I ever heard use it.

Joe epitomized the term "micro-management," orchestrating every waking moment of all things Sheratons, from how we got to and from each gig to organizing our weekly rehearsals and making sure our set lists reflected the top twenty radio hits currently in rotation at all times. He even had us wear matching bowling shirts with the band's name on the back and our individual names over the front pocket—which we were to wear *while loading our gear* in and out for each gig. How's that for hands-on management? As Chuck Sabatino put it years later, "Joe taught us how to be overly professional in an otherwise wholly unprofessional business."

Clothes were a big part of the professional persona. It was a long-held belief by generations of working St. Louis jazz musicians that you needed to look good to sound good. But for guys like us who came from pretty humble backgrounds, silk suits, mohair jackets, finely stitched dress shirts, high-end accessories like real leather belts and patent leather dress shoes—that kind of wardrobe was financially out of reach, as it was for most other local musicians. So the culture of buying contraband apparel was alive and well in the St. Louis music scene. And Joe Pokorney knew a guy.

Angelo—or "Ang," as he was known to his associates—was a local "fence," selling high-end, hijacked merchandise for pennies on the dollar. His place of business was a stool at the bar in the Club Imperial, where the band would huddle around Ang, perusing catalogs to pick out the whole look: matching suits, shirts, ties, shoes, belts—even down to cuff links. (Somehow, miraculously, thirteen custom-tailored suits would all be ready for pickup the next day. Don't ask me how.)

The Club Imperial was a venerable establishment that catered to a generally older clientele, mainly because it had a full liquor license (though I'm sure some of the crowd there had fake IDs). It drew a more racially diverse crowd, being closer to downtown, and had a more upscale, traditional nightclub decor and vibe that required its musical entertainment to reflect a sharper, well-dressed, more conservative image. Legendary local groups like Bob Kuban and the In-Men (who had a big hit at the time with "The Cheater"), Leo's Five, the Oliver Sain group, and Ike Turner's band had performed there regularly for years. (The Imperial was also where, in 1956, Ike Turner invited a young Anna Mae Bullock onstage to sing a song, which led to her joining the band, marrying Ike, and becoming Tina Turner.)

—

LIKE MOST PROMINENT ST. LOUIS BANDS, THE SHERATONS HAD DREAMS OF A NATIONAL hit single paving the road to greater success, but for the time being, all the success we concerned ourselves with was right there in the greater metro area: playing local clubs, with local Top Forty stations plugging the gigs. Other than the occasional drive down to Nashville to audition for labels—usually leaving behind a trail of markedly unimpressed A&R execs—we never really traveled outside our own limited turf. So you can imagine our excitement when we were offered the chance to perform in New York City.

It was entirely the doing of a wonderful man named Irv Satanovsky, who owned Northland Music Center, one of the biggest music retailers in north county. He supported so many young bands by generously making available the gear they needed, most times at barely above his own cost. Well, Irv went above and beyond for the Sheratons: he procured for us a major artist endorsement deal by way of sponsoring us in a national Vox Battle of the Bands promotion.

The competition selected one band from each of three regions across the country—East Coast, West Coast, and Midwest—and Jerry Jay and the Sheratons were tapped to represent the Midwest. We were to be flown to New York, where—outfitted with all our new Vox gear and our new threads from Angelo—we'd play at the 1967 Forest Hills Music Festival. Along with the East and West Coast finalists, we would participate in the final phase of the competition while opening that evening for the Doors and Simon and Garfunkel. Not a bad gig.

For most of us, it was our first time on a plane. I'm not sure what the other passengers thought as our whole group—like members of some cult, dressed identically in our three-piece blazer-slacks-cardigan "travel ensemble" that Joe had insisted on for the flight—took our assigned seats, essentially taking over the entire coach section. I remember the thrill of takeoff, feeling the power of four big jet engines push me back in my seat, and shortly after liftoff, I noticed our bandleader Jerry's wife gripping the arms of her seat as mascara ran down her cheeks with tears of terror. New York, here we come!

On the day of the gig, we had a photo session with the other bands, Vox corporate execs, A&R execs, radio personalities, and our sponsor, Irv Satanovsky, who accompanied us for the whole trip. Then on to our sound check. I was almost dizzy stepping out onto the biggest stage I'd ever seen, with huge lighting trusses and a giant house sound system. But we soon learned that of that huge stage, we'd been given only about ten square feet—not much room for a thirteen-piece band with fancy footwork. Still, we were confident that once those awesome stage lights came up and shined down on our little patch of real estate, we were gonna kill it. Just like every night at the Castaway!

Except . . . we went on early. *Really* early. It was still daylight, with hardly anyone yet in the venue. And those who were there seemed more interested in finding their seats than in listening to us.

For a lot of the guys in the band, it felt disappointing and anticlimactic. For Joe, however, it was worse. Joe saw a conspiracy at work.

"It was rigged! It was always gonna be those California bastards! Of course they get to play after dark, to a full house—under the lights!"

Yeah, Joe wasn't gonna see it any other way.

"I'm tellin' ya, those judges were psychologically impacted!"

Truth is, compared with the winner—a hip, counterculture acid rock band from the West Coast called Orphan Egg, who, for the record, were excellent—we must've looked like we got lost on our way to play some farmer's wedding, in our embossed tux jackets and patent leather dress shoes. The triumphant return we had all envisioned—local press reporting our major label record contract, crowds of adoring fans awaiting us at Lambert Field, photo spreads in *Billboard*, *Tiger Beat* . . . all of it—*POOF!* It was not to be. But as far as I was concerned, the whole experience still gave us some bragging rights.

—

THE FOLLOWING MORNING, CHECKING OUT OF OUR HOTEL, I WAS APPROACHED BY A gentleman who had been one of the judges the night before—one of maybe ten people to actually see our set. He had some nice things to say and handed me his business card; turns out he was an exec from Monument Records, a small but prominent independent label based out of Nashville, whose roster over the years included Roy Orbison, Joe Simon, and a young singer-songwriter named Kris Carson, who later used his real name, Kris Kristofferson.

He commented that while our band had played only hits by other artists, songs already familiar to the audience, the winners, courageously, played their own original material, which boded well for them. He pointed out that the Doors and Simon and Garfunkel had become hugely successful largely on the strength of their original music, which gave them a stamp of timeless originality. But more than that, it would ultimately reward them with a much greater revenue source than they could hope to get from artist royalties alone. He told me that record labels were increasingly interested in signing artists with their own catalogs of original songs and asked if I'd ever considered writing my own music. In truth, other than the little ditties I cooked up in the basement with my dad, I really hadn't. But this conversation was an eye-opener for me, and I resolved right then and there to commit more time and effort to writing songs.

The whole encounter was no more than a casual conversation, yet to Joe, still smarting from the sting of our loss, it seemed a threat somehow to his micro-managerial authority.

Back home, at the next rehearsal, he more or less confronted me and wanted to know exactly what the Monument exec and I had talked about. I told him our conversation, adding that he had given me his card and encouraged me (and any of the guys, for that matter) to send along any demos of original material.

To me it was all so academic, since I didn't have any songs at that time or any real reason to believe that I'd ever talk to the guy again. But Joe demanded that I turn over the guy's info and discontinue any contact, which kinda put me back on my heels. I was certainly aware of and appreciated how much Joe had done for all of us, but I didn't like feeling bullied. While I don't remember the exact wording, our heated exchange ended with me offering some version of "take this job and shove it," and I left Jerry Jay and the Sheratons for good.

From there, I played a few gigs around South St. Louis with a band called the Reeb Toors ("root beer" spelled backward, if you must know). I took over for their singer Sandy Guidry, who then went over to the Sheratons, replacing Jodi, who it turns out quit shortly after I left the building. The intriguing, never-ending musical chairs of 1960s St. Louis club bands.*

As for me, after having met that record exec, I began feverishly writing songs—not necessarily good ones, but the best I could come up with at the time. I never did, however, contact that Monument Records exec again.

—

NEXT, I LANDED AN AUDITION WITH THE DELRAYS, A WELL-KNOWN ILLINOIS BAND—WHO actually opened for the Beatles at Busch Stadium when they came through town on their first US tour. (Their manager was Nick

* Jodi went on to sing with a few jazz/R&B trios and quartets in some of the more upscale venues like the Adam's Mark Hotel. All who'd worked with her were shocked and deeply saddened to hear that she passed away far too early, not long after she started playing those clubs.

Charles, a DJ at radio station KXOK, which was sponsoring the Beatles' show, so . . . I'm sure that helped.)

On the day of my audition, I arranged with a buddy to drop me off in Jennings, Missouri, not far from Ferguson, where I was to hook up with Delrays guitarist Russ Bono, whom I had never met. From there, I would ride with Russ to audition for the group at their rehearsal in Belleville, Illinois.

Our designated meeting spot in Jennings was the Velvet Freeze, a local ice cream joint I was familiar with because it was just around the corner from the S&H Green Stamps where my mom worked. Now, Jennings was known to be a fairly rough Irish/Italian Catholic working-class neighborhood, and the few square blocks around the Velvet Freeze were particularly dicey—not a place generally welcoming to strangers, particularly if you were a person of color or a scrawny, oddly dressed, long-haired hippie-looking stranger like me. Even the short walk around the corner from the S&H Green Stamps store to the Velvet Freeze required vigilance and, if necessary, fleetness of foot.

So when a couple guys followed me into the ice cream store, I suspected this probably wasn't gonna end well, my only potential backup in the place being the short, sweet middle-aged woman behind the counter, asking me, "What can I get you, honey?"

With these guys breathing down my neck, standing on either side of me at the counter, I stared straight ahead at the menu on the wall, pretending to ponder the options, while actually pondering the odds of not getting my ass kicked. The commentary from these two nitwits was ramping up, until one of them reached over and not-so-lightly tugged my long hair and said, "Hey . . . My friend and I would like to see your vagina!"

Just as I was trying to think of a witty response—*BAM!* This sweet little lady slammed her hand down on the counter, scaring the living shit out of all three of us, and yelled, "Hey, you little cocksuckers! Leave him alone or I'm gonna come around this counter and beat the shit outta *both of yas*!"

They seemed to have had no doubt she meant it because they were out that door in a flash, and without missing a beat, she regained her composure, smiled, and softly repeated the question. "Now. What can I get you, honey?"

Still in shock, but much relieved, I ordered a large chocolate milkshake and thanked her for intervening.

"They know better than to mess with me," she said. "I know where they go to school."

Just then, in walked this tall, lanky Italian kid with long, wavy black hair almost down to his waist. I thought, "Jeez, this guy's probably got a life expectancy of about fifteen minutes around here."

First words out of his mouth: "Hey, Mom," as he leaned over the counter and gave her a big kiss. She then said, with a loving smile, "This is my son Russ."

Are you kidding me? The very guy I was there to meet! I thought, "He is either one unassuming badass, walking around here with that hair, or just lucky that everyone in Jennings is terrified of his mother."

He hugged his mom goodbye (I did too), and then Russ and I drove over the river so I could try to become the new lead singer for the Delrays.

I passed the audition.

CHAPTER 6

HIGH SCHOOL AND MARIJUANA (AND NOT NECESSARILY IN THAT ORDER)

Things were definitely going in the right direction; I was moving up the chain of bands that had rep and reach. The Delrays were known on both sides of the Mississippi, so I was now, for the first time, getting to play a little further away from home, mostly on the east side of the river in all the small towns of southern Illinois.

We even recorded a single—for Arch Records, a subsidiary of Stax/Volt Records in Memphis. It was a cover of the Burt Bacharach–Hal David song "(There's) Always Something There to Remind Me"—coproduced by DJ Nick Charles and a young guy from down-river in Memphis named Steve Cropper, already a celebrated tour de force as a writer, performer, and producer for Wilson Pickett, Sam & Dave, Otis Redding, Booker T. and the MG's, Eddie Floyd . . . you name it. (From the category of "small world": the horn section he hired for the overdubs on that recording was none other than the Memphis Horns, whom I wound up working with again a decade later while touring with the Doobie Brothers.)

As I was still fifteen at the time and without a driver's license, I would catch rides with the other guys, usually Russ or our bass player Dennis Ambry, who'd swing by to pick me up on the way to our gigs.

Of course, entering the McDonald house wasn't without its risks. While poor Dennis was waiting for me to get my stuff, my mom, whose overzealous hospitality could often border on hostage-taking, would endlessly ask:

"Are ya sure I can't make you a baloney sandwich, hon?"

"No, ma'am, thank you."

(Pause, and repeat.) "Are ya sure?"

"Uh, yes, ma'am. No thank you, really."

"'Cause I can make you a baloney sandwich real quick . . . You can take it with you . . ."

By the time we were pulling out of the driveway, my mom, ever determined, would be on the front stoop waving a baloney sandwich in the air. "Are you sure?"

I have to admit I always found it perversely amusing to watch my family's normal, daily dysfunction present itself to someone from the outside world. All I know is it wasn't long before Dennis began to call ahead while on his way to make sure I was ready to roll when he got there.

—

I TURNED SIXTEEN WHILE WITH THE DELRAYS, GOT MY LICENSE, AND WAS FINALLY ABLE to drive myself to the gigs in either my mom's or my sister's car, whichever one I could commandeer that night. At least now I could maybe ask a girl out on a date once in a while.

It had been a couple years since I last talked to Diane or her family. I had tried to date other girls a couple times—with no finesse and little success. And then, out of nowhere, there was Sue.

She was unquestionably beautiful and, delightfully, a bit strange—probably the only girl at McCluer High School who walked around with a two-foot-long pet iguana on her shoulder.

To this day, I still marvel at how hopelessly in love with her I fell. It happened so fast and soon, she was all I thought about all the time.

During school hours, I counted the minutes till every encounter we might have between classes; I had already flunked most of them, so she was really the only reason I still showed up.

I would have done anything for this girl. I probably would have even gotten a real job and given up those fantasies of someday going to California—if she'd asked. But thankfully, she never did.

Because she in fact decided to dump me—for a senior, who also happened to be the Missouri state wrestling champion. A guy named Al.

It was a hard pill to swallow. I don't think I even realized the extent of my depression, though I remember my family and friends seemed uncharacteristically concerned. My dad even made a point to come around and hang out with me a couple of evenings. That alone kinda got my attention.

I remember one night finding myself in the car with him at the 270 Drive-in Theatre when it hit me: "What the fuck am I doing at the drive-in movie . . . with my old man . . . watching a Dean Martin doubleheader?!" (*Rio Bravo* and some Matt Helm movie, for the record.) I didn't even remember us having driven there, only suddenly being there. It was like I'd just snapped out of a weeks-long blackout.

Though I was by this point no stranger to loss and heartache, it was as if I was still that traumatized kid, utterly lacking the skills or self-awareness needed to help me sort out the aftermath. I found myself unable to stop missing Sue and, as a result, narrowly avoided an ugly confrontation with her new boyfriend, who, it might be worth reiterating, was the state wrestling champ.

As much as I wanted to get Sue off my mind, the problem was: I kept seeing her. I had one class in the same room where she had a class immediately before. So, every day, she would file out and I'd stand there, mentally preparing myself: "Okay, just don't look at her . . . Just look the other way, for God's sake!" Of course, then she'd walk by and all the willpower in the universe wouldn't have helped me in that moment. To not look at her was impossible. I'd have given anything for it to have been otherwise, but I was powerless. And it apparently made her uncomfortable too, as she mentioned it to the champ, who then felt morally obligated to kick my ass.

Fortunately, my buddy Chuck Sabatino heard about it and, God bless him, stepped in to plead my case: "Hey, Al, listen . . . This guy doesn't mean any harm, he's just brokenhearted. He knows it's over. He's just having a hard time. Have a heart, man."

Well, it seems Al was a man not beyond reason and graciously called off the ass-whooping—with one final condition: "Okay, but you tell your friend to stop looking at her before sixth period!"

That seemed as good a time as any to make my final exit from academic pursuit.

—

STILL, AS MUCH AS I'D LIKE TO BLAME HEARTBREAK FOR MY GENUINE LACK OF INTEREST in scholastics, the truth was I just hated school with a passion. I hated the classes, which, due to my severe attention deficit, I couldn't keep up with to save my life. I hated the rigidity and the structure, and I really did not relish the whole social aspect of it all.

In fact, by that point, everyone who knew me had come to accept that whatever my future held, traditional higher education was probably not it. Even my high school principal suggested I look for some alternative ("Isn't there some kind of trade school for . . . what it is you do?"). In his view, I had already missed so much school that I had entered the realm of lost causes at McCluer High School, and honestly, I'd already decided to give up the ghost and just drop out of school altogether.

This greatly freed up my schedule to gig even more, which was fortuitous, because somewhere around then, I left the Delrays and joined an extremely popular and much busier group called the Guild, a resourceful bunch that had a sweet thing going—and was closer to home to boot.

Literally a couple of miles from where most of the band lived in rural Illinois, there was an old ballroom that was still in limited operation for local private functions, weddings and such. And occasionally the place was booked for some of the Stax/Volt artists who came through the area. A faded but still beautiful old art deco structure, the Collinsville Park Ballroom was at one time a hoppin' whistle-stop gig for the big bands of the '30s. In the lobby, there still remained the original jewel box marquee and relics from a bygone era—old photos, yellow and faded, of Benny Goodman, Paul Whiteman, Jimmy and Tommy Dorsey—like a portal back to its glory days.

The building was owned by an old guy named Al (not a wrestling champ) who was happy to make his money selling the booze, letting the band keep the door, which turned out to be pretty lucrative. People would drive in from as far as a hundred miles away in any direction—crowds of four hundred, five hundred, or more. Every Thursday night they would pack the place to hear this amazing cover band, known for their "vocalese" prowess on medleys of Beach Boys, Chicago, and Four Seasons hits.

The Guild were dazzling in their ability to meticulously re-create those records live. One of our vocalists, Denny Henson, handled all the high male falsetto parts—Frankie Lymon, Frankie Valli, and a pretty damn convincing Carl and Brian Wilson. I mean to tell ya: when we did "Good Vibrations," it sounded *exactly* like the record—even with our poor man's vocal imitation of a theremin (that electronic, high-pitched "sci-fi" sound). In our efforts to replicate these records live, we all had to be versatile instrumentally, so while I had up to this point been primarily a vocalist in bands, now with the Guild I was enlisted to play guitar as well as keyboards as needed.

—

THE GUILD'S RESIDENCY AT THE COLLINSVILLE PARK BALLROOM HELPED PUT THE VENUE back on the map. It gained the attention of the twenty-one-and-over crowd, and for the band, that place was a cash cow. We made enough on those Thursday night gigs that we didn't need to work the rest of the week, but we did anyway—most weekends playing every college hot spot we could find within a five-hundred-mile radius.

And the hectic schedule made downtime a most valuable commodity. Some of the band members lived in a couple of lakeside cabins where every week, after our ballroom gig, there'd be the "Thursday night open house" with lots of beer and as many people—especially girls—as we could invite.

When I was with the Sheratons, I was still underage and mindful of the fact that I was allowed to play most of those club gigs only if I was in the company of an adult—which most of the guys in the band were—and, of course, refrained from alcohol.

Now, with the Guild, it seemed like the door was opening to being a genuinely free "adult." And it wasn't long before I started to experiment, and soon enough, "more" always seemed better. If I finished a beer, I'd be sure to grab another one. If there was a bottle being passed around, I'd take a swig.

And then there was pot. It was the late '60s and pot was becoming a much more common part of the social scene. While I had tried it a few times before, my relationship with the stuff was about to become more of a daily ritual. In the warmer weather, we'd barbecue, play some horseshoes, and smoke some pot. In the colder months, we'd smoke pot, maybe play a quick round of ice hockey on the pond, go back to the cabin to warm up, listen to records, and . . . smoke more pot.

A lot of people would argue that marijuana is not addictive. If that's true, I for one definitely broke that mold. I really took to it. It wasn't long before I became one of those people who, when I wasn't smoking pot, was always thinking about smoking pot and—it goes without saying—always looking for it. I thought it improved my playing and creativity, enhancing my ability to write a great song articulating some deep and complex insight . . . or to just stare at an ant walking across the table. Honestly, I think it all came down to my growing need to escape, to disengage.

The truth was I wasn't comfortable in my own skin, especially in social situations. It seemed my subconscious thinking was: "If you got to know me, you'd be disappointed"—the belief system that had been quietly gnawing at me my whole life, a relentless feeling of being "less than."

One of my earliest memories of smoking some really good weed was at one of those lake-house parties. I remember standing behind a girl, mesmerized by her exceptionally beautiful long black hair, when, in my catatonic state, I noticed my hand, as if it belonged to someone else, slowly reaching out to touch her lovely mane. Before the situation could become any creepier, thankfully she turned around to the sight of me quickly retracting my hand, followed by my stumbling attempt to make conversation.

—

AT THE TIME, DRUGS SEEMED TO BE THE ANSWER TO MY LACK OF CONFIDENCE AND CON-stant state of anxiety. They seemed to fill that huge hole and, at least for the time being, served to save my sanity. I was unaware of how, in fact, they only heightened these underlying negative mindsets. I didn't realize then that drugs and alcohol would ultimately become the bigger problem. In hindsight, I think I knew subconsciously I had a propensity for substance abuse, even that far back. There may have been some even earlier clues.

When I was about four, I came down with what used to be called "the croup." My mother came home from the drugstore with a bottle of Cheracol cough syrup for children, which tasted like candy but contained codeine. She had just given me the allotted tablespoonful when the phone rang, and she set the bottle of cough syrup on the ironing board and proceeded to spend the next hour or so chatting on the phone.

With my mom in the next room, arms waving in animated conversation, I glanced over at the bottle and saw an opportunity for an extra little swig of this heavenly-tasting stuff. "I'll just grab one more gulp—no one'll be the wiser."

Well, even at four years old, I was about to exhibit the alcoholic behavior that bears the axiom "One's too many, a thousand's not enough!" Next thing I knew, the bottle was empty. I went and sat in the living room, waiting for my mom's wrath. It wasn't long before, through my groggy stupor, I heard her scream, "Michael! My God, did you drink this whole thing?!" I wound up in the emergency room having my stomach pumped, but . . . surely feeling no pain.

—

SO, CLEARLY, I ALREADY HAD A NATURAL PREDILECTION FOR ENJOYING TOO MUCH OF A good thing, and when I was playing with the Guild, it didn't help that I was now making stupid money. I was sixteen, still living at home. My mom had been working ten-hour days as long as I could remember, struggling to just feed us. Even with Kathy and me as teenagers bringing in what we could to help, for a long time it was still tough just to keep the house and stay afloat. But now I was regularly making upward of $350 a week—cash! A couple thousand bucks in today's money, which seemed like a fortune to us back then. Even after taking out some for my few essentials—gas, food, clothes, musical gear, and family car maintenance—I was still able to give my mother most of my weekly earnings. And with that, I bought my freedom. In exchange for my greater financial contribution, my parents adopted their own version of "don't ask, don't tell": the less my mother had to ask my father for money, the less he was inclined to tell her his opinion about anything.

I don't remember why exactly I parted ways with the Guild. I somehow felt like I wasn't a good match for the group and was already thinking about California pretty seriously—once again, one foot out the door.

So Delrays buddy Russ Bono and I, along with my two original bandmates from the Majestics—Pat Molloy and Bob Bortz—reunited, forming a band called the Blue.

We found our way into the stable of artists being booked by the Blytham Ltd. agency, based in Champaign-Urbana, and we were soon hitting the road for college towns in the greater Midwest: northern Illinois, Indiana, and even some teen clubs in Wisconsin, where the beer-drinking age was eighteen. We found a niche in the nightclubs and discotheques that seemingly couldn't get enough of our goofy, eclectic song list.

Purposely genre-less, we were just having fun at this point, playing music to dance to, with no discernible intention of developing a professional persona as a group. We weren't trying to be hip. Our set list was an unapologetic indulgence of our favorite pop music—from Ray Charles to the Ronettes to Dion and the Belmonts. From the Animals to Bobby Darin to Dionne Warwick. We were no jam band. Fats Domino, Del Shannon, Sly Stone, the Everly Brothers, and every obscure Motown and Stax/Volt song we could find—the less well-known, the better. Such was our quiet rebellion.

In some ways, I think it was a backlash to all the time we spent trying to keep up with the musical trends. We kinda didn't care about that anymore. If we could just roll on to the next gig in our Econoline van with just enough room for our gear and the four of us and our roadie—even if one of us had to lie across the equipment in back for the hundred or so miles—we were happy just having low-overhead fun.

In our typical dysfunction—barreling down the highway, usually late for the gig, over the speed limit, with overdue registration or expired plates, possibly a taillight out—we were obvious prey for small-town speed traps where state troopers lay in wait. With usually little or no money between us, we'd plead our case, explaining that if we could just get to our gig, we'd then come back with the cash to pay our fines. Once in a while, some sympathetic trooper would agree to the deal—but it would require holding on to *one* of us till the others returned with the money. And so it was that our beleaguered, solitary roadie, Scott, would regularly become our human collateral, spending a day or two in some county jail awaiting our return. (Truth be known, he was good-natured about it, and frankly looked forward to his inmate perk of Big Macs and fries at the county's expense.)

One slightly more professional high point for us was the recording of a four-track demo at Golden Voice Recording Company, which was actually a one-man operation in a small cinder block structure in the middle of a cornfield in Pekin, Illinois. In addition to covers of Ray Charles's "I Don't Need No Doctor" and the Ronettes' "Be My Baby," we also recorded two original songs of mine: "God Knows I Love My Baby" and "Fools in Love."*

—

THESE WERE THE DAYS OF THE SUMMER OF LOVE AND WOODSTOCK, AND FOR A WHILE, everyone, it seems, was embracing the peace-and-love vibe. In May 1970, we were invited to play a Memorial Day weekend extravaganza near Heyworth, Illinois, billed as the "Incident at Kickapoo Creek." Depending on who you talk to, it was "just a good bunch of kids having fun" or "an absolute mess!"

Headlining the carnage were Canned Heat, B. B. King, Delaney & Bonnie & Friends (with fellow St. Louis native Bonnie Bramlett), and the Paul Butterfield Blues Band (featuring saxophonist David Sanborn, another St. Louis homeboy). Among the dozens of other acts on the bill was our band, the Blue, along with a lot of our college-bar-band buddies, such as REO Speedwagon, the One Eyed Jacks, and, as it happened, my friends the Guild.

---

* These were the famous "lost tapes" that my bandmates talked about for fifty-some-odd years, in our minds growing ever more mythic in status—until we heard them. During the writing of this book, my old friend John Baruck found the tapes while cleaning out his attic and made copies for us all. I have to say, listening to the recordings again, in spite of their obvious unpolished nature, was a wonderfully nostalgic trip back to that moment in time.

Treating it as one of our usual hit-and-run gigs, we didn't arrive till the last day. By contrast, my entrepreneurially inclined sister Kathy and her friend Sandy went up a couple days earlier with coolers filled with hundreds of sandwiches they had made, calculating that they would make a fortune selling them to the crowd of stoned and hungry revelers and, of course, more than pay for their trip.

Well, by the time the band and I pulled in, we found Kathy and Sandy backstage, both tripping pretty good, as they—along with just about everyone else there—had been unwittingly dosed. (There was always some character dropping acid into the watercooler or other people's drinks at these types of events.) The two of them were grinning like Cheshire cats as they explained how, in the spirit of peace and love, they'd decided to just give all the sandwiches away. So much for entrepreneurial spirit.

I soon discovered that somewhere over the course of that day, not long before we were set to go onstage, I had been dosed too. I don't remember much from that point on, just the physical acid rush I felt as we started to play, and vague, random images of the sea of humanity before us—certainly the largest audience I had ever played for.

It wasn't till around noon the next day—when I had sufficiently come down and found myself standing naked up to my waist in Kickapoo Creek, playing Frisbee with some other naked people I didn't know—that I realized the festival was over. The stage was being torn down and the crowds were gone, nothing left but trash as far as the eye could see. I was able to spot my clothes lying on the creek bank (thank God!), and as I slowly dressed myself, I began to discover how badly sunburned and dehydrated I was. So when I saw a warm, open Coca-Cola next to my clothes, I figured it must have been mine at some point and took a swig, only to discover that a huge bee had taken up residence in the can. I managed to spit it out, but not before the thing stung my upper lip—from the inside. With the band having oil-spotted me the day before,* I proceeded to hitchhike the four hours or so back to Ferguson—disoriented, fat-lipped, and severely sunburned in some rather unfortunate places.

—

THIS EMERGING LIFESTYLE THAT I SHARED WITH MY FRIENDS MEANT BEING ON THE ROAD a lot, and that suited me just fine. My life was, after all—as it had already been for the previous five or six years—entirely and solely about playing music.

Still, even with this single-minded focus, I was well aware that fate might be the deciding factor in what lay ahead. The Vietnam War was raging by now, and while I had no interest in participating, being a bar musician was not exactly a legitimate draft deferment. So I tried to take it one day at a time. However, between my quietly escalating substance abuse, penchant for self-destruction, and reasonably good chance of getting drafted, I was kind of in a race with the devil.

And then fate did indeed intervene.

---

* When you've lingered too long at a pit stop, you might emerge to find the band and vehicle gone, leaving nothing but an oil spot on the pavement. Hence the term "oil-spotting." (It was also an indelicate means by which certain band members were fired.)

CHAPTER 7

LA CALLS

The Blue regularly performed at a club in downtown Champaign called Chances R, which had always been ground zero for the local college crowd. A ’60s hot spot for hippies and jocks that had only recently ceased to employ dancing go-go girls, it had morphed into being a more notably hip music venue.

A local musician friend, Barry “Foz” Fasman, had sent—unsolicited—that demo tape we made (“God Knows I Love My Baby” / “Fools in Love”) to a successful LA record producer he knew named Rick Jarrard. Rick had produced such groundbreaking albums as Jefferson Airplane’s *Surrealistic Pillow*, Harry Nilsson’s *Aerial Ballet*, and José Feliciano’s *Feliciano!* (which included the hit single “Light My Fire”). As he happened to have grown up on a farm near Champaign, he had his brother Ray Armstrong come down to catch one of our sets. (Why the different last names? I know not.) Well, Ray came down to see us and was evidently impressed enough to suggest his producer brother come down to hear us while home visiting the family for Christmas. Rick did come by and apparently liked my voice.

When I first started singing with bands at fourteen, besides being infatuated with Ray Charles—his sound, his soulfulness—I was trying my darndest to sound like Mitch Ryder and James Brown, really any of the great screamers of the time. However, after a lot of gigging in smoke-filled clubs, I found that I started to lose my voice more often. In my efforts to emulate these guys, I was doing more damage than anything else, and ultimately, I had to find a way to develop a range where I could sing with some passion and not strain my vocal cords quite so much. I started to learn that the voice is a malleable instrument that you negotiate with along the way, and I developed a kind of "fifth gear" half-voice that allowed me to sing with some power in the upper ranges. So by the late '60s, I had already begun to sing a bit more like the way I do today.

—

UPON HEARING MORE OF MY ORIGINAL MATERIAL—MOSTLY BALLADS AND MIDDLE-OF-the-road pop ditties, which came in closer to Gary Puckett and the Union Gap than the Rolling Stones or John Mayall—Rick presented me with the idea of signing with his newly formed independent production company. The plan was he'd shop a deal with a major label like RCA, with whom he had a long-standing relationship, which would hopefully result in my coming out to California to make a record. Pretty exciting stuff!

My first concern, however, was the dilemma this presented regarding my band, as the offer obviously didn't include them. But in my naive way of thinking, I figured, "Hey, if I get lucky enough to make an album with a major label like RCA, well, who knows . . . Maybe by the time I get back to St. Louis, I'll already be on the radio, at which point I'll just scoop up the band, and, full sail, we'll be on our way!"

I had no real experience with contracts or deals or anything like this, but our band did have Blytham Ltd., our booking agency, right there in Champaign, the three principals of which were: Bob Nutt, who started the company; John Baruck (later the manager of Journey and REO Speedwagon); and a young guy from the small neighboring town of Danville, Illinois, by the name of Irving Azoff.

Irving was nineteen when he started at the company, and he already displayed the great promise and killer instinct that only a few years later would define him as one of the dominant players in the music industry, managing such artists as the Eagles, Dan Fogelberg,

Steely Dan, Jimmy Buffett, and Joe Walsh. As Bob Nutt put it: "I hired Irving because I was afraid not to."

By the time we worked with him, Irving was already a partner at the agency, and he was fantastically persuasive. (How persuasive? Put it this way: I not only played his younger brother Ronnie's bar mitzvah in 1969 but also Ronnie's wedding a decade later.)

I took the contract Rick and his team offered me and ran it by Irving, which was probably RCA's biggest fear. Those guys seemed to sense that Irving's artist-centric philosophy was not in their best interest, so they actively tried to discourage me from sharing the contract with him. But I did, and Irving's advice was "Don't sign it. You're gonna get where you need to go. Don't rush into this—because it's not a good deal."

But I felt I had to take the deal—who knew if I'd ever get this chance again?

Irving understood, but reiterated, "Whatever you do, don't turn over your publishing to these guys. You keep that. That belongs to you and your heirs forever."

Per his advice, I did make a feeble attempt to separate that from the recording contract and retain ownership, or at least to make a separate publishing deal. I remember telling one of the executives at RCA, "If it's okay, I'd rather leave my publishing out of the deal." To which he replied, "Oh, no, we can't do that. We can't legally put out your album unless we have the publishing." Which I suspected wasn't true, but I didn't really understand what I was giving away. Thus furthering my education in the music business.

—

AS UNPREPARED AS I MIGHT HAVE BEEN, I THINK SUBCONSCIOUSLY I WAS DRIVEN BY A much more powerful motivation: something like guilt. I think I still believed that aside from my own ambitions, I might also prove something to my dad. Despite his disapproval of my intense, singular focus, and his frequently expressed fear that I might be headed for the disappointment of not "making it," I still felt I owed it to him somehow to live out this dream. I still believed somewhere down deep that my success was something I could share with him, that I might finally get his approval with this endeavor in a way that nothing else would. That it might somehow be the culmination of that bond we formed years earlier through music.

As for my mom, she was totally on board with me going off to become a "radio star," maybe even more determined than I was. At this point in her life, California represented the promised land. The plan, as she often made clear, was that I would someday be successful enough to move her and my sisters out to the West Coast with me and, in the bargain, allow her to leave all her disappointments behind—a failed marriage and the hardships of raising three kids on her own. And I understood that; I think all of us were trying to leave some kind of broken existence behind us. Whatever traits I inherited from my mom, the one that may have best served me was her stubbornness, her never quite taking no for an answer. In my haphazard pursuit of a career, sometimes the only thing that sustained me against continual setbacks and storms of self-doubt may have been that determination I got from her.

If nothing else, I owed my mom for keeping my shoddy school attendance our secret, not to mention her unconditional love in spite of my less-than-stellar track record as a person. I felt I had to honor her desperate need to believe that my talent would take care of us all someday.

—

AND SO IT WAS, WITH SOMETHING CLOSE ENOUGH TO MY PARENTS' BLESSING, THAT I would go off into the abyss of an uncertain future. And after all, what choice did they have, really? It wasn't like I was turning my back on some other promising career. I'd shown absolutely no aptitude for anything else. I certainly didn't have the grades or the financial means for college, with its potential military deferment. If anything, I think my dad viewed the possibility of me getting drafted as the most promising of all my prospects at this point. Before I left, I shared with him my concern that all my plans could go up in smoke if I got drafted, to which his response was short and sweet: "Well, if so, it's sure to make a man outta ya." I'm sure he meant that to be encouraging.

So, in August 1970, before what would have been my senior year in high school, I happily accepted the plane ticket RCA sent me—and the $3,000 advance, most of which I gave my mom to keep the house running in the absence of my gig income—and packed up for California. And by "packed up," I mean some jeans, T-shirts, underwear, socks, a toothbrush, and the Frye boots I was wearing at the time. That was it.

Before I got on the plane, I called a couple of people to say goodbye, and when one of my friends asked, "So, when are you gonna be back?" it was only then that it hit me. "Um . . . I don't know that I am coming back." I hadn't thought it through that far. I could see only what was immediately in front of me: I was gonna get on that plane and go to California to make a record.

Beyond that, I had no clue.

CHAPTER 8

CALIFORNIA DREAMS AND A COUPLE OF NIGHTMARES

I had a lot to ponder on that night flight to LA. I was excited, filled with anticipation for a chance to prove myself, but professional aspirations aside, it seemed like the wreckage in my personal life was more than enough incentive to get away.

After I finally got over Sue, it wasn't long before I rebounded and sought the comfort and refuge of a lovely young girl, a beautician named Maryanne, who I believed loved me just as I was. But until I had something to show for myself in this life, I didn't believe the person I was deserved that. In my subconscious but inevitable way, I was setting the stage for yet another untidy ending.

That was kind of my thing. Though I couldn't see it clearly then, this was actually the messy nexus of my ambition and my emotional insecurities; I was that guy whose overblown ego was in a pitched battle with his inferiority complex. I feared that allowing myself to consider other people's feelings too much might get in my way, might make me blink at the wrong time. Even as a little kid, I had the idea that no one knew what was best for me but me. No one could do for me what I might be able to do for myself—if I just stayed detached enough to move at will, quickly and unencumbered. And so leaving town seemed the only option for someone like me.

Then came the announcement: "We're beginning our descent into the Los Angeles area." There it was, rolling beneath me. More lights than I had ever seen in one place at one time. (The New York skyline had been pretty impressive too, but that was a daytime flight; it didn't look like this.) LA at night! As far as the eye could see.

I was met at the airport by Rick Jarrard's brother Ray, and on our way to his apartment, where I was going to be staying, we took a detour to swing by the Strip. That legendary section of Sunset Boulevard back then was populated by an edgy confederacy of strays, which made for great people-watching: runaway flower children, tourists, and no shortage of radiant, mini-skirted California girls. We cruised along with the other gawkers in their souped-up muscle cars and lowriders—those chariots of Mexican American culture showing off their hydraulics and musical car horns. It was unlike anything I'd ever experienced back in the Midwest.

I remember passing the Whisky a Go Go and P.J.'s, legendary venues that I recognized from the covers of live albums recorded there by Johnny Rivers and Trini Lopez. I recall hearing some music that I faintly recognized at first, until I looked up at the nightclub marquee: "Moby Grape—One Night Only." It seemed so surreal and wonderful, this magical place where all my daydreams actually lived! I was nothing short of mesmerized by the giant billboards heralding forthcoming album and movie releases and couldn't help but fantasize about seeing my own album release announced on one of those billboards someday.

At that moment, Ferguson felt a million miles away.

—

RAY WAS NOT ONLY NOW MY ROOMMATE, BUT HE ALSO WORKED FOR HIS BROTHER RICK, so we spent a lot of time together. Ray's life, to my eyes, seemed really structured. For starters, he was ex-military, very neat, and showered first thing every morning. I wasn't and didn't. I woke up late and wore the same clothes as long into the week as I thought I could get away with.

That first morning Ray left a note for me: "Meeting with Rick. We'll meet back at the apartment around noon to start looking at songs and plans for the week ahead." So I hit Reseda Boulevard on foot, looking to grab some food, and found a quaint little adobe Mexican food stand called Taco Bell. (They didn't have those in Missouri, so I assumed this was the one and only.)

As I ate my tacos, I could barely make out the base of the foothills through the haze and smog (another thing we didn't have in Missouri). I felt a sense of adventure as I romanticized being in the shadow of what I thought were the mountains of California, eating what I also thought was authentic Mexican cuisine. It wasn't until the seasonal rains cleared the air later that year that I even saw the San Gabriel Mountains surrounding the San Fernando Valley. At least by then I'd realized that there was a Taco Bell on virtually every corner.

—

MY FIRST DAY OF RECORDING FOR THE LABEL WAS AT ITS STUDIOS BACK DOWN IN Hollywood on Ivar Avenue and Sunset Boulevard. This was before the days of private designer lounges in studios. The lounge at RCA was just a small indentation off the entrance lobby, with two vending machines: one for soft drinks and the other for coffee, with separate buttons dispensing cream and sugar. (That was new to me.)

LA proved full of surprises at every turn. During a break on my first day there, I went to get a cup of coffee, and as I approached the machine, a tall, slender, gray-haired man had his back to me while he retrieved his coffee. Appearing less than enthused with the tepid, lumpy concoction he held in his hand, he said, "Hmm . . . this should be interesting." I thought, "Why does that voice sound so familiar?" While stirring his coffee, he turned around and gave a cordial smile. Oh my God, it was Gregory Peck! We chatted a bit, and he shared that he was there recording some dialogue, auditioning for the New York stage production of *Man of La Mancha*. I was struck by how genuinely nice he was. I remember thinking, "If my mother were here, she'd probably be offering him a baloney sandwich by now." Gregory Peck and I wished each other luck and returned to our respective studios. Welcome to Hollywood.

—

CHIEF AMONG HIS MANY SKILLS AS A RECORD PRODUCER, RICK JARRARD HAD A PARTICUlarly discerning ear for songs. Whether it was reimagining older, even somewhat familiar songs with a surprising choice of artist or finding new, as yet undiscovered material, he had a certain knack for pairing the right material with the right artist—a valuable skill to hone if you're in the business of producing records.

If proof were needed, I would point out the track he selected for me to record on day one: an impressive demo he had gotten from the publisher Dick James Music in London, a song by a relatively unknown British songwriting team: Elton John and Bernie Taupin. It was musically very much in the gospel tradition, which appealed to me, and had very clever lyrics, using current events of the time as spiritual metaphor. The song was "Take Me to the Pilot." Not a bad first at bat. Of course, it would soon be a monster hit for Elton John, but this was months before his debut album was released, and as it turns out, the demo was in fact the actual track from the album—a point the publisher failed to mention. So that took care of any designs we may have had for that particular song, but hearing my demo of it sealed the deal with RCA's A&R department. I officially had a recording contract.

—

IT WAS SUBSEQUENTLY DECIDED THAT WE'D DO AN ENTIRE ALBUM OF MY ORIGINAL songs—it having already been negotiated that my publishing would be split between Rick Jarrard Productions and RCA's publishing arm. I felt a bit fleeced at the time, but looking back, given the quality of my compositions, they quite possibly got the short end of that stick.

At eighteen, as a writer, I was particularly inspired by songs like Tom Jones's "It's Not Unusual" (written by Gordon Mills and Les Reed) and two great Burt Bacharach–Hal David tunes, "Reach Out for Me" and "Walk On By"—all songs that had chord progressions, voicings, and rhythmic variations more sophisticated than what was usually found in most pop music of the time. Bacharach and David were such prolific and monumental composers. I consider them right up there with Richard Rodgers and Oscar Hammerstein, George and Ira Gershwin—pillars of what I think of as "classical" American music. My songwriting back then was, at best, a poor man's attempt to emulate those guys.

Very often, when I'd start sketching out a song, sitting with a guitar or at the piano, I wouldn't have any words in mind at all or even an idea of what the song was about, just a random group of phonetically comfortable words. Sometimes they weren't even words, just *sounds* I'd make over a fixed chord progression, while fleshing out some vague melodic ideas—moving up a third, down a third, etc.—till I found the right melody with which to build the different sections of the song (the verse, chorus, bridge). Then I'd listen back on my black-plastic Panasonic cassette player and hope to get clues from my mumblings as to what words might work. But lyrics would often start off as just filler for me. My priority would be what phonetics worked well, and I'd figure out how to make sense of them later.

—

IF MY WRITING LEFT MUCH TO BE DESIRED AT THIS POINT, RICK JARRARD, AT LEAST, brought a lot of expertise to making the album. Not much expense was spared on this project. Besides the beautiful, lush orchestrations on every track—written by the very talented Perry Botkin Jr.—the rhythm section Rick assembled, I would soon come to learn, was an impressive group: Ron Tutt on drums, Jerry Scheff on bass, and James Burton on guitar. Collectively they were known as the TCB Band and had played with Elvis during his Las Vegas residency. (You can see them featured on the *Live in Las Vegas* special he recorded there.) They were also part of the expanding A-list of LA session musicians stemming from the original Wrecking Crew, who played on virtually every record coming out of LA in the '60s produced by Phil Spector, Bob Crewe, Al De Lory, or Brian Wilson. From the Beach Boys, the Ronettes, Sonny and Cher, Glen Campbell, and the Mamas and the Papas to the Monkees and Boyce and Hart—these were the guys you heard playing on those records.

Throughout the recording of my album, the lineup of musicians would vary depending on who was in town. Many of the guys were still splitting their time between doing sessions and playing network variety TV shows or the primo live touring gigs with the likes of Elvis or Neil Diamond. So here's me, eighteen years old, just having rolled into town, playing piano on recording sessions with icons like Hal Blaine, Max Bennett, John Guerin, Louie Shelton, Dean Parks, and Al Jackson Jr., singing with vocalists like Clydie King, Gloria Jones, and Kim Carnes.

In my effort to rise to the occasion, I may have been a little overly enthusiastic. It was drummer Ron Tutt who gently made the point that relaxing a little bit might help more than anything: "Hey, Mike, it's not like the first one to get to the chorus gets a prize." I was the proverbial bull in the china shop, or, as Randy Newman once described his own experience upon singing backgrounds with the Eagles, I was "the fat kid jumping in the pool and splashing everyone who was having fun up till then."

We finished recording the album around Christmastime 1970, and I was also working during that time as a pianist on recording sessions for some of Rick's other artists, like David Cassidy and Jack Jones, which was at once thrilling and terrifying. I knew there was absolutely no reason for me to be playing on any of those sessions (not even my own) other than the fact that Rick seemed to have some confidence in me and also perhaps felt somewhat responsible for helping me stay alive while living in LA. He generously paid me union scale on all the dates, which allowed me to join Local 47 and eventually helped me get a decent car through its credit union. (David Cassidy and Jack Jones, by the way, both recorded a couple of my early compositions, which only seems all the more remarkable in hindsight.)

Were it not for the learning environment Rick Jarrard Productions afforded me, there's a good chance I would never have gotten the studio experience that turned out to be so strategic going forward. It was where I first developed any real piano chops. In light of my challenged capacity for rudimentary learning, this situation worked for me, as I was always someone who learned better on the job.

—

IN FURTHER INTEREST OF KEEPING ME FISCALLY AFLOAT, RAY AND RICK AT ONE POINT introduced me to an ad agency executive from Chicago whose firm, J. Walter Thompson—a giant in advertising—handled the Lavoris mouthwash account. Being a fan of Rick's work, he had approached Rick to produce the music for a Lavoris commercial.

It was forward-thinking for the time, really, as the jingle industry and the pop record business were virtually two different worlds back then. Yes, Barry Manilow had famously found great success writing commercial jingles prior to breaking out as a recording artist, and some artists, like Herb Alpert, Patti Austin, and Paul Williams, had a foot in both worlds. But still, it was rare. I'm sure the guy envisioned one of Rick's more iconic artists, like Harry Nilsson or José Feliciano, singing in his Lavoris commercial. But . . . he got me.

When Rick asked me to write the music for and sing the jingle, I was thrilled to get the gig, of course, but less thrilled with the lyrics they gave me to work with. And I told the ad exec as much.

"Are they kidding with these words?"

To which he responded, "Yeah, I know. They're god-awful!"

Well, I came to find out later that he had actually written them himself. I didn't know whether to feel bad for having been so brutally honest or feel duped—because it wasn't until we were all on board that those lyrics were sprung on us. But that's what the agency had signed off on. So I sat down to the business of writing a short jingle. It's sixty seconds—how hard could it be?

Well, then they gave me a timing grid, something I had never heard of. It was basically a sheet breaking down—to fractions of a second—all the cues that needed to be met. You wouldn't think a sixty-second spot could have too many, but there were enough pages of them that I actually resorted to reading Earle Hagen's book on film scoring.

We recorded the music, and the finished commercial made it to national television. It ran for a few months, and I made about $3,000 in AFTRA royalties, which, given my low-rent lifestyle, put me in the black for the rest of that year.

As for the lyrics, I'll let you be the judge: "Get Lavoris, with pucker power! Put some excitement in your mouth!" Practically R-rated for 1970. And hands down the hardest lyrics I've ever had to set to music.

—

IN THE MEANTIME, LIFE WAS GOOD. I WAS YOUNG, SINGLE, AND LIVING ON MY OWN IN California. Sometimes flush, sometimes broke—nothing new about that to me. But being away from my family was a new kind of existence for me—and very liberating. I was just beginning to find out who I was by myself, maybe for the first time, which in itself was cathartic.

Still, there was no shortage of opportunities to get into trouble. Ray and I, when we weren't working, were just two young guys in pursuit of the next party. LA was a heightened experience in many ways—good and bad—and along the way, there were parties on private beaches with incredibly spoiled, rich twentysomethings who were roughly my age but lived lives so vastly different from what I knew in Ferguson. There were a couple of brief affairs with "older women" in their late twenties—studio receptionists and secretaries of record execs, women who were much more worldly than myself; I'm not sure exactly what they got out of the deal. But for this nineteen-year-old, it was certainly a welcome learning curve.

—

RAY AND I ALSO HAD A FRIEND BACK THEN NAMED JIM HILTON, WHO HAD ONE OF THOSE random strokes of luck that are the stuff of music business legend. As the story was told to me, Jim had been working in a recording studio as a staff technician/engineer, which turned out to be the right place at the right time.

After the not-uncommon drama played out, in which the band he was recording fired their producer, it fell to Jim to mix the last remaining track: a song called "In-A-Gadda-Da-Vida," a seventeen-minute-long ditty by Iron Butterfly that became one of the biggest hits of the decade. And as a result, Jim was awarded a credit as producer on the single and a sweet royalty.

So by the time we met him, he was living in a pricey bachelor pad with a fancy, fully stocked bar and an overheated swimming pool, which, for us, became party central. Jim had it all, including a fantastic pot connection. Even so, and notwithstanding his signature silk bathrobe and ascot that he liked to wear at his *soirees*, Jim, as far as I could tell, was just a really nice guy who was shy around women, and Ray would just tease him mercilessly.

Being the somewhat hapless bachelors, Ray and I would occasionally wind up with houseguests from hell. There was one crazy duo from some desert truck-stop strip club that Ray had met in his previous travels, who came to Cali to overstay their welcome at our apartment. We weren't exactly heartbroken when they discovered the greener pastures of our friend Jim's bachelor pad, with the private swimming pool where they could while away the hours nude sunbathing. That situation suited them just fine, as it turns out, and of course Jim thought he'd died and gone to heaven. Seizing our chance to escape, we left soon after introducing them that first night, as an inebriated Jim waved goodbye, a splashing martini in hand, and gave us a gleeful thumbs-up while dancing off with his two newfound friends. Ray and I figured: what Jim doesn't know yet hopefully won't kill him.

Well, after two weeks of what must've seemed like a booze-fueled skinny-dipping marathon, we heard that Jim finally encouraged them to move on. When we went to check on him, he looked like a frightened house cat: still alive, but certainly the worse for wear.

Like I said, some of it was good, some of it . . . not so much. But it was freedom, and that felt good.

—

OBVIOUSLY, I WASN'T OVERLY HOMESICK. BUT HOME WAS APPARENTLY MISSING ME. MY mother did a pretty good job of reminding me that my leaving had financial consequences for them, and as soon as I was on my feet a little, they would still need my help. My immediate and extended family had always survived by communal effort. It was what we were used to and, for most of my adolescence, the only way we could manage. Our grandmothers raised us while our mothers worked; it was all we knew.

Personally, I would have been happy to just send money home; I was enjoying my independence. But given my mom's fervent wish to someday move to California, and after all her hard work and sacrifice, who was I to not help make at least one of her dreams come true? So, while Rick and RCA engineer Rick Ruggieri were busy mixing and finishing the album we had made, I bought a ticket home for the holidays to start the process of my family's migration west, driving my sister's car from St. Louis back to California—with my dear old grandmother Genevieve riding shotgun. Having been a city girl most of her life, she was so excited about making the trip out west. We weren't even out of Missouri when, upon seeing a herd of dairy cows, she exclaimed, "Oh, look—buffalo!"

My sister Kathy flew out later—for free, a perk of working for Ozark Air Lines at the time—and together we found a house that could hold everyone. We put down a deposit, along with first and last months' rent, on a newly built two-story California contemporary house—nicer than anywhere we'd lived up to that point in St. Louis. It was to be home for me, my mother, my two sisters, and my grandmother. Kind of like *The Beverly Hillbillies*—without their millions.

—

UPON RETURNING TO LA, I GOT TO HEAR THE FINISHED MIX OF THE RECORD FOR THE FIRST time—and it was thrilling! It wasn't but a month later that I held a pressed vinyl single in my hands, a rerecording of the simple demo Rick first heard, the one I recorded with the Blue out in the Illinois cornfield. With this highly polished Motown-esque production, lushly orchestrated with brass, strings, and female background singers, it was a different animal. To be honest, at the time I thought it might have even lost some of its original charm, now buried under this wall of sound. But seeing my name on a major record company's label was a transcendent experience:

RCA RECORDS

"God Knows (I Love My Baby)"

Writer—Mike McDonald

Artist—Mike McDonald

Wow! What next? Spins on the radio? Climbing chart positions? I even heard a test market spin on a Top Forty station out of San Diego before I had even submitted the album art. The DJ did the big buildup over the intro and everything—just like I'd always fantasized. It was all working out beautifully!

Until later that week, when the album was scrapped and I was dropped from the label. Having hung so much of my future on this project, it was a gut punch for sure. It seemed no one else was nearly as excited about the project as I was. My quickly rising star came crashing down to earth.

But Rick still believed in me and did his level best to convince me this was just a bump in the road. And though I appreciated his optimism, I saw other examples of where that road could lead, ones that hit a little closer to home for me.

One night, Rick and I had dinner on the Sunset Strip with John Rosica, who at the time was head of promotion at Bell Records. Afterward, as we were walking to our car, a pathetic figure emerged from under a stairwell, startling us as we passed by. Stumbling and distraught, he appeared to have been severely beaten up, covered with cuts and abrasions, his face all swollen, nose broken, eyes blackened, and his shirt bloodstained.

The guy asked John for a few bucks, reporting he'd been mugged, his wallet and money taken from him, but John's expression told a different story. As we walked away, he explained that he knew the guy, who had not long before been a very well-respected musician and even played with Buffalo Springfield on their rise to great success, but was now on the street, a hopeless addict, sleeping under the stairwell there in the parking lot.

I'd be lying if I said that didn't jolt me a bit. I found myself, in that moment, trying to reconcile my own increasing dependence on alcohol and weed, wondering just how far away I was from this guy's experience, if we all might not be a little closer to falling through the cracks than we think. My dad's suggestion of a plan B suddenly didn't seem like the craziest idea.

—

BUT IT WOULD ALL DROP ON MY HEAD LIKE A TON OF BRICKS—LITERALLY—A COUPLE OF weeks later when the biggest earthquake in fifty years hit the San Fernando Valley. While I was out surveying the damage around us, my sister Kathy made the instantaneous decision to go back to St. Louis and was already starting to pack by the time I got home. I tried to talk her down, but with each aftershock she was only more convinced it was time to leave LA.

My instinct was to stay, but the reality was RCA had dropped me and I was out of money. It had taken all we had, collectively, to set up the family's move to California. As for a plan B? Nada. There was none. My dad was already on a flight to LA to help drive us all back to St. Louis. Believe me, if I'd had any options, I'd have used them. The thought of returning to Ferguson with my tail between my legs was the last thing my already shaky self-esteem needed at this point in my life.

My dad, the ex-Marine, was convinced that this normally three-day drive should take no more than two, with the three of us driving in shifts: one drove while the other two slept sitting up in the moving car—for two thousand miles.

As long as the drive was, it felt even longer because, though he didn't come right out and say it, I was only too sure, the whole way back, my father was thinking, "I hope you're done with this bullshit."

CHAPTER 9

ONE HIT SHY OF A ONE-HIT WONDER

I'd left for California on the tailwind of a great promise to find my fortune, and now I returned home with nothing to show for it.

I did finally take my father's advice to go down to take the dreaded GED High School Equivalency Exam—more for his peace of mind than my own—and he was more than happy to make that appointment for me. As far as difficulty and aptitude level, the test was something a moderately clever chimpanzee would be hard-pressed to fail.

For a while, that was the most productive thing I'd accomplished since being back. Truthfully, it wouldn't have been a stretch for me to have just stayed on in St. Louis; I'd always loved the place and the guys I'd grown up playing music with. In fact, I did get together with some of my old bandmates in different fleeting configurations and work some one-off gigs. I even made some new alliances; my old friend Steve Scorfina introduced me to an amazingly talented singer-songwriter, Michael O'Hara, and his brother Leon (who also happened to be Chuck Berry's son-in-law). We did some gigs together with Michael's band Spoon River, playing some of his powerful, gospel-oriented original music.

But I was clearly out of the loop at this point. My sister was nice enough to lend me her car for the occasional gig, and on a good night I might make enough money to fill her tank with gas and maybe buy myself a couple of drinks, which was increasingly becoming my go-to in finding my comfort zone. Because, good friends aside, I never felt more like a square peg in a round hole. I felt exposed back home. In California, I was out and about in clubs and bars, hanging with people who really hadn't known me long and had no real stake in my actual well-being. But ironically, those had become the places and people with whom I'd grown more comfortable. Being back home in Ferguson, I felt under constant scrutiny and comfortable only with those who clearly shared my problem—like my buddy and fellow musician Dan, a bright, mildly mischievous individual whom I'd always admired for his intellect and offbeat humor. We began our friendship in high school along with a group of friends, some of whom I'd known since grade school, but we were all getting too old to hang out and run around Ferguson. All of us fancied ourselves on some path to the future, but we were actually busier getting stoned and losing traction.*

—

CALIFORNIA WAS, OF COURSE, STILL ON MY MIND, BUT I HAD NO REAL PLAN OR MEANS TO get back there—though that would change when I got a call from Rick Jarrard. He thought I should come back out, as he'd further developed his relationship with Bell Records and was hopeful I could sign a deal with them, and till then, he would throw some session work my way with a couple new artists he was developing for the label.

He mentioned that Ray was back east checking on the family farm and would be driving out to LA if I wanted to hitch a ride. As I was a little short on plane fare, this might have been my only shot to get back to the promised land. So after just a few months floundering

---

* It would be a few years before my friend Dan finally turned his life around, ultimately becoming quite successful in the field of drug and alcohol counseling and, to this day, a shining example for the rest of us.

in St. Louis, I took that ride back to California with Ray. We drove for three days straight, listening to whatever radio stations we could pick up, and somewhere in Oklahoma we found ourselves arguing over the merits of Bill Withers's new release "Ain't No Sunshine." (I for one thought it was a beautiful reinvention of traditional blues making it onto mainstream radio; however, the drum break refrain of "I know, I know, I know, I know . . ." was apparently lost on Ray.)

And it was on that drive west, in a coffee shop in Colorado just off Interstate 70, that I got another piece of impactful news.

It was the morning the military draft lottery was published, and I braced myself to see what fate had decided for me. With eyes toward another chance at a possible solo record and a second shot at finding work back on the West Coast, I couldn't bring myself to look at those lottery numbers printed in black and white right there in the *Denver Post*. I handed the newspaper to Ray and asked him to read it to me. This would be either my biggest moment of relief or just another one of those gut punches. Lo and behold, my birthday, February 12, drew #340—well beyond the numbers that would be called up for service that year. I was in the clear. But I had to have Ray read it to me three times before he finally put a finer point on it: "You're not goin'! Fuckin' relax!"

I just couldn't believe it. I'd already, on some level, made my peace with the possibility of being drafted. I certainly didn't want to go into the army, but it had been in the back of my mind for so long that I had come to accept the idea that my life could very possibly be interrupted, all my plans upended once again. After all, I was nineteen and healthy, and wouldn't it just be my luck? So many of my friends who opposed the war just as I did had stood steadfast by their conviction. Some had pulled all kinds of shenanigans to get 4-F status—taking LSD before reporting to the draft board, showing up for their physical in a dress—or had fled to Canada. But I knew that was not going to be my story. There was too much in my history that would not allow me to do that.

It wasn't that I was afraid to disagree with my dad on such hot-button political issues. Oddly enough, on this one we were in solidarity; he didn't support America's involvement in Southeast Asia either. But my lifelong respect for his service as a Marine seemed to overrule any chance that I wouldn't go if called. His example had made it clear to me early on that most of the men and women who laid down their lives in service of this country likely were pacifists at heart, and I can only assume I would have been like the many who, in spite of their ambivalence, would answer the call out of respect for those who'd gone before.

That being said, it was with enormous relief that I continued along with Ray as we made our way through Colorado, stopping off in the High Rockies at idyllic Estes Park, where he was to visit a couple of songwriters Rick was hoping to sign.

These two guys were real-life singing cowboys who, like most songwriters, made their living doing anything other than songwriting—a sad statistic but nonetheless true. One of the guys was a fast-draw performance artist who by night would dazzle onlookers in various saloons with his stories and Colt six-shooters; the other was a performing singer-songwriter a few evenings a week in the same bars he drank and played cards in by day. Both also worked on and off as hired hands on some of the large ranches up there.

The place was so beautiful, and it was easy to romanticize the whole lifestyle—so much so that if I had been alone on this trip and didn't have work waiting for me in LA, I might never have made it back down that mountain. I'd always loved the idea of living in nature. (The closest thing to a plan B that I ever remotely considered was answering one of those magazine ads saying "You Can Be a Forest Ranger.")

—

UPON MY RETURN TO CALIFORNIA, IT WASN'T LOST ON ME THAT I WAS LUCKY TO PIECE together this second chance, and I knew I had to put my shoulder into it a bit more this time. I was determined not to return to St. Louis until I had something to show for my efforts.

I gladly resumed working on recording sessions for some of Rick's other artists, among them a young ingenue singer-songwriter from New York named Amy Boersma. She had been slated to be produced by Brian Wilson for Brother Records (the Beach Boys' label)—a project eclipsed by Brian's deteriorating health and the label's subsequent turmoil. Rick had just signed her to Bell Records, and I was assigned the enviable task of rehearsing with Amy, playing piano and writing out chord charts for her songs in preparation for her upcoming recording dates.

Did I mention she was awfully pretty? I was infatuated from the moment I saw her. I distinctly remember she had this colorful, well-situated patch on the inseam of her jeans that I tried my best not to stare at. Plus, she had a boyfriend.

But more striking than anything was this angelic voice, distinguished by an intermittent sexy "break," a breathy quality that was a wonderful and unique part of her style. She even recorded one of my early tunes on those sessions, a song called "It Don't Matter Now,"* which wound up as the B-side of her first single release. (The A-side was a song called "We're Half Way Home" that she wrote with her sister, Sherry.)

The best part of those sessions, beyond getting to listen to Amy's gorgeous voice, was getting to know her, her sardonic sense of humor and infectious smile. It seemed the more she hurled her sarcasm my way, the more fond of her I grew.

After about a week of our preproduction rehearsals, we met with my friend and copyist Dave Bachaus at his house in Pasadena to finalize the charts. (As a copyist, his job was to make pretty all my chicken-scratch chart notations.) Driving home that night, still

---

* Alison Krauss would cover the song years later.

hardly knowing each other, I felt a growing attraction to Amy as we made small talk—"What a pretty view it is from the Pasadena hills all the way to Hollywood . . ."—all the while thinking, "Damn! I wish she didn't have a boyfriend." Sadly, as fate would have it, after her recording sessions, but for a few random encounters, we mostly lost touch with each other over the next few years.

In the coming months, my mom and sisters came back out to California. My younger sister Maureen enrolled and finished high school in Sunland-Tujunga, a small community north of the San Fernando Valley, while my sister Kathy and I once again secured a house for rent—not quite as nice as the last California house, but the rent was reasonable and it sufficed.

I wasn't there full time anyway, as I was working more and more in Hollywood and Orange County, and couch surfing was becoming more or less a lifestyle, since the drive back up the mountain just to crash at my mom's to do laundry and raid the refrigerator seemed to work better as a biweekly event rather than a daily routine.

—

THE EARLY '70S WAS A HIGH POINT OF SUCCESS FOR THE RECORD INDUSTRY. IN THE EARLY 1960s, the industry revenues were still based largely on the sale of singles. But with the advent of concept albums like the Beatles' *Sgt. Pepper's Lonely Hearts Club Band* and the Who's *Tommy*, album sales greatly increased and labels found their revenues skyrocketing. Consequently, there was now a lot of money being thrown around, grooming the next wave of burgeoning artists and bands. New artists and their managers could procure hefty advances to go rent a house, write songs, and record a lot of debut albums—many of which never went anywhere. But what that meant for me and so many other musicians was there was a lot of work. About this time, I started branching out doing more studio work as a background vocalist and playing piano on the odd track date here and there. Outside the LA recording scene, I kept busy playing club gigs around town and the surrounding counties. This was back in the days when musicians actually got paid for playing clubs—not that the money was always that easy to get ahold of. Band reps and club owners were by nature moving targets. It was not uncommon for the club owner, at the end of a night's performance, to pull the old scam: "Hey, I gotta do the books back in my office, but why don't you come back tomorrow afternoon and I'll have your dough." Knowing that game of cat and mouse all too well, we usually made it clear that we were "happy to hang" as long as need be till the bookkeeping was finished. A typical club owner response at this point might go like this: "Sure, fellas . . . Let me have one of the girls set you up in my private booth with some drinks"—where, conveniently, we wouldn't see the owner's car pull out onto the street. Though we'd usually catch up with them at some point and get paid, it was many times an exercise in tenacity.

By the end of '71, into '72, I was gradually becoming a part of a larger pool of club musicians that kept a sort of musical-chairs turnover when it came to the almighty "casual club dates." We rarely rehearsed, as we were all familiar enough with at least a couple of sets' worth of dance favorites in this newly emerging disco era (before club DJs replaced live bands)—songs by War, Stevie Wonder, and Wilson Pickett, along with the more contemporary Tower of Power, Steely Dan, the Doobie Brothers, and the Eagles. And if we ran out of songs in the course of an evening, we'd just tell the audience that we had a "request" for something we played earlier—until the club owner got wise and fired us.

This alliance of rotating players worked well for all of us; it was understood that if a better-paying gig or session came your way, it was an acceptable practice to call in a sub to take your place. Most of the subs were part of this unofficial pool of musical talent anyway, so as your circle of friends widened, you knew who was proficient and possibly available. Unlike back in the Midwest, where you were usually committed full time to one ensemble and getting a sub too often carried a certain stigma of unreliability, out in LA it was usually a smooth process. I was a sub for other guys often enough, and it taught me to be a quick study when needed.

I played more than a few well-known country bars in LA during the '70s—the Palomino, the Round Up, the Sagebrush Cantina. In later years, my sisters Kathy and Maureen—both talented vocalists with their own career aspirations—played them too, along with their respective bands, and I would sit in with them from time to time. Kathy's band, Prairie Siren, even did a residency at a gay country bar called the Rawhide.

One of my favorite country music gigs in those days was working with Merlin Moran and His Rinse Water Band. Merlin had secured a gig as the house band at the renowned Aces Club—a nightspot in the more industrial part of the city near the airport, then having recently reopened after a string of parking lot homicides.

It was there that I became familiar with the Bakersfield songbook, all the great Buck Owens and Merle Haggard tunes, not to mention music from Nashville—Waylon Jennings and Willie Nelson, George Jones, Patsy Cline, and Tammy Wynette. The Aces Club had been a whistle-stop for many country music legends over the years, but now the new owners—a retired couple who had sunk their life savings into the place—were licensed to operate only after hours, more or less creating a stable for creatures of the night.

In this new (and soon to prove ill-fated) enterprise, the evening would usually start slow, though there were never more than five to ten people in the place during the "peak" of those wee morning hours (and that included the owner and his wife). During the first set, around one a.m., things were fairly tame, usually just an older couple—the "Arkansas kid" and his wife, Gladys—who had the place to themselves and would glide across the dance floor unencumbered as if on a cloud, he in his blinged-out cowboy shirt, Gladys in a flowing, wagon wheel–embroidered square dance dress and rhinestone-studded dance slippers, and both wearing little neckerchiefs. As they floated past the stage, they would give an elegant wave to the band, like square dance royalty. Western dancing was their life, and this place, along with the band, was—at least for the first set—all theirs.

However, the later it got, the weirder the clientele. Like the guy at the pool table who enjoyed hurling the cue ball across the room when he lost a game. Or the guy who'd hold court at the bar, loudly airing his grievances about a wife who needed to understand "who's boss!" The ranting would carry on until the owner, losing his patience, would make "the phone call" to the guy's wife, who would shortly afterward show up and unleash a quick but decisive volley of blows with her purse, leaving her big-shot husband humiliated and crouched under the bar, the barstool his only shield against her flurry of kicks and strikes to the head. When she felt her point had been sufficiently made, she would stoically restrap the purse over her shoulder and, without a word, walk to the entrance and wait without turning around. Then came the awkward moment when our hero would crawl out from under the bar and, without a shred of dignity left, hurry to open the door for her and sheepishly follow her to the car.

—

AT ONE PARTICULAR CLUB GIG REHEARSAL, BOBBY FIGUEROA, A GREAT DRUMMER AND vocalist, happened to mention that later that afternoon he was going to audition with Steely Dan, one of my all-time favorite groups (then and still now). I was so jealous! How did somebody get that lucky?

We all had our eyes on the horizon, looking for that big tour or recording project, but it was sometimes these seemingly insignificant, casual LA club dates that were the very vehicle that led to those greater opportunities—which is what happened with one gig that magically fell into my lap.

My friend Brandy Bento, a terrific bass player, had been contracted to put together a band for a better-than-normal-paying gig: a Christmas wrap party for the cast and crew of the TV series *Emergency!* on the Universal lot. Sounds great. Count me in.

But then she landed a much better, potentially long-term union gig in Vegas that she couldn't turn down. So she asked me to take over the task of putting a band together for the wrap party. However, knowing all too well that procrastination was one of my more distinct character defects, she made a point to impress upon me the importance of not waiting till the last minute.

Which of course is exactly what I did. No more than a week out, I panicked and shared my dilemma with the only musician I'd procured for the gig so far, my sax player friend Steve Leeds. Me and a sax player—not quite the band anyone had in mind. The gig now only days away, with no gear or time to rehearse even if we had the rest of a band, Steve sensed my rising anxiety.

"Don't worry," he assured me. "My brother can help us find some gear, and I know some cats. They're involved in an album project right now but mostly tracking during the day, so there's a good chance they'll be free that evening."

"Really? That's great!" (If it all actually works out.) I thought it prudent to mention, since these guys sounded like highly paid session musicians, that the money was probably much less than what they were used to.

"Don't worry about that," he told me. "These guys will probably do it just for fun."

Okay . . . too good to be true. But even if that all panned out, I was concerned there wasn't much time to rehearse. Steve actually scoffed at that point.

"Mike, these guys don't need to rehearse. We'll just make a list of songs and what keys we're doing them in . . . a rough chord chart and . . . go."

Well, okay! We might've just snatched victory from the jaws of defeat here. Over the remaining few days, going through my record collection to try to develop a set list with chord charts, my panic level started to rise again as I realized that I had never done a gig where I was the only vocalist, and I only vaguely knew the lyrics to some of these songs.

Thankfully, and miraculously, the gig went off without a hitch. We wound up playing more than the two hours I'd planned for, the last hour just jamming on our favorite old blues and R&B songs. The spontaneous musical interaction between us was extraordinary; these guys were exceptional players and extremely inventive. My buddy Steve had somehow managed to wrangle together in this eleventh hour: Jeff Porcaro on drums, his brother Mike Porcaro on bass, Kent Henry on guitar, and a friend of the Porcaro brothers who sat in on a few tunes that evening by the name of David Paich, who later, along with Jeff Porcaro, would become a cofounder of Toto.

Besides my gratitude for them coming to my rescue that night, they were also all just a great hang, and I have to admit I was impressed by their unflappable confidence. It was obvious that these were some up-and-coming cats.

In between sets, while having a smoke out in back of the soundstage, I remember Jeff Porcaro talking about a track he had just cut earlier that day with Steely Dan. (What—*another* fucking guy who gets to play with Steely Dan?!) The song he referred to would become the title track of *Pretzel Logic*, an album that I couldn't have known then would figure heavily in my future, and all by way of this fortuitously random encounter.

But first, I had some personal issues to work through.

CHAPTER 10

WHAT COULD POSSIBLY GO WRONG?

I remember sitting in a parking lot in front of the Bank of America in Burbank in my beat-up '61 Ford Fairlane with the badly oxidized red paint job, having my usual lunch of Ding Dongs and a Diet Dr Pepper. I'd been running errands that day like picking up my old Wurlitzer electric piano from the repair shop and doing some laundry, while, as always, putting off other expenses—like repairing the flat tire in my trunk. The bald spare would have to last me a couple more days.

It was then I noticed a guy in a three-piece suit, who I presumed to be an executive from the bank, taking a smoke break. My thoughts drifted toward what it must be like to be that guy, with all that responsibility and structure in his life. Compared with him, I must have looked like a lost cause . . . Then it hit me: compared with him, I *was* a lost cause! Everything I owned in this world—the complete sum of my existence—was parked there in front of that bank. My piece-of-shit car, my piece-of-shit Wurly, the clothes on my back and some miscellaneous laundry . . . Oh, and not to forget, the Ding Dongs and Diet Dr Pepper.

Not yet even twenty, my life at that time was beginning to show all the stress cracks of futility. I was, to say the least, a two-legged red flag to any woman with the slightest modicum of common sense. Still with no place of my own, I was gaining a rep with my friends as a serial couch surfer; my only experiences with a real bed at this point were thanks to the occasional kindhearted waitress who thought I might be good for *something*. I was down to being able to afford only one actual hot meal a day and struggling, frankly, to see the romance in my footloose, fancy-free musician's lifestyle.

—

IT'S NO SECRET THAT DRUGS AND ALCOHOL WERE A PREVALENT PART OF THE LA MUSIC scene then, especially the new kid on the block: cocaine. My introduction to the stuff was by way of one of those aforementioned kindhearted waitresses. As I recall, that first time I didn't really notice much of an effect, which to my way of thinking only meant: "If at first you don't succeed . . ." The next time, it was a fast track to a delusional level of self-confidence, and I would spend the next ten years chasing that dragon.

While I personally couldn't yet afford the luxury, I couldn't help but notice that there was a certain extra measure of cool to those who *could*. Coke was becoming currency. It was one thing to show up at a session on time; it was another thing to show up with a little blow in your pocket. Nothing would ingratiate you more with the other musicians on the floor than offering to those inclined a little bump before downbeat.

Aside from its desired effect, I discovered that cocaine opened the door to further substance abuse, as I soon experienced the need to *counter* the very effect I was seeking. Suddenly, with too much of a good thing, I needed to take the edge off with barbiturates and increased alcohol consumption—not to mention I was smoking three times as many cigarettes while doing coke.

As common as drug use was then, I don't know if everyone was struggling like I was. I couldn't tell you how many times I passed out, threw up, got lost, woke up not knowing where I was, or some combination of all the above. I lost count long ago. Eventually, as my drinking escalated, I started to experience grand mal seizures—complete loss of consciousness, uncontrollable muscle spasms—all a result of alcohol toxicity, whereby your neural messages all trigger at once and, as it was explained to me, the switchboard that is your brain overloads and shorts out. In many cases, unless someone else was there to witness it, I wouldn't even know these incidents happened, so they were likely more frequent than I even realized. The seizures were also responsible for some bouts of memory loss, which I wasn't aware of until an emergency room doctor asked me what year it was and I had no idea. All I ever remembered was waking up exceptionally groggy and having, at some point in the night, pissed myself.

—

AS IF MY PERSONAL DRUG USE WASN'T ENOUGH OF A PROBLEM, I "WISELY" TOOK ON THE role of errand boy for a girlfriend who sold a little cocaine on the side. I'd help her out from time to time delivering small amounts to her friends, many of whom were studio musicians. At one point, I remember thinking, "I came out here to be part of this recording scene as a musician, but lately it seems the only sessions I'm going to are when I'm dropping off a couple of grams of coke to the horn section."

This was a short-lived enterprise, however, because once again, if there was a way to fuck up a good thing, I'd find it. Early on in our symbiotic relationship, my girlfriend asked me to pick up a small amount of all-but-pure cocaine from this guy Roy (not his real name)* at his apartment in Beverly Hills. I was to pick up the coke and bring it straight back to her, where she would "step on it" (cut it with B_{12} powder) and turn, say, half an ounce into an ounce, thereby yielding a small profit margin for herself. As I say, this was no cartel-size operation.

Now, I had met Roy a few times before, so he knew me and trusted me and invited me in to enjoy a little "taste" before I left. In

* Okay, yeah—that was his real name.

fact, he'd usually insist on that; he was a nice enough guy, kind of chatty, though who *isn't* after a couple lines of cocaine.

Roy was a brainiac, kind of a bookworm, and if you were a client, he liked to have you sit while he chemically tested the stuff in front of you with his chemist's paraphernalia; he was nothing if not proud of his product's quality, not to mention his vast collection of succulents and shelves full of rare and wide-ranging books, which filled the apartment. I was, of course, happy to participate in this ritual, confident that indulging this professional courtesy would in no way deter me in my courier duties.

Unfortunately, on my way back to my girlfriend's apartment, I got the idea in my head that it'd be nice to take the edge off a little with a shot of whiskey. So I drove to a little restaurant-bar in Hollywood, a well-known watering hole frequented by musicians and entertainment industry types. While there at the bar, I ran into a bass-player buddy of mine who was doing well at the time, playing with several big-name artists like Bobby Darin, Glen Campbell, and Roger Miller, all of whom had big network weekly variety shows and Vegas residencies and toured year-round.

Turns out one of his superstar employers was about to meet him there for dinner and my friend invited me to join them, whereupon I made the stupid mistake of mentioning that while I'd be happy to sit for a drink or two, I couldn't stay long as I was on a "special mission" for my girlfriend. I realized too late that I'd already said too much.

Of course, a stiff double shot of whiskey was never known to greatly improve my judgment either. So, feeling a little stingy, I thought, "Well, surely it couldn't hurt to share one little bump with my old friend before his boss gets here. There's so much here, no one will be the wiser." (It was that same old skewed cough-syrup logic that landed me in the emergency room at four years old.)

Well, things went downhill fast once our third party showed up ("party" being the operative word here), and . . . I'm not totally sure exactly what followed. I just know we ended up in a stall in the men's room with his boss, a really engaging and funny guy who kept us in stitches for hours, stopping only periodically to ask, "You got a little more of that?"

Before the evening was over, the three of us couldn't feel the roofs of our mouths and there were certain consonants we could no longer pronounce. By this point, pretty much all of this stash—which was not mine—was gone. I now had to face my girlfriend and explain what happened to her much-anticipated delivery. And that was pretty much the end of my career as her drug mule.

—

I WAS EVENTUALLY FORGIVEN, AND ONE NIGHT NOT LONG AFTER THAT, WE WERE SCHED-uled to play at the Troubadour, backing up a friend who was showcasing his new album on Capitol Records.

The afternoon of the show, I happened to be babysitting my girlfriend's five-year-old daughter while she ran some errands. I was sitting in her living room watching television, with the little one happily drawing pictures next to me at the coffee table, when suddenly there was a knock at the door. There was something about that knock . . . And as I walked up to the door, I could hear a couple of male voices talking to one another in hushed tones.

Rather than just opening the door, something told me to look through the peephole—where I saw three or four guys standing on the stoop and down the stairs. In that moment, the odds of these guys *not* being narcs seemed slim to none. My hope that they might be Jehovah's Witnesses was dashed when they indeed identified themselves as LAPD.

I cracked the door slightly, thinking I would appear more cooperative, but as I explained that the woman who lived here wasn't home and that I was just the babysitter, they burst through the door, pushing me back over the coffee table. As the lead detective started to pull his weapon from behind his back, I immediately put my hands up in full compliance, while subtly gesturing with my head to make him aware of the little girl, hoping to appeal to his better nature and hopefully not further traumatize the child.

Luckily he reacted favorably; he apparently saw no need to draw his weapon and even smiled and acknowledged the little girl in a friendly tone. He then calmly asked me if there was a friend or family member who could come and get her, as I would most likely be going to jail if they found any drugs. They found only a small amount of marijuana in a shoebox lid on top of the fridge, but that was probably enough.

They continued to ransack the apartment in search of more drugs and were growing visibly disappointed, as I'm pretty sure they were informed this would be some big-time bust. My girlfriend happened to come home around this time and called a friend in the building who was the regular babysitter, and she, fortunately, was able to come take the little girl while the two of us were both handcuffed and read our Miranda rights.

Down at the now familiar Van Nuys precinct, our one phone call was to our friend's manager, explaining that more than likely we'd be unable to do the showcase that night. A couple of hours later, he very impressively bailed us out just in time to do the Troubadour gig, and he even got us an attorney, who in the coming days was able to get our felony charges dropped to misdemeanor possession. All in a day's work for a good rock and roll manager.

—

I WAS SENTENCED TO ONE YEAR'S PROBATION, AND SINCE THE LA COURT SYSTEM WAS SO overwhelmed with petty drug arrests in 1972, anyone who was a federal employee in any capacity and so inclined could volunteer to be a probation officer in LA County. So it came to be that I met Ray Paul, a contractor for the federal government's involvement with the military-industrial complex—and my new probation officer.

Probation back then consisted mostly of just staying out of trouble and periodically checking in with your PO. But it also required me to attend individual counseling and group therapy sessions a couple of hours a week, usually consolidated into one day. We would take a lunch break between sessions, at which time I'd go down to my car and drive around the north Valley, smoking a joint with the windows down (one of which was off its track and always down anyway). Then I'd scarf down a cheeseburger on my way back to the shrink's office and do a quick hit of spray deodorant to my clothes and hair, which I kept in my car in case I ever got pulled over. From there I'd do my best to not look too high.

Ray had a few other requirements of his own: I had to go to some extra group therapy sessions he hosted with his wife, Aida. And, oh yes, help him landscape his yard. He also suggested I attend a few AA meetings.

The first one he took me to was a men's group in the federal building in downtown Van Nuys, a good reminder of the hours I'd spent in the nearby precinct. Most of the attendees were guys Ray knew from working in that very building, many of them coming directly from work, still in suit and tie. I, on the other hand, walked in wearing a worn-out jean jacket and beat-up Frye boots with long hair and a beard. As I walked to a vacant chair at the far side of the room, one of the attendees muttered, "Jesus—it's Charlie Manson." I felt more than a little conspicuous, once again not-so-slightly "other than."

—

RAY PAUL AND I COULDN'T HAVE BEEN MORE POLAR OPPOSITES. HERE WAS A FEDERAL employee, a suit with a high-level security clearance, and me, a nineteen-year-old pothead musician with delusions of grandeur, barely making enough money for one meal a day and gas—and I had the gall to be suspicious of his intentions.

But on the other hand, I just had a feeling that somehow, he might know something, some "enlightenment" that I'd missed or had possibly been avoiding my whole life. He impressed me with his honesty and hard-won humility. Ray was a scrappy, type A kinda guy who grew up at the end of the Great Depression on New York City's Lower East Side. Like me, he had suffered from the consequences of his self-centered obsession and resulting poor choices, and like me, he had a one-size-fits-all answer for dealing with his problems—simply put: once you do enough damage, you move on. Whether it comes in the form of a transfer application, a divorce, or, as *my* pattern was, looking for the closest emergency exit and slipping away by whatever means possible and with the least amount of confrontation. That was familiar to me. It's all the same shit, that pattern of "doing the next geographic."

In this odd pairing, I was ultimately given one of the greatest gifts I'll ever receive, when Ray, the most unlikely person I would ever look to for advice, pointed out that *I* was the problem. It wasn't the fault of random bad breaks or people, places, and things out of my control. No doubt, shit happens. But it was how I reacted and eventually dealt with it all—that's where my real problems began, and the responsibility for what happened as a result of that was mine alone. I'd never learned to be at peace with myself, and at the time I first crossed paths with Ray Paul, I was obviously not yet ready to do the hard work of getting there.

Despite that, some good luck was nonetheless around the corner.

CHAPTER 11

STEELY DAN AND THE (ALMOST) MURDER OF AUNT MAME

In the spring of 1973, about the time my probation period was over, I was starting to make a little more money. Studio work was picking up for me somewhat, so I was able to procure a loan through the musicians' Local 47 credit union and buy an only slightly used Ford Pinto and a slightly newer Wurlitzer electric piano. (I was still unable to afford a Fender Rhodes, considered at the time the new standard.) And by nights, I had a regular gig playing with a band at the Trojan Room in Glendale, a small neighborhood bar holding maybe fifty people max.

Then one day, my friend Brandy called to tell me that Jeff Porcaro was trying to reach me. I hadn't heard from Jeff since meeting him at that great wrap-party gig more than a year earlier and had no idea what this could be about.

Turns out Steely Dan were rehearsing for a tour to promote their new album and were looking for someone to handle some keyboards who could also sing some background vocals—and Jeff had recommended me, which blew my mind! He was actually calling from their rehearsal to ask if I wanted to audition. I said, "Sure! When?" And he said, "How about now?" I threw my Wurlitzer into my Ford Pinto and hauled ass down to Modern Music rentals and rehearsals in Hollywood.

My anticipation/anxiety as I drove down there would be hard to measure. Steely Dan had become my favorite group since the Beatles. Their unique mix of jazz, rock, and R&B influences and their experimental recording techniques had raised the bar for pop music. They had already had some big radio hits with "Do It Again," "Reelin' In the Years," and, now, "Rikki Don't Lose That Number," the first single from their new album *Pretzel Logic* that was getting traction on the radio. So for me, this had all the makings of an opportunity almost too good to be true.

I was greeted at the rehearsal hall by their stage manager, Warren Wallace, whom I would describe as a fairly dynamic personality—the kind of guy that if there was a fight on the other side of the bar that had nothing to do with him, he'd jump tables just so he could get in on it.

Warren and road manager Gary McPike helped me load in my meager amount of gear and hooked me up. I met everyone that first day: Donald Fagen and Walter Becker, drummer Jim Hodder, guitarist Denny Dias, percussionist/vocalist Royce Jones, and the legendary guitarist Jeff "Skunk" Baxter. I remember Jeff Baxter as being immediately engaging and funny. He was sporting a black eye, apparently received during a basketball game earlier that day at the Hollywood YMCA with some of his NYC crew, which he wore like a badge of honor. When I naively asked about the "Skunk" moniker, he said, in an exaggerated New York accent, that it came from "an indiscretion in my youth." Since no one else seemed to require any further explanation, I thought it was best left alone.

Donald and Walter were, of course, the founders and creative epicenter of the ensemble, but they were hardly the rock gods you would imagine. More like a comedy duo from the Catskills. Donald had the physique of an eighty-year-old woman, and Walter, with his intellectual aura, gave off more the vibe of a lab technician working on some nefarious government experiment. They had been playing together since their college days and had by now developed their own sense of humor and irony based on their mutual distrust in human nature (especially record execs and lawyers).

The band behind them was, by this point, set in place; some members were newer, and a few had been involved since the band was first formed a few years earlier. I was, at that moment, the only real question mark.

I must admit, it's with a certain astonishment that I look back on that audition. I hadn't had any time to prepare in advance for it, and I realize now that I was learning all the tunes on the spot—keyboard parts and background vocals. And these were not simple songs: "The Boston Rag," "King of the World," "Bodhisattva" . . . Steely Dan songs have lots of moving parts—sophisticated chord progressions and complex harmonies—not the kind of songs I was used to playing, which were generally three- or four-chord songs that were often interchangeable.

I'm pretty sure it wasn't my fair-to-middling piano chops that got my foot in the door, as Donald was an exceptionally talented and formally trained pianist, having faithfully studied jazz greats like Bill Evans and Earl Hines. Clearly, he didn't need my help there. But with me playing keyboards, it freed Donald up to play more synth and not worry as much about the piano comping underneath. It meant he could be "up front" a bit more. I think what really got me the gig that day was the fact that I was able to hit the high harmonies in a relatively full voice. Donald and Walter seemed to appreciate that.

—

IF MY LIFE EXPERIENCE HAD TAUGHT ME ANYTHING UP TO THIS POINT, IT WAS TO ALWAYS brace myself for disappointment. But this audition seemed to be evolving into a full-blown rehearsal. I didn't want to read too much into that, because there had been no clear affirmation like "Congratulations, you got the job!" I did get a nod and a wink from Jeff, which was reassuring, but nothing from Donald and Walter. They didn't say anything. But the fact that nobody had tossed me out of there yet seemed like a good sign. Usually an audition like that could last fifteen minutes, a half hour . . . maybe an hour, tops. But Donald kept teaching me one song after another—and after five or six hours, somewhere along the way, I had apparently managed to enter the world of Steely Dan.

We continued rehearsals for the next couple weeks at Modern Music and played our first gig in Glendale at a club called the Sopwith Camel, a large old ballroom with psychedelic lighting and an actual antique biplane hanging from the ceiling over the dance floor. All the managers and record execs were there that first night, as was an ounce of premium blow, conspicuously piled in the center of a coffee table in the dressing room, compliments of who knows who. So a few of us indulged our tendencies toward excess, and as a result, the song tempos that night were a little on the bright side. Our second appearance was a live radio broadcast in LA, and then we were off to begin the tour.

In my early band days, "touring" meant driving everywhere, all of us in one van, and when we weren't sleeping on people's floors—usually of charitable waitresses or appreciative customers from the club—we might stay in, say, a Holiday Inn, but all of us in one room. Now, with Steely Dan, we not only flew (commercial), but we all had separate hotel rooms (still mostly Holiday Inns, though). And we had a road manager, Gary McPike. What a luxury to not have to worry about where we had to be next or how to get there. That job fell to poor Gary, and I'm sure for him, a lot of times, it was like herding cats. For example, early on in the tour I hooked up with a woman who turned out to be more of a problem than I had anticipated. A heroin addict / dealer friend of a friend, she picked me up at the airport and duped me into coming along with her to one of her "drops" on the way to the hotel, and the next morning, I had trouble convincing her it was time to leave. With the band already loaded up and waiting downstairs and Gary banging on my door, I remember thinking, "I'd better get my act together before I get myself canned."

One of our early dates was at the Masonic Temple in Detroit. I was already enjoying the camaraderie and settling into an easy friendship with the band and crew, and while sitting in the dressing room before the show, a few of us were looking out a second-story window, watching some eye-opening inner-city street activity below, when suddenly another window at the back of the room shattered with a deafening crash, and a bleeding arm from outside the building wrapped itself over the sill, through the sharp, jagged glass. After struggling to pull the rest of his body up, a teenage dude attempted to hoist up a friend with his other arm. Both had somehow scaled the wall to the windows above and almost made it into the room.

But just as this kid called to us for help, the dressing room door burst open and three of Detroit's finest rushed in and started billy-clubbing the two kids, who then dropped back down to the alley below, leaving everyone else in the room stunned as the cops, without a word, just exited the room. And now . . . showtime!

—

DONALD AND WALTER WERE NEVER GREAT FANS OF TOURING, BUT IF THEY WERE GOING TO do it, their creed was: "It better be comfortable, and we better have top-notch production"—starting with their sound system.

They stipulated they wouldn't use the house systems available in most venues or rent equipment from regional sound companies, which was the norm for most touring bands at the time. Those systems were typically mono, less than high-fidelity—more midrange-y, with a less defined, booming bass range. Donald and Walter were looking for more of a live audiophile experience.

So they sought out an independent company with a more cutting-edge design. Enter Dinky Dawson, a brilliant veteran audio engineer from Scotland with impressive jet-black mutton chops, who, having worked with the likes of Fleetwood Mac, the Byrds, and the Kinks, came on board with his latest state-of-the-art sound system design for the Steely Dan tour. And impressive it was.

By the time we played Boston, it had become obvious even to me that what the audience heard out front was much more compelling than what we were hearing in our monitors onstage. Though my understanding of audio technology was limited at best, Dinky was kind enough to explain it all . . . slowly.

The traditional view up till then had been that you couldn't have a giant stereo front-of-house system in a large venue setting because the two different sides of the house would hear only half a mix, especially those seated in the first ten to fifteen rows. Dinky didn't agree with that theory, and he created his own setup, which consisted of about a hundred small speakers stacked into two towers powered with modified stereo amplifiers, crossovers, and graphic EQs assembled to his own specs. The result was that it greatly enhanced the live audio experience for the audience, and he could integrate and utilize his stereo design in the band's unique musical arrangements.

For instance, he used the stereo panning capability to great effect during the intro of the evening's first song, "Bodhisattva." When the opening two-bar synthesizer glissando would sweep "right" to "left" and back again across the audio spectrum, many nights that effect all by itself would bring the audience to their feet. It was in the bag before we even got to the first verse.

—

ONCE WE GOT TO NEW YORK, IT WAS CLEAR WE HAD REACHED THE LAND OF THE DAN. THE band's turf, so to speak. The fans there exhibited an almost proprietary familiarity with the band. "Rikki Don't Lose That Number" had reached the Top Ten on the *Billboard* charts, and hitting the stage was like being the home team that just won the championship. For Steely Dan, playing New York City was a most welcome home game.

We had been on the road for a few weeks when, passing through the Midwest, we stopped in my hometown of St. Louis to play the venerable old Ambassador Theatre on Seventh Street. I had a great time before the show seeing old friends and family who dropped by the hotel to visit, but as much as I love friends and family, this was a bit of an overload. By the time everyone left my hotel room, I needed a break. So I lit up a joint and turned on the TV to chill before the sound check and show, when the phone rang. I picked up, assuming it was our road manager, but I couldn't quite hear the voice on the other end with the TV blaring in the background.

"Hello?! Shit! Hang on! Fuck, this TV is so *fucking* loud!"

I turned down the TV and returned to the phone to hear a frail little voice. "Mike? Hello, honey—it's Aunt Mame."

Didn't see that coming.

"Oh jeez, Aunt Mame. I'm so sorry! I thought you were some guy I work with. How are you?"

Her voice teeming with excitement, she said, "I'm comin' to see you tonight!"

I should mention Aunt Mame was in her early nineties, living at the Hotel Alverne, a senior facility not far from the theater. Still, this was downtown St. Louis, a bit of a dicey neighborhood, and by the time we took the stage, it would be late at night for a woman even remotely her age. So I did my best to lovingly discourage her, explaining also that it would be "really loud," which I don't believe she quite grasped. "Loud" to her would be, like, a door slamming.

Not only were *we* pretty loud, but our opening act was Montrose, one of the loudest bands in rock and roll. I thought this might not be a good night out for my Aunt Mame; she'd be dead in her seat before I could get to her. But there was no stopping her. She was coming, hell or high water. I was at least able to convince her to let me arrange to have my cousin Bill pick her up. She agreed to that much.

Cut to: I'm backstage before the show, doing an interview for the local TV station—"Local musician Mike McDonald comes to town performing tonight with Steely Dan" and all that. Which would of course normally have excited me no end, but the whole time I was distracted, worrying about my Aunt Mame. At the risk of seeming rude, I explained my dilemma to the interview crew and excused myself just in time to hear the thunderous downbeat of the opening act through the floor. Now I'm running up the stairs, striding three steps at a time. I burst into the lobby to see my cousin Bill and an usher holding what looks like my great-aunt under her arms, her feet literally dragging behind her across the carpet. "Oh, God. I knew it. We killed her!"

I rushed up to them, looking for signs of life. When I got to her, she looked up into my face, still trying to hold her ears—Ronnie Montrose's thundering guitar in the background—and smiled and said, "Oh, hi, honey."

Okay, so now greatly relieved that she was still alive, we found her a comfortable chair in the lobby, and I assured her that Bill would take her home, to which she replied, "No way! I'm staying to hear you!"

And like a champ, she stayed till the bitter end. It seems the opening act wasn't exactly her cup of tea, but she reported later that she did enjoy Steely Dan—with one constructive criticism: "That 'Dan' fella sings too much. He should let you sing more."

I laughed, took her hand, and gave her a kiss on the cheek—and that would be the last time I saw Aunt Mame.

—

ON TO KANSAS CITY, AND AFTER SOME DATES OUT WEST, EVENTUALLY BACK TO CALIFOR-nia. Our final US date would be on the Fourth of July at Santa Monica Civic Auditorium. All of us were in a rather celebratory mood, as this was, after all, our last night of the tour, and the party atmosphere was a notch or two above normal. Our truck driver, Jerome, normally a shy, soft-spoken man, like most of us probably had one too many in the dressing room that night. Now, encouraged by Donald and Walter, it was decided that he'd take the stage as the impromptu MC for tonight's performance.

Jerome was on fire, ramping up the crowd's anticipation for what they were about to experience, like a slurring Baptist preacher. "So let's hear it now for . . . the Magnificent one! The Stupendous one! The Pontificant one! The Proliferant one! . . ."—and whatever other adjectives he could invent on the spot—finishing with: "The ONLY one! MR. STEVIE DAN! . . . *or whatever* . . ." (trailing those last two words off mic while actually belching). The crowd erupted, and then, for what might well have been the last time for me, we dropped into the intro of "Bodhisattva."

—

I HAD A VERY INTERESTING MOMENT AFTER THE SHOW THAT NIGHT. I HAD INVITED MY former probation officer and mentor in recovery, Ray Paul, and his wife, Aida, to the performance. My rationale was that this was a gesture of appreciation for all he'd done for me up until recently: getting me through my legal obligations and helping me rein in my drug and alcohol use (relatively speaking) long enough to get back on my feet. My deeper motive, however, was for him to witness how well it all turned out for me.

I still remember the look on his face as he came back to the dressing room and glanced down at the beer in my hand. There was no judgment, no comment, but I sensed his concern. And despite my cavalier attempt to pass it off as insignificant, the moment was seared into my memory that night, like an ominous warning of what was to come.

CHAPTER 12

THE DAN'S EUROPEAN ADVENTURES

I hated to see the tour end but felt like I had truly experienced something so worthwhile and had learned so much from getting to know and perform Donald and Walter's music. It was, for me, an incredible education.

There had been talk throughout the tour of doing some more dates in Europe, but once again, if experience had taught me anything, it was: "Don't hold your breath." Besides, even if the band did go, there was no guarantee that I'd be part of it; the band had had a different configuration of musicians for every tour they'd done up to then.

The tour, as much fun as it was, started to feel like a dream I'd had, and whether I would ever see any of those guys again was anyone's guess. There was also the somewhat depressing irony of finding myself back at the Trojan Room in Glendale, playing Top Forty sets that included—adding insult to injury—a few Steely Dan songs. One week, playing to sold-out crowds of ecstatic Dan fans; now, back playing to a few disinterested regulars at the corner bar.

Then I got a call from the band's management.

"Donald and Walter would like to know if you'll be available for some dates in Europe coming up. It won't be for a couple of months, but the guys would like to offer you a monthly retainer till then."

I couldn't believe it! A retainer? I'd only heard of such a thing, where you actually get paid to just hang around and be available. I tried to wrap my head around the roller coaster ride I seemed to be on of late.

European departure day came. Jeff Porcaro picked me up—in a limo, no less—and then we headed to Donald's, where he and Walter joined us for the ride to the airport. It was typical miserable LA gridlock all the way there, but listening to Donald and Walter attempt to "read aloud" the mind of every truck driver who stared down into this limo full of scrawny, long-haired weirdos provided more than enough entertainment value.*

As excited as I was about my first trip to Europe, I was a bit anxious about the flight itself. I had flown a handful of times, but sitting on a plane for ten hours? Over the Atlantic Ocean? That frankly scared the hell out of me. So a friend of mine offered me a pill.

"Just a muscle relaxer," she assured me.

Well, it was Placidyl, strong enough to knock out an elephant. I don't remember even making it to the ticket counter, much less boarding the plane. Nowadays I'm sure they wouldn't even let someone board in that condition. But to give credit where it's due, once again our road manager Gary "the Hammer" McPike, a championship-level persuader, somehow got me on the plane. All I know is when I came to, I was on the tarmac at Heathrow.

On arrival in London, we hit the ground running. Donald and Walter were swallowed up by A&R people and press, so the rest of us hit the streets in search of all the wonders of London.

Jeff Porcaro and I wandered off to check out Carnaby Street—the hip fashion destination of the mods and the rockers—and some other more upscale men's shops that carried Italian suits and accessories. (Jeff bought himself a nice suit and got fitted; it was still a little beyond my budget.)

---

* Years earlier, while they toured as part of the backup band, Jay and the Americans lead singer Jay Black, noting their dark and acerbic wit, dubbed Donald and Walter the "Manson and Starkweather of rock 'n' roll."

After we wandered around that part of London, we followed a recommendation and had lunch at a brand-new spot that had just opened to rave reviews. It was purportedly the only place in London where you could get a real American hamburger. Back then, hamburgers in London had the taste of minced meat, and Coca-Cola was always served at room temperature, so we were excited to discover this new place: the Hard Rock Cafe, the first of what soon became the huge international chain.

I still remember the unique ambience of the place. The music was untypically loud for a restaurant, and while we enjoyed our "American" cheeseburgers, the great-sounding in-house stereo system played a brand-new Joni Mitchell track I hadn't heard yet, "Free Man in Paris," whose lyrics resonated with me in that moment. I was feeling pretty "unfettered and alive" myself.

—

WHEN WE MET OUR UK CREW AT REHEARSAL THE NEXT DAY, WE WEREN'T SURE WHAT TO expect, concerned that perhaps the techs might not be on par with the crew we had in the States. Turns out there was no need to worry.

In rehearsal we met Chris Adamson and Phil McDonald (no relation), who, along with a couple other Brits, impressed us greatly. The crew was incredibly proficient and savvy. These guys were used to playing venues a couple hundred years older than the United States itself, often performing feats of daring to make sure the show went on unhindered. Like the night Chris Adamson stacked and then climbed road cases to open a window high above the drummers in an effort to relieve the hundred-plus-degree temperature onstage. Since it had been painted shut, he broke the glass pane using nothing but his elbow wrapped in towels, like some swashbuckling daredevil, releasing much of the stifling heat before the drummers passed out.

Then came our first London gig, at the Rainbow Theatre. The British audience was so responsive! They seemed as excited to be there as we were. There are recordings of that gig I've heard in recent years that brought me right back to that moment and the excitement we all felt playing in London for the first time. Even on tape it's palpable.

After that gig there were a couple more days' worth of interviews and scheduled TV appearances for Don and Walter—something they particularly hated and had for the most part successfully avoided at home. On top of that, Donald came down with strep throat. So in order to "recuperate more efficiently," they convinced the record label to rent them the private penthouse suite at the upscale and boutique Blakes Hotel.

Their new quarters were accessible only by a private elevator in a separate lobby, both of which required a special key. So the boys now had a cloistered enclave from which they then proceeded to cancel all gigs and TV appearances for the following week. This of course sent the record company and management (not to mention promoters) into a frenzy, prompting one of the management partners to fly from LA to London to do damage control.

Band and crew, meanwhile, were still staying at the more traditional Curzon Hotel, and having just been informed we now had the week off, Royce Jones, Warren Wallace, and I found a reputable, off-property fluff-and-fold laundry and a pub that served classic English fish and chips, both highly recommended by our British crew. (Fast food and cheap laundry service—pretty typical day off in the life of traveling musicians worldwide.)

We didn't do much that next week. I know we went to some local clubs and heard a few local London bands—couldn't tell you the names. I do, however, remember that we all got sick in some form or fashion—some of us from jet lag, some from Indian food. My particular illness was a bit more exotic.

Back then, before you traveled abroad you had to get multiple shots, one of which was a smallpox vaccine, and before the most recent political controversy over vaccines, we never questioned the mandates for such precaution, although we knew there was always that one-in-a-million chance that you'd get some adverse side effect. Well, guess what? In this case, I was that one in a million. I woke up in London one morning to find these hideous sores on my arms.

So the record company sent me to this guy who was apparently one of London's premier "rock docs." His office looked more like a trendy nightspot than a medical practice. The doctor himself was a handsome middle-aged guy with longish silver hair, wearing an ascot and a double-breasted jacket with flashy gold buttons, and his beautiful medical assistant, in her short mini-skirted nurse's uniform, looked like she'd stepped right out of every adolescent boy's sexual fantasy.

Then there was me, sitting there somewhat mesmerized by the whole scene, with my arms on fire. The doctor took one look at them and calmly said, "Oh, yes . . . I see . . . How are you sleeping?"

I said, "Well, I've been so jet-lagged that frankly my body clock's a little confused, but more importantly, I just don't know what *this* is."

He repeated, "Hmm, yes . . . I see. Quite. But . . . how are you sleeping?" This guy seemed overly concerned about me getting sleep.

"Pretty good, I guess . . . I'm sleeping okay."

"Are you sure?"

"Yeah, I'm fairly sure."

He then paused and tried an only slightly different approach. "Let me ask you this: Do you need anything for sleep?"

Ahhh . . . Okay, well, if you put it that way. "Sure. Why not."

Shortly thereafter, I left with a tube of skin salve and two consecutive prescriptions for quaaludes, the first of which he filled right there on the spot. Obviously acquainted as he was with the recreational habits of musicians, I guess he just presumed I'd be happy to have a pocket full of 'ludes, which were enormously popular back then. They gave one a sense of euphoria and heightened all the pleasure centers in the brain, making them the party drug of choice in those days.

Back at the hotel, I gathered a couple of my colleagues to share the news of my latest acquisition, and it wasn't long before the first script was duly distributed.

Alas, the other consequence of 'ludes was they made you stupid. The next morning I woke up facedown in a small puddle of skin ointment that I must've tried to apply the night before. Dragging myself to my feet, I found a note that had been slipped under my door: Donald and Walter were inviting us all up to their penthouse for a "strategy meeting." Sounded like fun.

We were instructed to meet in the Blakes Hotel bistro at noon, where Jeff Porcaro would bring us up to the room, as he had been given the key to the magical private lift. We were specifically instructed to not mention any of this to the promoter's staff or Dan's management, which was kind of awkward since seated right next to us at the bistro that morning were the promoter's rep, some record company execs, and one of Steely Dan's two managers, Joel. (They both shared the same first name, so I couldn't tell you which Joel it was.) They were all hoping to talk to Donald and Walter—if they could only get the front desk to put the call through to their luxurious lair. The hotel staff had been instructed by the boys to hold all calls.

Joel, already suspicious of our presence, asked that if we happened to talk to Donald or Walter, to please let them know that all parties concerned were anxious to speak with them. We promised we'd mention it and then, somewhat sheepishly, left and walked across the street to the private lobby and took the lift to see them.

Any intention of forwarding that message was completely forgotten the moment the lift door opened directly onto the living room of this multi-bedroom, executive, deluxe penthouse suite—a vast expanse taking up the entire top floor, with private balconies, a fully operational chef's kitchen, and lavishly mod European-chic/bachelor-pad decor; it looked like how I'd imagine James Bond's honeymoon suite.

Upon entering, the atmosphere got even more surreal: flouncing across the living room were a handful of young ballerinas doing their stretches, pliés and jetés, or whatever they were. I wondered if I had mistakenly strayed onto the set of some Fellini-esque film, but soon learned that the girls had come with Walter's mother, a very cordial and interesting woman. She at first presented as your friend's seemingly normal, all-American mom, but was also, as it turned out, something of a bohemian. She had spent the last twenty-five years or so traveling throughout Britain and Europe, randomly taking up residence in abandoned estates or vacant commercial spaces where she made a living teaching ballet. And now she was here, with her small traveling band of nubile students, preparing for yet another impromptu class.

As they warmed up, Walter's mom invited us to share some of the wonderful spread she'd prepared for us all: an array of exotic charcuterie and cheeses, and something I'd never seen before called "hummus." As I understood it, she and Walter had not communicated since sometime back in his early teens, and she had apparently just shown up here in London, unannounced, to lay eyes once again on her son.

Walter, for his part, was sitting on the floor, stereo headphones on his head and his bass in his lap, playing along with a Frank Zappa record. Donald, somewhat amused by our reaction to all this, from a relaxed pose on the couch, asked, "Hey, is Joel still down there?"

Then I remembered: "Oh, yeah! Right! He wants to know if you're coming down."

Donald then yelled across the room. "Hey, Walter! Joel wants to know if we're coming down!" Walter didn't answer or even react (what with "Weasels Ripped My Flesh" blasting in his headphones), so Donald looked back at me with a faint chuckle and said, "I guess not."

—

BY THE END OF THE WEEK, WE WERE SET TO FINISH OUT THE REMAINING DATES AND MAKE up what we could before our visas ran out. Joel made a couple more attempts to engage Donald and Walter, who continued to successfully avoid him, refusing to even talk with him.

It came to a head a couple of days later when Joel, acting on a tip, showed up unannounced to the hotel coffee shop where Donald and Walter and a few of us were having a late breakfast, and as soon as Walter spotted him, he jumped into action, summoning over the nearest busboy.

"Hey, how would you like to manage our band?"

The poor guy spoke no English and could only smile and nod agreeably. No matter.

"Great! That settles it," Walter said, glancing at the guy's name tag. "Felipe, you are officially our new manager."

Felipe glanced back and forth between Walter and Donald, somewhat confused, but still managing a polite smile. Now, as those two hurriedly got up to leave, Donald chimed in, "Welcome aboard, Felipe."

Poor Joel had just reached the table in time to say, "Guys, we gotta talk," when Donald informed him that any future discussions concerning Steely Dan business should be taken up with their new manager, Felipe, who stood there stoic and silent, his eyes now darting back and forth between the three of them.

I couldn't say for sure how long Felipe served as the band's "manager"—probably not much after lunchtime—but I know that over the next two weeks, if my memory serves, we went on to play Leeds University, the Manchester Apollo, and the Empire Theatre in Birmingham, then on to Amsterdam and Copenhagen for our final show of the tour at Tivoli Gardens.

That was a magical night. At the last hint of dusk, the beautiful lights spelled the park's name over the entrance and lit up every ride and attraction inside. The strange mix of popular songs and carnivalesque music that played throughout the park further added to the dreamlike ambience. I recalled hearing of Tivoli Gardens as a kid and it always sounded like it was straight out of some fairy tale, and here I was, playing with Steely Dan! Talk about surreal. Who'd have imagined that a random recommendation from a friend I'd met just once a year and a half earlier, on a gig that was itself pretty random, would lead to this beautiful and bittersweet summer night in Copenhagen. Though I couldn't have known it then, that show would be the last time I'd walk onstage with Steely Dan for many years to come.

—

WHILE KILLING SOME TIME WAITING FOR OUR CONNECTING FLIGHTS HOME AT LONDON'S Heathrow Airport, Walter and I were talking about our plans back in the States, and I mentioned that I was going to start looking for a place to live so I could relinquish my title as Couch Surfing Champion of Los Angeles. Killing a couple of birds with one stone, he suggested that I might want to house-sit his apartment for him while he was in New York for the next week or two.

He had this vintage 1930s-era apartment in Venice Beach, which back then was a pretty rough area, populated mainly by artists, musicians, and heroin addicts. So he was happy to have someone keep an eye on it for him, which made me feel better about taking him up on the offer.

It wasn't a pretty place by any means—kind of old and dingy. (This was before vintage appliances were cool.) But it was a great musician's apartment, with a crazy component stereo system connected to giant electrostatic speakers that Walter had rigged together, guitars lying around, and an extensive and eclectic album collection to listen to. And it was a chance for some solitude—until he got back, anyway. So I dropped my suitcase full of dirty laundry from the tour on the floor, and as I looked out the grimy old casement windows at the glistening ocean and the iconic Santa Monica Pier, I thought, "Hey, not too shabby."

And then, because this is how life likes to throw you a curve sometimes, I woke up later that night to discover, to my horror, I had crabs. Remember those? Not only not fun but, in my particular situation, not exactly the place I wanted to make this discovery. I was appalled to think this newfound trust and friendship was now in jeopardy. Walter, not just a friend but also my employer, was now the guy I had to call and admit to having crabs—while staying in his apartment!

The next day, I was already well into the drill of multiple medicated shampoos and laundry loads of all sheets and linens on the hottest possible settings. I was about to fumigate the entire place when Walter called: turns out he had them too, as likely did most of the band and crew. Given our constant close proximity on the road, it would be hard to know who got 'em first. Kind of the rock and roll version of head lice at a preschool.

—

WITHIN THE FIRST FEW WEEKS OF BEING HOME, THE BAD NEWS CAME LIKE A LIGHTNING bolt: Donald and Walter were disbanding the group. I found out while spending a casual evening with Denny Dias at his apartment, watching him chop some coke on a mirror for close to an hour. (Denny was meticulous in all things.)

As upsetting as it was to hear the band was being dissolved, it kind of fit into my fatalistic belief that there was nothing good that couldn't go south.

As drastic as the change was for all of us, it was no doubt more devastating for the original band members—Denny, Jeff Baxter, and Jimmy Hodder—though I remember being struck by Denny's somewhat philosophical take on it all; he seemed to understand it on another level, that this change was a natural step in Donald and Walter's artistic evolution. They would reemerge as a duo that would tour no more, concentrating instead solely on making records, for which they would summon the best musicians available for the specific needs of each track as they saw fit.

It's fair to say that Walter and Donald's subsequent body of remarkable work was a direct result of this new approach, markedly distinct from the albums they had recorded as a larger group. Now freed from the rigors of touring, these projects, stemming from longer and more intense periods of songwriting, would produce the iconic gems on future albums that have since become Steely Dan classics.

Donald and Walter—along with engineer Roger Nichols and producer Gary Katz—were, more than ever, keenly determined in their further pursuit of natural sonic quality. *Katy Lied*, for example, the first album of this new direction, was just such an experiment. Unlike convention at the time, it was recorded without the use of post-equalization of any signal path; all the sounds of all the instruments and vocals were solely a product of microphone choice and placement. Little or no signal processing took place between the listener and the microphone diaphragm, in an effort to achieve the most pure and natural-sounding recording possible.

I was thrilled to be asked to participate in the making of that album, singing background vocals on a few tracks, the first of which was a tune called "Bad Sneakers." That was also the track where Donald and Walter first experimented with the idea of using me to sing *all* the harmonies and having me double myself, making my vocals more of a singular "instrument," as opposed to just blending in with a group of background singers. This technique produced a textural effect, a kind of ethereal resonance, and it was an approach they would use again on songs like "Rose Darling" and a particularly difficult harmonic exercise for me on a song from their *Aja* album called "Peg."

The background chorus on that one was a challenging cluster of close harmonies that made it difficult for me to keep pitch, so I suggested to Donald that he teach me each part one at a time and allow me to record them individually, without hearing the closest interval I was harmonizing to. It wasn't till I finished doubling the last part and heard him play it all back together that I could appreciate the subtle harmonic personality of the background vocals to "Peg."

Just getting to hear and be a part of this great new music in its early incarnation was thrilling. Over the years, much has been said about Donald and Walter's "perfectionism," which I think is an unfair assessment. Admittedly, there was no shortage of ball-busting in their pursuit of getting everyone's best performance. Walter, for example, might wait until the end of a take, hit the talk-back button, and offer something encouraging like, "Gee, I remember liking the sound of your voice much more on the last sessions." He might have been serious, for all I know, but I just took it in the spirit of his good-natured New York hazing. Having said that, still, it was a thrill knowing that my voice might soon be embedded into these wonderful new tracks that I was hearing for the first time.

—

THOUGH THERE WOULD BE NO MORE LIVE PERFORMANCES BY STEELY DAN FOR SOME TIME, remarkably they remained Top Forty radio darlings for the next twenty years or so. I believe in their own way they sort of opened a portal, setting the stage for a larger audience to readily embrace a more sophisticated, jazz-oriented sound, and in so doing, they greatly broadened the concept of what had been considered mainstream, contemporary music. That their unique and beautiful recordings repeatedly made it onto the *Billboard* Top Ten was, by any measure, an impressive phenomenon.

Getting to work on their subsequent albums, like *The Royal Scam* (being encouraged to step out and ad-lib a bit on "Kid Charlemagne"), *Gaucho* (singing the signature background part on "Hey Nineteen," with the lyric "The Cuervo Gold, / The fine Colombian, / Make tonight a wonderful thing"—an accurate description of the changing times and fading lifestyle we were living), and *Aja* ("Peg" and "I Got the News") will always remain highlights of my career.

But in the summer of 1974, with Steely Dan, for all I knew, now behind me, I was hitting the bricks again—playing the LA clubs and a few scattered sessions here and there . . . Now, at twenty-two, my future felt once again, at best, uncertain.

CHAPTER 13

MICHAEL AND WALTER'S NOT-SO-GREAT ADVENTURE

I had, at least, found my own place to live by then.

For seventy-five bucks a month, I rented a garage apartment in Burbank, emphasis on "garage." I mean, it was literally a garage behind the house owned by two very kind middle-aged women. Slab floor, a fold-out couch, an old refrigerator, two cinder blocks and a board to hold a small black-and-white TV, a reel-to-reel tape machine, and a hot plate. That was all there was. The only sink was in the small (likely out of code) bathroom/shower where I shaved and did dishes.

By then I remember feeling like it was time I gathered myself and looked a bit more closely at my rudderless existence. My various on-and-off girlfriends at the time would probably have unanimously agreed. By this point, I was smoking pot first thing in the morning, and by noon I had already found an excuse to augment my frame of mind with at least a couple of beers. Coke for musicians at my economic level was still a bit of an extravagance, so if I was to enter that world, I needed to be a little creative.

Once, while I was house-sitting for my now ex-girlfriend, who, with her young daughter, was out of town visiting her parents, Walter called me inquiring about our old friend Roy, the coke-dealing horticulturist. Walter had been to Roy's with me before, and though he was duly impressed with Roy's library and succulent collection, this was not our collective focus.

Now, given my history of clear thinking and making healthy choices, it's a cinch I was about to do neither. Instead I decided that this was one of those times you gotta spend a little money to make a little money, as they say. What better recipe for disaster than a quick drug deal involving, right off the bat, two people prone to excess. So taking what little money I had left from the last Steely Dan tour, along with some cash that Walter kicked in, we embarked on a monumentally painful and colossally stupid escapade.

Our plan was simple: we would buy about a half ounce of some of that exceptionally pure cocaine from our old friend Roy and cut it in half, which would still be much better than most coke on the streets of LA—the idea being we would not only make some easy money (selling only to our friends, completely under the radar) but end up with a fair portion of blow for our own recreational consumption, free of charge. And since the apartment I was watching had a professional-grade scale and a large dining room table, this seemed like the perfect venue to pull off this caper. The obvious jeopardy I was putting my ex-girlfriend in, not to mention my inability to use cocaine in moderation, apparently never entered my mind—or Walter's either, for that matter. After all, it was a fairly simple plan. What could possibly go wrong?

Well, true to form, of course we snorted most of it before even getting around to cutting it, let alone selling anything. In fact, other than getting up to pee, we never left that dining room table. After a couple harrowing days of molar grinding and tequila-fueled aimless discussions about everything from music to possible wood nymph sightings in Laurel Canyon, or whatever stupid shit other people have said while high on cocaine, we were left with little more than a gram or so—not exactly enough to qualify as "inventory."

So, in an attempt to bring this disastrous folly to a close, I sent Walter home with most of what was left of the blow. Financial investment having already been forsaken, and now left alone with this mess to clean before my ex's return, I downed one last shot of Cuervo and smoked my second-to-last Marlboro Red, saving the last one for the morning to enjoy with my coffee till I could buy more. I decided that the unholy mess we'd made of the apartment—the overflowing ashtrays, the nearly empty fifth of tequila, and the pitifully sad remnants of cocaine that remained on the scale's porcelain plate or spilled across the dining room table—could wait till tomorrow. I should get some sleep. Again, not one of my better choices.

A couple hours later, just before dawn, still lying awake in bed with my heart pounding out of my chest, obsessing on that last cigarette, the unmistakable red light from a police car began streaking across the bedroom walls. I could hear car doors slamming and radio dispatches accompanied by voices outside. So I jumped to my feet, and outside the bedroom window I saw a couple of cop cars, and before I could get a handle on what was happening, there was a loud knock at the front door. *Shit!*

I stumbled, bouncing off the walls down the short hallway to the living room while trying to put on my pants, when there was another even louder knock. "Los Angeles Police Department!" I hesitated for a brief second, glancing over at the remaining blow and paraphernalia still sitting out on the dining room table, realizing that taking the time to deal with it was not an option, and if they were here to bust me, they were coming in anyway. So I decided to wing it and resigned myself to my fate, which would most likely be my imminent (now second) arrest in the same apartment belonging to this poor girl whose only crime was to trust me once too often. She hadn't been gone more than a couple days, and I'd already created this absolute shit show, with unthinkable consequences.

I opened the door and was practically blinded by a flashlight shining in my face.

"Are you Mike McDonald?"

In my adrenaline rush, shock, and confusion, I managed to mumble, "Uh, yes . . ."

Next question I heard: "Does this belong to you?" as he redirected the light onto the face of the guy in custody next to him . . . Walter! The cop then explained that he had gotten a 911 call about "some crazy dude" across the alley knocking on windows calling my name. "He tells me he was here earlier tonight and got confused when he returned and couldn't remember which building you lived in."

"*Yes!*" I jumped in, tap-dancing as fast as my brain would allow. "Yes, that's right. He was here earlier. Boy, he sure looks to be in rough shape now. Uh . . . thank you, Officer! I promise I'll keep him here till he sobers up."

At this point I wasn't sure what I was even saying. All I knew was that for some reason, thankfully, they hadn't tried to enter the apartment. The cop informed me that I'd better damn well keep Walter under wraps and that he didn't want to have to return tonight for any reason. I dragged Walter back into the apartment, the front door closed, and after what seemed like an eternity filled with more radio dispatches and police chatter, the cops finally drove away. Talk about dodging a fucking bullet. I turned to Walter.

"What the fuck! I mean . . . Jesus! What were you thinking? After four a.m.—knocking on windows?"

Walter just responded with a nervous giggle. "I know, right?"

Standing there staring at Walter in disbelief, to be honest I didn't know whether to be pissed or just laugh. What I did know was that the prospect that I might still be holding is what drew him back out into the wee hours, because I was just that pitiful myself. Disgusted with both of us, I just rolled my eyes and pointed to the scale, then threw some blankets and a pillow on the couch for him while he began to make short work of the remnants of cocaine still on the plate.

When I headed off to bed, Walter was finishing off the tequila, playing an unplugged electric bass. For how long? I don't know. All

I know is he was gone in the morning when I woke early and began to clean up the mess we'd made before my ex returned. The nosier neighbors in the complex, of course, later made a point to inform her of the late-night visit from the LAPD. When she asked about it, I just explained that some crazy guy was knocking on windows across the way and the police wanted to know if I heard anything. She said that it made her all the more glad I was there to keep an eye on the place. In that moment, the only response I could think of was to quote my friend Walter. "Yeah, I know, right?"

In the aftermath of all this excitement, I returned to my pathetic garage apartment, where I sat for a few hours in solitude with a new pack of cigarettes, consumed by that all-too-familiar depressing, gray mental wasteland that always came at the end of every binge till I could hopefully once again sleep it off.

In the coming weeks, however, fate would intervene once again, this time in the form of a phone call from Jeff "Skunk" Baxter.

CHAPTER 14

MEET THE DOOBIES

In the year since Steely Dan jettisoned the band, Skunk had been on the road playing with everyone from Elton John to the Doobie Brothers, and somewhere along the way he got word to me that the Doobies might have a temporary need for my services on keyboard and vocals.

The Doobies started in 1970 as an obscure local band playing biker bars in the hills of Santa Cruz and San Jose, California. But by this point, early 1975, they had become one of the biggest touring bands in the world, riding the wave of several platinum albums, whose sales were driven by enormous hit singles like "Listen to the Music," "Long Train Runnin'," and "Black Water." It was a moment of almost unheard-of good fortune that I was invited to step on deck of this already phenomenally successful musical enterprise.

This opportunity only arose from the untimely misfortune befalling Tom Johnston, their guitar-playing lead singer and one of their principal songwriters, who, after the stress of nonstop touring, decided to take a hiatus for health reasons. The band needed someone to fill in, if only for the short haul. They still had two great guitar players in Skunk and Pat Simmons, but since they had never toured with a keyboard player, it seemed like an opportune time to introduce one to their live show, especially since Bill Payne's keyboard figured so heavily on some of their biggest hits. Also I think Jeff had suggested that my singing might come in handy.

The catch was I had to be on a plane the next morning to fly to New Orleans and go right into rehearsal. Unlike my first Steely Dan encounter, this wasn't so much an audition as it was a case of Jeff Baxter vouching for me and putting on the line his belief in my ability to show up and do the gig. I'll always be indebted to him for that.

I mentioned that I was at that moment a little low on cash for such a trip, but Jeff explained that the ticket would be waiting for me at the airport and that, going forward, my salary would be $1,500 a week—plus a nice per diem, which was just extra cash for expenses—starting when I got there. This was more than I made with Steely Dan in a month! (None of us got rich touring with the Dan—not even the Dan.)

So I jumped on a plane and, less than twenty-four hours later, walked into a rehearsal in downtown New Orleans, at a venue the band had played the night before called the Warehouse. It was there I first met the guys: drummers Keith Knudsen and John Hartman, Pat Simmons, and bassist Tiran Porter. They were a road-hardened bunch of musicians for sure, all of them unique personalities, and as the new guy, I found myself surveying the landscape, trying to get a sense of the group dynamic: Skunk was his usual effervescent self, Tiran gave off a vibe one would associate more with a college professor than your typical musician, Keith and John were cordial and good-natured, and Pat, without making any effort to portray himself as such, struck me as having a leadership quality that the other guys seemed to recognize.

The stage plot was an impressive sight, with two elaborate drum kits on risers, one on either side of an elaborate array of miscellaneous percussion instruments—congas, a bongo rack, a bell tree, and a giant Chinese gong—placed strategically center stage.

We wasted no time diving into the material, starting with the stuff I was somewhat familiar with: "Black Water," "Long Train Runnin'," "Listen to the Music" . . . songs I'd been playing at the Trojan Room in Glendale just a few weeks earlier. By the time we got to their newest single, an older song by Motown artist Kim Weston called "Take Me in Your Arms (Rock Me a Little While)," I started to really appreciate the energy that the band had infused into their version and, frankly, into the live performances of all their songs. The double-drummer concept was like a human power plant; their precision and the energy it produced was mightily impressive. This was no nightclub act!

With just two days' rehearsal, I managed to get a handle on all of the Doobies' roughly two-hour-long show, taking sufficient notes, but more so tapping into my years of club experience, which did come in handy here. I'd become a quick study and developed a somewhat enhanced power of retention (which, I'll be the first to admit, ain't what it used to be).

—

TWO DAYS. THAT WAS IT. NOW WE HIT THE ROAD. MY DAD WAS LIVING IN NEW ORLEANS at the time, so I made arrangements to meet him for lunch the next day, and from there we would drive together up to my first show with the band in Shreveport. Armed with nothing more than the address of the venue and a Rand McNally book of road maps, we managed—without too much trouble—to find the place: a gigantic circular arena, designed more for sports events than concerts. Finding the backstage door was a little tricky on a round building. After walking around the perimeter a couple of times, pulling on several locked entrances, my dad began to wonder if maybe we had the wrong place—until we finally stumbled upon the stage door by the loading dock, which was exactly where we had parked in the first place.

The difference between playing these songs with the band at the smaller rehearsal hall the previous day and running the material down in this cavernous, empty concrete arena—with sound system and audience seating completely circling a huge stage, the closest bandmate at least ten feet away, and playing at about three times the volume—was, at first, daunting.

After sound check we sat down to an amazing four-course dinner prepared by the band's traveling professional chef and social director, Dan Fong (who would go on to become one of the more iconic rock and roll photographers of the '70s). This feast was a far cry from the bag of Lay's or Doritos with an overcooked hamburger that was heretofore my experience of backstage fare.

I wondered that whole evening what my dad was making of all the machinations and sheer size of this traveling road show, twenty-some-odd people, all with their own very specific tasks and areas of responsibility, scurrying about. I couldn't tell if he was as impressed as I was or just wondering, "Who's paying for all this?"

Phil Basile, the road manager, invited my dad to sit on the side of the stage during the show, and since no one knew who I was, it was safe for me to walk up there with him while the house lights were still up and wait for the band to come out. It wasn't till the house went dark and ten thousand people jumped to their feet in a single deafening roar while we took the stage and the drummers rolled through the intro of "Jesus Is Just Alright" that it occurred to me: the last gig my dad had seen me play was at the Panorama Lanes bowling alley in Belleville, Illinois.

Having listened to their music only on the radio, I can tell you that playing live with the Doobies was an altogether different and more visceral experience. By the time we launched into "Take Me in Your Arms," I felt like I was strapped to the nose of an Atlas rocket. As I started to sing the lyrics written on scraps of paper taped to my piano, I could only hope that I sounded reasonably confident. That song—my first lead vocal ever with the Doobies—got a response from the audience that was enthusiastic enough, though understandably peppered with more than a few people yelling, "Hey, where's Tom?!" Pat Simmons, who had, in Tom's absence, become in effect the band's new front man, introduced me to the crowd.

"On keyboards—Michael McDonald!"

Nice to hear, but a little strange, as I had always been "Mike." No one had called me "Michael" since the nuns in grade school. But the next day, the rebranding continued as the local reviewer identified the strange new guy singing some of Tom's songs as "Michael McDonald." As the tour went on, Pat continued, every night, to introduce me that way, as did every subsequent reviewer. And so it was from that point on, I officially went from "Mike" to "Michael."

—

THAT FIRST NIGHT WAS AN UNUSUAL MIX OF ADRENALINE, ANXIETY, AND MELANCHOLY when, shortly after the show, I said goodbye to my dad, as the band rolled out and he drove back to New Orleans. It seemed over the years after he and my mom split that we never got to see each other nearly enough, and I always looked forward to every opportunity I had to be with him. Though I wished we had a little more time to visit, it was with a certain sense of satisfaction after the excitement of the evening's events that I hoped he might be somewhat impressed or at least reassured that I was on the right path.

As we set out from Louisiana across Texas, it was not lost on me that the tour route was a well-worn path for this band and others in their genre, guitar-slinging rock and roll bands like ZZ Top, the Allman Brothers, the Marshall Tucker Band, and Lynyrd Skynyrd. The Doobie Brothers were consistently well received by the sold-out crowds in ten-to-fifteen-thousand-seat arenas, a following they had worked hard to build, sometimes playing over two hundred shows a year.

While their earliest tours meant spending hours and miles in a cramped Winnebago, the Doobie Brothers that I joined were airborne in an older Convair twin-engine prop plane (owned by Seals and Crofts) and would soon have their own small fleet of planes: two restored '50s-era Martin 404s—one for the band, one for the crew (the *Doobie-liner* and the *Crewbie-liner*). They, too, were double-engine prop planes, not designed to fly at higher altitudes, but they *were* designed for comfort, with spacious executive interiors: captain's chairs, long leather couches, and booth table arrangements—good for eating and poker games.

Smoking marijuana was a normal ritual that seemed to accompany whatever function we were performing as a band. We smoked at recording sessions, at rehearsals, and throughout any given day while out on tour. It always seemed to make the tedious parts—being locked in a fluorescent-lit studio room for hours on end, the monotony of endless hotel check-ins—more bearable. We never left home without it, and if we ran low while away, there were always plenty of reputable drug dealers in any given city who, anticipating our arrival, would find their way to us.

A lot of the bigger dealers seemed to move around with impunity, although I'm sure coming to our shows was about as close as they cared to be to all the off-duty cops working security that night. On occasion, these dealers would show uncanny imagination and initiative by way of greasing the palms of the hotel staff and finding their way into our rooms before we even arrived, for the purpose of leaving some of the more Class A drugs—cocaine and heroin—stashed behind picture frames or taped under toilet tank lids. They were well acquainted with those of us who might require such service. The traveling rock bands and their crews rolling through town were not just a welcome influx of cash for these guys but also a chance to party like a rock star after the gig, back at the hotel.

Still, the next day, it was back to business as usual for us, and that next plane ride was always part of the workday ahead. We typically spent every morning the same way: once on board, while drinking a lot of strong coffee and smoking pot all the way to the next town, we'd plug our headphones into a multi-junction device connected to the plane's sound system and listen to a cassette of the last night's show. Listening every day to the same two hours of music you had just performed hours before might seem like the tedious part I mentioned earlier, but it was in fact an important exercise for us and something I always looked forward to. You never knew when you might hear something you tried last night and know better than to ever try again, or, even better, something interesting that someone played in passing that might be expanded upon as more of an overall arrangement idea—something we could, and many times did, try out at our next sound check. Time well spent, we thought, in an ongoing effort to maintain and oftentimes improve the quality of our live shows.

—

OUR DAYS ON THE ROAD WERE TYPICALLY LONG AND WOULD INVARIABLY END BACK AT the hotel bar, where we'd sometimes sit in with the local lounge band and drink enough liquid courage to talk to the local girls. Our interactions with some of the local *guys* were not always as pleasant, like the time in Huntington, West Virginia, when some redneck businessman made an offhanded racist comment in the elevator, whereupon Memphis Horns saxophonist Andrew Love knocked him out cold, leaving him lying there, halfway out of the elevator. From our rooms, for hours afterward, all you could hear was the dinging of the bell as the elevator door kept bouncing off the guy's unconscious torso.

Everyone from the band and crew to the pilots, truck drivers, and office staff were good-hearted, hardworking folks, and I liked them all. Some of the crew, great musicians themselves, had along the way developed valuable technical skills and experience—knowledge about repairing, modifying, and maintaining professional gear, which enabled a band like us to sustain the forward momentum of touring.

We all seemed to merge seamlessly, all of us having in common this penchant for life on the road. It felt like most of us might be running from something, whether it be childhood trauma or just the boredom and stagnation most adults settle into after high school and college. A few of the crew had been to Vietnam, and this lifestyle was made to order for them, just as that constant motion seemed to be cathartic for my dad after World War II. We rarely slowed enough to let the demons catch up with us, and when they did, we'd just get high. For most of us, this was our version of running off with the circus.

Early on, one of the big attractions for me of being in a band—beyond the music and the overdose of male bonding—was that it was a great way to avoid "maturity" and still get paid. But I would learn in time that part of that was my genetic predisposition to substance abuse, which was as much a catalyst as any love of music. Any profession where drinking alcohol is seen as relatively normal can offer a kind of camouflage for those of us with addictive tendencies. And after initially observing this band and this crew, I wondered if perhaps my concern about my own substance abuse was overblown. I started to think maybe all I ever really needed was the right gig, with an organization like this one, where everyone's day started with a little hair of the dog in a stiff cup of coffee and a big fat doobie. I mean, after all . . . it's right there in the name.

Though it wouldn't be long before I started to become "that guy"; I was the standout even in *this* environment of two-fisted drinkers, the one who had to be escorted to his room at the end of the night.

—

WE FINISHED OUT THE THREE TO FOUR MONTHS' WORTH OF DATES I'D BEEN HIRED FOR, and during that time I'd met some big-time promoters, record company field reps, and regional promotion guys who took partying to a whole new level, like it was their job, which, you could argue, it probably was. And there were some legendary ladies in every town who seemingly never missed a rock concert by anyone within a hundred-mile radius. They were often fondly remembered for their wit and poise as much as their beauty, not to mention their encyclopedic knowledge of where the great local bands played. Most of them, I felt, harbored dreams of settling down—getting married, having children, and living happily ever after with some rock star. I think they just had a little trouble making up their minds as to which one.

We ended the run with a gig in Honolulu, which was booked, I believe, for the sole purpose of underwriting two weeks of R&R for the band and crew on the island of Kauai. By now we'd grown thick as thieves and were, to say the least, a little worse for wear. I hadn't ever been on a tour that long or intense before, with so few days off. I wasn't sure I remembered how to live a normal, stationary life anymore.

I held no expectations of staying with the group for any extended period; that's not typically the way these things work out. Usually you'd get a great gig like this with a great band just before they break up. All I knew was I had a gig that required no audition and provided a salary that was more than I could ever ask for. So I was grateful—for however long that played out.

But then Jeff Baxter informed me that the band would like me to consider staying on indefinitely, even after Tom's return. I, of course, was thrilled, though I couldn't help but wonder if anyone had run this by Tom.

I hadn't met Tom yet; all I knew about him was his music. And since he and Pat Simmons had been the band's core composers up to that point, I don't think the audiences ever stopped anticipating Tom's return. Even over the next couple years of his absence, I'm sure they remained ever hopeful that he might rejoin the band onstage once again.

At this point, I wasn't yet an official Doobie Brother, but I also wasn't a temporary sub anymore either. I had somewhat graduated to being more of a fixed sideman on an extended salary. And truth be told, I would've been happy to sing backgrounds and play piano with the band in that capacity for as long as they'd have me.

I remember one night, just after that first run of dates and after I'd been asked to stay on with the band indefinitely, we were rehearsing in San Francisco at the Winterland Ballroom. We were staying at the Miyako Hotel in Japantown. Jeff Baxter and I were smoking a joint before heading down to dinner, and as we sat in his room talking, he pointed out that our current salary was about fifty grand a year, which was a lot of money then and certainly a lot to me. There were years where if I was lucky my annual salary added up to about five grand. Sitting in the room that night, Jeff put it another way. "Man, think about it. You're making the starting salary of an executive at IBM—playing rock and roll music!"

That should have been an exhilarating moment of realization, bringing with it a feeling of accomplishment. But given my penchant for insecurity, as soon as he said it, a deep sense of dread and fear came over me. I didn't feel like I was capable of anything deserving of that kind of compensation. My deepest sense of who I was told me once again that it surely wouldn't be long before everyone realized I was a fraud. I almost skipped dinner to go back to my room, where I could turn out all the lights, get in the fetal position, and shake for a while—till I remembered the little bar in the lobby just outside the restaurant, where I could find my usual immediate remedy for anxiety: a drink. Maybe six.

CHAPTER 15

DOOBIE OR NOT DOOBIE, THAT IS THE QUESTION

Upon returning to LA, the band was scheduled to embark on a new album, and again, I didn't presume that would involve me. But Pat Simmons had mentioned to their producer Ted Templeman that he thought I might bring something to the project as a vocalist and keyboardist. Though for me, the thought of filling Bill Payne's shoes was, to say the least, daunting.

As a piano player, I was basically self-taught, my only formal lessons being those nights with Tom Hanlon early on (if you don't count my cousin Peggy Doyle teaching me, at the age of five, how to bang out the Marine Corps hymn with one finger). When I moved out to California, I also had some lessons with a lovely Frenchwoman who would use a ruler to lift my wrist into proper position. Needless to say, we weren't a good fit.

I had learned to expand on the basics as I went along—mostly from watching other keyboard players, not the least of whom was Donald Fagen, who taught me how to voice simple chords, making them more harmonically appealing and transparent. Still, with Donald doing all the heavy lifting in Steely Dan, my keyboard duties were more or less "as needed" and not as vital. However, now, with the Doobies, I was the sole keyboardist, and I felt I really needed to up my game.

So I started taking lessons from a gifted pianist and teacher named Fletcher Peck, a veteran New Yorker who used to play in the orchestra of *The Jackie Gleason Show*. He was a fun, irreverent character who immediately seemed to understand my lack of attention span for formal, rudimentary training. He sensed I didn't like to go the long way around for anything and made a point to feed me the information I most wanted to learn: a little guidance in terms of chord voicings, substitutions, progressions, reharmonizations . . . that kind of thing. He did, however, give me the dreaded *Hanon: The Virtuoso Pianist* book of exercises to teach me better finger independence (a book that's been gathering dust for fifty years).

A lot of the experience was about unlearning some bad habits. For starters, I needed to do more with my left hand. I've found that people who teach themselves to play can get a bit simplistic and heavy-handed in the left hand, playing simple one-note patterns or a lot of octaves. In my early songwriting days, I was always emulating bass guitar with my left hand, to give the idea of what the syncopation of an actual band might sound like. But as I developed as a piano player, I learned to use my left hand to expand the chord voicings and not leave it all to the right hand to carry.

I also had to learn how to be more efficient with the physical *mechanics*—the way your hands and fingers actually strike the keys. I've always been a banger, and over the years it has steadily ruined my shoulders and hands. I had to learn how to use my arms and fingers more economically and creatively, and maybe even my wrists. (Could be that French lady with the ruler was onto something after all.)

—

KEYBOARD LIMITATIONS AND ANXIETIES ASIDE, IT WAS STILL TERRIBLY EXCITING TO have Ted reach out to me and talk about the upcoming session. Ted's casual corporate style and demeanor in those days—white tennis shorts, cashmere sweaters draped strategically over the shoulders—may have been in sharp contrast to the long-haired, unshaven, counterculture image of the typical '70s independent producer, but he nonetheless had almost supernatural instincts in the studio. He had been a member of an earlier Warner Bros. band, Harpers Bizarre, famous for "The 59th Street Bridge Song (Feelin' Groovy)." It was common at the time for record label staff producers, once they got a few hits under their belt, to ultimately create their own independent production company. Ted, on the other hand, was very much a company man; he saw his future in the A&R department at Warners as vice president. Though he started his producing career with the Doobies, he later went on to produce such diverse and classic artists as Van Morrison, Nicolette Larson, Captain Beefheart, and Van Halen. His brilliance at deconstructing our arrangements and then reconstructing them in a better form was an invaluable key to our success in the studio, and we all understood how lucky we were to have his guidance.

Personally, I was thrilled to be any part of this upcoming project, and as the new guy, I certainly wouldn't have had the balls to suggest any of my original songs for the album. But it turns out Tiran Porter had played Ted a demo he and I recorded while hanging out at his house, a song of mine entitled "Losin' End." It's not a song I would have ever imagined the Doobies doing, but to my surprise, Ted was intrigued by the idea, and so that would be the first song I ever recorded with the Doobie Brothers, for an album that would eventually become *Takin' It to the Streets*.*

As for the title track, it was actually a song I'd started writing a couple of years earlier, on my way to a gig at a club in Orange County, south of LA. The original germ of the idea emerged from conversations I had with my younger sister, Maureen, who, like most of her college-age contemporaries, had grown very socially conscious. A

---

* I would later reimagine "Losin' End" at a slower tempo for my solo album *If That's What It Takes*.

true product of their time, they were growing more keenly aware of things like rural and inner-city poverty, the exponential growth of economic disparity, the ever-increasing number of Americans falling through the ever-widening cracks . . . We would find ourselves talking about the hope of a more equitable society, and the hard truth that progressive change like that historically never came easily.

As idealistic and overly intellectualized as the subject may sound, it struck me, one evening driving to that club gig, that it might be just the right lyric subject matter for this gospel-inspired chord progression I had been tinkering with. I had always wanted to write what I felt could pass for a traditional gospel song; that style always held a powerful attraction for me. I also suspected the lyric content might be a conversation whose time had come.

Musically, I started with the piano intro/verse, followed by the ramp-up to the chorus, and the lyrics came pretty easy for those first two sections. "You don't know me, but I'm your brother . . ."

For the chorus, I felt it should just kind of sing itself when I got there. However, initially, the title was elusive; "Falling Through the Cracks" just wasn't gonna pay off. I quietly messed with the idea after quickly setting up my piano before downbeat at the club. The elements of the song kept playing through my mind. And then later that evening, while behind the wheel on the way home (as would often happen), it came to me: "Takin' It to the Streets." By the time I got home that night, I all but had a new song.

For the longest time, I imagined what it might sound like with a rhythm section and choir, recorded live in some church. But now, playing with the Doobies, with the door wide open for me to present any and all musical ideas for this project—and the fact that I didn't have many other songs to offer—I nervously played down the idea of "Takin' It to the Streets" for the band. I must confess, it wasn't until I heard Pat, Tiran, Skunk, Keith, and John's driving percussion, along with Bobby LaKind's signature conga part on the intro, that I started to feel the song's potential in a new and exciting way. I remember listening to the first playback of that track and having that euphoric moment, thinking, "Damn, that shit sounds good!"

What I can tell you for a fact is that a few months earlier, driving home from a club gig in my Ford Pinto with an idea that existed only in my head, I couldn't have imagined in my wildest dreams that this song would so profoundly change my life.

—

ANOTHER LIFE-CHANGING COMPOSITION FOR ME WAS "IT KEEPS YOU RUNNIN'." THAT song was the miraculous result of my one day's attendance at the Dick Grove School of Music, a master class held in a small office space on Ventura Boulevard.

On that particular day, the instructor, Mr. Grove himself, who was an accomplished jazz pianist, was talking about passing chords and standard jazz chord progressions. He demonstrated how beautiful compositions, like Jerome Kern's "All the Things You Are," are often built on what might technically be considered a series of passing chords, changing keys, creating the basic harmonic body of the song.

That one-hour class kind of blew my mind wide open; almost every song I wrote after that—especially songs like "It Keeps You Runnin'," with its chromatically descending II–V passing chord progression—was directly influenced by what I learned that day. As for the lyrics on that one, they were just about the fear of re-experiencing heartbreak in the past and the natural reluctance to ever letting oneself be vulnerable again.

One never knows what good fortune might come from any composition.

The day we recorded "It Keeps You Runnin'," Carly Simon happened to come by the studio to see Ted, as he was scheduled to produce her next album. She was sitting in the control room, seemingly impressed with the track we were cutting, and that led to her later cutting the song herself on her next album, *Another Passenger*—using the Doobies as the rhythm section. (And, it turns out, that set the stage for the two of us to collaborate again down the road.)

The *Takin' It to the Streets* album was recorded in the summer of '75, our first experience of long, extended night sessions—trying to get as much done as possible before we hit the road again. I remember having to take catnaps on the floor of the studio, trying to catch up on lost sleep. It was there, at Warner Bros. studios (formerly Amigo Studios) in North Hollywood, a facility capably managed by audio engineers Lee Herschberg, Chet Himes, Donn Landee, and Mark Linett, where I would spend much of my time in the days ahead.

It was also where I met Tom Johnston for the first time, when he came in to record his song "Turn It Loose." I remember thinking the song had that distinctive energy and cleverness that were signatures of Tom's writing—songs like "Listen to the Music" and "Rockin' Down the Highway," to name a couple.

I'd like to say I didn't worry too much that Tom might resent my even being there, that I chose to focus instead on what I might be able to bring to the song—but that would be somewhere short of the truth. It was too easy for me to give at least some credence to my paranoia. In my mind, I was sure he must've been thinking, "This guy's no Billy Payne!"

But if Tom was less than impressed with my contribution to the track, he didn't let on, and he seemed to be every bit the nice guy everyone described him to be. Still, what impressed me most was that for all his physical health challenges at that point, on that day he still rose to the occasion and gave a hundred percent effort.

Being in the studio with the band on that first album, I came to meet so many talented people, artists who ended up impacting my career in the most positive ways. Like the day my old friend Michael Omartian, a session piano player whom I'd worked with on some Rick Jarrard sessions years earlier, happened to be working in the studio down the hall. He asked me if I'd pop in and sing a line or two on a track he was producing for a newly signed Warners artist, a singer-songwriter from Texas by the name of Christopher Cross. The song, "Ride Like the Wind," would be the first release from his debut album, which went on to sell over six million records and win multiple Grammys. (I got a lot of mileage out of that half hour of work: the line "Such a long way to go" would—fortunately or unfortunately—become a favorite with drunken Michael McDonald impersonators for years to come. And it was used in a very funny *SCTV* sketch where Rick Moranis, striking an uncanny likeness to yours truly in his full fake beard, sprints into a recording session to sing that one line, running back in each time it repeats, then jumps into his idling vintage convertible and races off, presumably to record yet another background vocal for someone else.)

—

SINCE STEELY DAN'S *KATY LIED* ALBUM, I HAD BEGUN TO GET MORE WORK AS A STUDIO background singer, on tracks such as Elton John's "Victim of Love," Bonnie Raitt's cover of Del Shannon's "Runaway," Little Feat's "Red Streamliner," and Jimmy Webb's "Old Wing Mouth," to name a few. This was a time when vocal harmonies were as prominent on pop records as they'd ever been—think of groups like the Eagles, Orleans, America. And despite all the shit I'd later take for singing on seemingly everyone's tracks, I have to say: I really enjoyed it. There was a certain romance to it for me—like getting a front-row seat to something special, my personal *20 Feet from Stardom* experience. It was a thrill to hear these tracks before they were even mixed and to meet these wonderful, impressive artists, including then up-and-coming singer-songwriters like Lauren Wood and Tim Moore.

I think most would be surprised if they knew how many iconic singers did vocal background sessions in LA during the '70s. While on any given session they may have been singing in service of some other artist, they were all exceptional artists themselves, and I felt privileged to be accepted into that group, invited to sing alongside the likes of Luther Vandross, Howard Hewett, James and Phillip Ingram, Siedah Garrett, Bill Champlin, Timothy B. Schmit, Mike Finnigan, John Townsend, Kim Carnes, Bonnie Bramlett, Patti Austin, David Pack, and Kenny Loggins, just to name a few.

Among the more memorable perks of hanging around Warner Bros. studios during the recording of the *Takin' It to the Streets* album was playing one-on-one basketball with James Taylor. There was a hoop and backboard in Studio A, and upon being the first of our crew to arrive one day, I discovered James in there shooting some baskets. He was there to work next door in Studio B on his *In the Pocket* album and, as it turns out, also the first to arrive. He joked about how pathetic it was that we were the only ones there. After all, what self-respecting rock musician shows up early to his own session?

As we hadn't officially met, I shared how much I admired his work, how I'd listened to his prior album, *Gorilla*, in my car every day for the last year. I have to admit I was a little stunned when he bounced the ball across the floor to me, but no lack of athletic ability on my part was too humiliating for me to miss this opportunity to have a conversation with the man himself.

As James actually made a few shots (and I mostly chased the ball around the studio), we made small talk about everything from the perils of coming up with enough songs for a whole album to living in California—a subject on which we shared differing opinions. He was typical of most people I'd met from the East Coast. I sensed that he missed it and maybe found West Coast culture lacking, whereas I, like so many others from the Midwest, would have happily stowed away on a manure truck just to get to California.

The Warners studio is also where I first met Lenny Waronker and Russ Titelman, two of the most respected producers in the business, who worked with James Taylor on those two iconic albums, adding to their impressive list of accomplishments (they had also worked with Randy Newman, Ry Cooder, Rickie Lee Jones, George Benson, and Eric Clapton, among countless others). Lenny and Russ would soon turn out to be significant players in my eventual solo career.

—

BUT FOR NOW, AT THE CLOSE OF THE *TAKIN' IT TO THE STREETS* PROJECT—WHICH TOOK close to six, seven months, all told—most of us seemed pleased with the results, and I for one was feeling exhilarated.

As for Tom Johnston, I don't know that I'm the person to speak to the matter of his possible ambivalence about this project. On the other hand, I couldn't help but feel somehow responsible. The group that he had founded with Pat and then left for a short while had changed—not surprisingly, since his contribution and presence had always had such a formidable impact. So his absence was palpable to any ardent Doobie Brothers fan. His voice and songs had been—and always will be—such a signature of the band's sound. So in that temporary vacuum a shift of sorts was inevitable.

A lot of people have credited me with—or accused me of—single-handedly changing the band's sound. But my take on that is it mostly had to do with the conspicuous void left by Tom's brief departure. From the beginning, the band as it was, with Tom and Pat being the main writers, created a fairly eclectic and diverse songbook, experiments in everything from psychedelic folk rock and slack-key instrumentals to funk blues rock.

Now, in Tom's absence, all the band members—Skunk, Keith, John, Tiran—in their own way, out of necessity, contributed something to this new scattering of musical directions. However, I believe it was Pat's profound influence on the band's music from the beginning that was a sustaining force as much as any musical contribution made by any of us.

As I say, it's not my place to speculate on Tom's personal feelings about this album, but suffice to say some of the material wasn't necessarily anything Tom would have envisioned. Not so much the songs "Wheels of Fortune," "8th Avenue Shuffle," or even "Takin' It to the Streets," but some of the others we were experimenting with, like "It Keeps You Runnin'" and "Losin' End," which leaned more pop/R&B rather than the guitar-centric blues rock the group had largely been known for up till then.

But I can only speculate that these shifts in musical directions might help explain Tom's subsequent focus on a solo album—and increasingly limited participation with the next two Doobie Brothers albums.

—

AS FOR ME, I COULD HAVE LANDED IN A LOT OF PLACES AND EVEN BEEN GIVEN SIMILAR opportunities, but it didn't escape me that here I was, in what I believed was the best spot to be—with this label and this A&R department that were largely responsible for some of America's best established and emerging artists. Warner Bros. Records, through the leadership of Mo Ostin, Lenny Waronker, Russ Titelman, and Ted Templeman, had built a remarkable roster of artists: Joni Mitchell, James Taylor, Randy Newman, Van Morrison, Emmylou Harris, Fleetwood Mac, Bonnie Raitt, Gordon Lightfoot, Rod Stewart, Van Halen, Aerosmith, George Benson . . . The walls of the offices and the hallways in between were covered with the gold and platinum commemorative albums that represented some of my favorite music.

One day, after a visit to Ted's office, I was amazed to see a large billboard in front of the Warners complex in Burbank promoting the release of *Takin' It to the Streets*, with a giant image of the album cover that must have been a couple of stories high. What an amazing sight! I happened to have a big roach in the ashtray of my car (nothing unusual there), so I parked in front of the billboard, lit up, and sat there staring at it for about a half hour. I thought back to how dazzled I was by all those billboards I'd seen on Sunset Boulevard that night I first arrived in LA, only a few years earlier. As much as I might've fantasized such a thing, I don't know that I ever actually, truly believed that one day I'd see one promoting an album that I was even remotely involved with. But . . . there it was.

Having spent so much of my life feeling like the guy "least likely to succeed," always dreading that inevitable question "So . . . what have you been doing?"—suddenly, awash with feelings of validation, I finally had a worthwhile answer.

Later a friend of mine told me about first hearing "Takin' It to the Streets" on the radio. He was driving with a couple of his buddies, all of them already fans of the group. As the DJ announced "a new song by the Doobie Brothers!" he reached for his car radio in anticipation and cranked the volume. As the song's intro began, they all looked around at one another, perplexed . . . till one of them broke the silence with "What the fuck is *that*?!"

My friend wasn't really clear as to whether that reaction was a positive one . . . or not so much. Nevertheless, that proverbial train had officially left the station.

CHAPTER 16

LIVIN' ON THE (IT'S NOT MY) FAULT LINE

"Takin' It to the Streets," the title track, went on to be a moderate Top Forty radio hit—my first ever—and the album overall received a lot of support from FM radio. So we spent the entire next year more or less following the sun—touring steadily across the United States, Australia, and Asia, where fandom took on a whole other thing. I remember in Japan, there were fan club "welcoming parties" at every train stop, the sounds of excited screams and camera shutters clicking as we made our way into the waiting cars. A poor man's *Hard Day's Night*, perhaps, but indulging myself in the band's popularity—on the other side of the world!—and finding a crowd of people who even knew who *I* was . . . was a strange but gratifying experience.

We also made stops in Hong Kong and Bangkok, which provided a more sobering perspective. This was 1976, not long after the Vietnam War, and the refugee crisis gave the impression that the Southeast Asian world was collapsing. In Bangkok, we saw whole families living on the street. No matter which way you walked, it seemed the entire world was walking in the opposite direction. While out exploring with Pat one afternoon, I almost had my pocket picked by a kid not even ten years old. Barely sensing something, I reached around and grabbed a small wrist whose hand was holding my wallet. I snatched it back and then watched a small group of laughing street urchins disappear into the oncoming wave of humanity.

One of my saddest memories of the city is seeing a young mother holding an infant on her hip while begging at tables inside a small Thai bistro. The infant, crying with its little hand stretched out gesturing, couldn't have been more than eight months old, already proficient at begging on the street.

Yet even in this sad chaos, Bangkok exuded an undeniable beauty and charm.

After experiencing the strict social norms and the traumatized economic conditions of Southeast Asia, Australia seemed like a whole other planet. We got to experience the magic of Sydney Harbour from a beautiful chartered sailing yacht—a prophetic moment as possibly my first actual "yacht rock" experience. (And for the record, I get that the term was originally meant to be somewhat dismissive, and my first impression upon hearing it wasn't necessarily encouraging, like being relegated to "oldies radio." Still, both of those monikers more than helped to keep our music alive in minds and hearts over the years and have practically become musical genres of their own, so . . . no offense taken.)

Back in the '70s, traveling to all these exotic locales I had only heard about was a real eye-opener for me. And when the album itself went platinum, having sold over a million copies, it felt like I had been jettisoned into the fourth dimension. At this point, I was enjoying all these experiences, traveling the world—and getting paid for it! It would be a while still before I got home and could process my newly (somewhat) upgraded economic status and enjoy the subsequent lifestyle—for better or for worse.

—

AS WE STARTED COMPILING POTENTIAL SONGS FOR OUR NEXT ALBUM, I MADE A cassette recording of a chord progression I was playing around with. All I had was a roughly sketched-out melody—no lyrics except one four-word phrase, a placeholder serving only to point to where I thought the chorus could begin. Ted, bless his spot-on producer's instincts, heard the tape and the phrase—"You belong to me"—and instantly said, "You should have Carly Simon write the lyrics to that." I thought, "If only."

So Ted sent Carly the tape, and in no time, she sent back the original cassette and the beautiful lyrics she'd written in longhand, and thus was born "You Belong to Me"—without the two of us ever once sitting in the same room or even talking on the phone. She just took the vague melody I offered and sent back these well-crafted lyrics that instantly felt perfect the first time I sang them. All that was left was to go in and cut the song with Ted and the Doobies.

The Doobies' version was a mild FM hit for the band, but Carly's version a few years later, produced by Arif Mardin, was a bona fide Top Forty radio hit. "You Belong to Me" went on to be covered many times, by such wonderfully talented artists as Anita Baker (produced by Phil Ramone), Jennifer Lopez (on an album produced by Cory Rooney), and Chaka Khan, who did a gorgeous, funky version (produced by Jimmy Jam and Terry Lewis). The song proved to have some legs, for sure. And to think it might never have been born had Carly Simon not happened to drop by the studio that day, all those years earlier.

—

AS WITH EVERY ALBUM, COMING UP WITH ENOUGH SONGS THAT YOU FEEL ARE GOOD enough is never an easy process. The way it usually worked at that point was: one of us would bring in a song and teach it to the band, and we'd come up with an arrangement away from the studio, usually at our band enclave up on the Northern California coast, a big old 1920s-era Mediterranean house that the band owned collectively. Our live-in housekeeper, Terry, would look after the place in our absence and make sure we were fed while there rehearsing in the main house, and we augmented the garage area to accommodate our equipment storage and crew's workshop. It was there we'd compile our versions of the songs, sometimes for weeks, and then we'd head into the studio in LA—where Ted would mercilessly tear into our arrangements. We'd typically rearrange the song right there on the floor, more often than not ending up with something much better than what we had just spent weeks rehearsing.

It was altogether a necessary but stressful undertaking, especially for someone like me, for whom self-doubt and shaky self-esteem were default settings. I truly didn't know if I was coming up with anything decent. I wasn't even so sure about "You Belong to Me" when we first recorded it, to be honest.

One particular bright spot: Ted thought we should include one Motown song on the album and suggested Marvin Gaye's "Little Darling (I Need You)" (written by legendary Motown composers Holland-Dozier-Holland), which turned out to be one of the few tracks from the album to chart—and for me, the first of what would be many covers of Motown classics, music that has sustained and inspired us all for years.

But overall, other than writing with Carly and recording a Marvin Gaye song, I don't have particularly fond memories of making that album, certainly not of the lingering (if only imagined) tension I felt surrounding the subject of the band's musical identity, which seemed to be very much in question at the time for those of us involved.

When the album—now titled *Livin' on the Fault Line*—was finally completed, we went up to San Francisco (our inspiration for the title) and did a day of photo shoots for the back cover, in locations around the city. But we started the day with some quick publicity shots at SIR Studios, where Tom Johnston was the last to arrive—with a bang.

The rest of us were already being positioned against the wall for the first of those shots. Upon entering, Tom, every bit the "Born to Be Wild" biker visage, greeted the group with a warm "How's everybody!" and then unsheathed a large bowie knife. The second his arm rose to throw the thing, we all instinctively scattered and dived for cover. Of course it was all in good fun (I chose to believe), but I couldn't help but notice that it stuck in the wall closest to where Jeff Baxter and I were standing.

In hindsight, I regret that I never really took the opportunity to venture into a deeper conversation with Tom during the recording of that album. I felt, even then, that we had a lot more in common than we had differences. The more we got to know each other from then on, the better friends we became, and have remained so to this day. But at that point in our history it was awkward, and the right moment just never seemed to present itself. I had at times sensed his frustration with my contributions to his songs when we were tracking. I remember being almost relieved at one point when, while critiquing my piano part on one of his songs, Tom broke the ice by saying, "That sounds like something my sister would play." But at least from then on I knew I could count on Tom to be honest with me.

It would be my guess that in the end, it was the making of this album that pushed Tom a bit closer toward his final decision to exit this band—the band that he'd started with Pat and John Hartman all those years ago.

But if he needed one more reason, the last straw might well have been the band's appearance on *The Dinah Shore Show.* Dinah was a delightful host with much charm and probably the only person on earth who could coerce us into a skit where she played Snow White and the Doobie Brothers dressed up as the Seven Dwarfs. Call me crazy, but I think that might have pretty much cinched it as far as Tom's departure from the band.

That memorable appearance, it should be noted, was a suggestion of our unorthodox publicist at the time, David Gest—a dedicated and inventive PR man who actually had many different, successful careers but is probably most widely remembered for his brief marriage to Liza Minnelli. David was a colorful character we were all quite fond of, though not always delighted with his suggestions. It was David, after all, who masterminded the Doobies' appearance on the '70s sitcom *What's Happening!!* Remember that show? Featuring the lovable characters Dee, Raj, Dwayne, and Rerun? Yup, the Doobies were on there. A very special two-parter, no less. While TV sitcoms like that might have been taboo for any self-respecting rock band in the '70s, being on the show did, crazily enough, endear the band to a whole new generation of fans.

—

AS FOR THE ALBUM ITSELF, IT DIDN'T SEEM LIKE ANYBODY WAS ALL TOO PLEASED WITH *Livin' on the Fault Line*—except maybe LeVar Burton. I'd met the talented actor at a party, and the first words he said—or should I say *sang*—to me were the very highest notes of "You Belong to Me," the part that goes "*Tellll hiiiiiiim* . . ." That's how he opened the conversation, before proceeding to express his appreciation of the song. I must admit that was an encouraging moment for me during a period of nagging doubts, because so many other people—critics included—felt the album wasn't our best work. It seemed to them the direction we were taking—slightly more jazz oriented and perhaps a bit more mellow—was too much of a departure. It might have seemed like we were trying to see how many chords we could put into one song or how many times we could change key, while a large part of the Doobies' faithful following just wanted more of the energetic, roots-oriented, guitar-driven rock and roll that made the Doobies popular to begin with.

And with the exception of "Little Darling," this album proved to be not so radio-friendly. Consequently, the label was not all that excited about it either, as it sure didn't sell a whole lot of records—barely five hundred thousand, fewer than half of what our previous album had sold. It felt like we were down for the count.

But then, as the poets say: shit happens.

CHAPTER 17

MINUTE BY MINUTE

Still smarting from the tepid response to *Livin' on the Fault Line*, the only thing we felt we could do was to collectively make an earnest effort to win back some of that audience on our next album. We each felt some responsibility to try to make it right, and amid that pressure, there was an undeniable atmosphere of internal strife building within our ranks. And I will be the first to claim my share of the blame in that department. I began to take my insecurities out on the other guys more regularly during the next round of recordings.

For starters, Jeff Baxter and I seemed to be butting heads more often—no doubt a result of my domineering attempts to dictate the parts I felt he should play. At the very least, it seemed like our perspectives as to how to move the band forward were at odds: I wanted to approach the songs and the arrangements from a more straight-ahead R&B perspective, whereas Jeff always seemed to want to explore a more harmonically progressive approach. I remember, for instance, on "Little Darling," Ted suggested we have a sax solo, an idea I liked. Jeff, however, had orchestrated a rather elaborate guitar interlude for him and Pat to play. Jeff won that one—and to his credit, it was always a big moment in our live show that highlighted his and Pat's impressive abilities as guitarists.

In hindsight, it was silly to let petty musical discrepancies become actual resentments. We all came from diverse musical backgrounds—which, it could be argued, was one of our strengths as a band. But that also required a lot of give and take. To be sure, our experience up till this point had made us, above all else, good friends with a common goal. But during this period of real or imagined pressure, it became too easy for me to transfer my frustrations onto others. Looking back now, I think what I secretly feared, once again, were my own shortcomings; I worried I wasn't delivering the goods. Or worse, that I was single-handedly taking the band down the shitter. So if a song wasn't working, I would naturally place blame on the drummers or the guitarists or the sound engineer . . . or the janitor, for that matter. I don't think anyone involved would argue the point that I was no picnic to deal with at the time.

To add to this festival of merriment, we were also on the road during this time, as touring and recording always overlapped a bit in the Doobie schedule. We normally traveled through the summer and fall months, without fail, to take advantage of the warm weather. And struggling to finish our albums in the short time frames allotted in between live dates, we often ended up finishing vocals and other miscellaneous overdubs out on the road—at A&R Studios and Right Track Recording in New York, FAME Studios in Muscle Shoals, Curtom (Curtis Mayfield's studio) in Chicago, and, if we were near Memphis, Willie Mitchell's Royal Studios (on Willie Mitchell Boulevard).

During those hectic summer months of 1978, I was technically single: dating some (which necessitated yet more creative juggling) but officially living alone. And frankly, between our touring schedule and trying to finish the new album literally on the run, having no official significant other to consider was probably a blessing in disguise.

A little better off financially at this point, I bought myself the quintessential "house in the hills"—a modest ranch house advertised as a bachelor pad—for reasons I couldn't explain other than it had a Jacuzzi and pool. I found some cheap furniture to fill the place but did indulge myself with a brand-new seven-foot Yamaha grand piano that sat in the living room with expansive windows looking out on a spectacular view of the San Fernando Valley.

In time, and with the help of Grey Ingram, the Doobies' front-of-house engineer, I put together a small four-track studio in one of the bedrooms, where Pat and I wrote and recorded a demo of "Dependin' On You," which became a track on that next album. Most of the songs I composed over the next few years were born at that shiny grand piano in the living room.

As organizational skills were never my strong suit, I was also managing to give less than my full attention to another commitment I had taken on: producing an album for Amy Boersma, the beautiful young singer I had met when I first came out to LA. We had lost touch over the years—somewhere along the way she had changed her professional name to Amy Holland—and she happened to come to one of the Doobies' shows at the Forum in LA, where she sent a note back to say hello.

When we first met, working for Rick Jarrard, I was nineteen, and she was all of sixteen and had a boyfriend to boot. So though I had developed quite a crush on her, nothing came of it at the time. But I legitimately loved her voice, and I'd thought once or twice that if I ever got the chance to produce an artist myself, she would be someone I'd love to work with. And now, out of the blue, she reached out. I figured that had to be some kind of sign.

So that hello soon evolved into a collaboration: I agreed to produce, with Patrick Henderson, what was to be her first solo album for Capitol Records. But between interruptions for my Doobies schedule and my prodigious lack of focus, progress on her album was slow going.

I did try to focus on as much songwriting as I could fit in while home. Songwriting can be a challenging and elusive enterprise. For reasons I've never been able to fully understand, I've found that some songs come easily and quickly, while others . . . not so much.

Like "What a Fool Believes."

—

THAT SONG WAS CERTAINLY WORTH THE WAIT; IT'S BY FAR THE MOST SUCCESSFUL AND widely recognizable song I've ever written. But that one was not a fast or easy delivery.

I started with nothing but that verse piano riff. People have pointed to that riff as iconic, and for a long time in the '80s, it was widely copied, or "lifted." But to be honest, it's a kind of syncopation and bouncing staccato rhythm I had heard a million times before in gospel music and '60s pop R&B records.

Anyway, that's all I had at first, along with some words I jotted down on the back of an envelope on a flight from New York back to LA: "She came from somewhere back in his long ago." At that point, I was just poking at the idea of how two people could look back on the same event with two completely different perspectives. That's all I had.

I played that rough, still-unfinished sketch of the song idea for Ted Templeman in his office one day, and his immediate response was "That's a hit!" And to his everlasting credit, he stayed on me about it for weeks and months. "I'm tellin' ya, you gotta finish that one!" And each time, I reassured him I would. But alas, it stayed unfinished for the longest time. Until . . .

Months later, my Doobie brother Tiran Porter told me he happened to run into Kenny Loggins, whom I had never met but long admired, from his days with Loggins and Messina and solid compositions like "Danny's Song" and "A Love Song" to his newly established status as a solo artist with songs like "Celebrate Me Home" and "Why Do People Lie." Kenny was writing some of the more musically sophisticated songs out there. And now, to my surprise and good fortune, Kenny expressed an interest in writing with me and gave Tiran his number to pass along. I was beyond excited.

Kenny and I made an appointment to get together at my house to write, and when the day arrived, I was anxiously at it early, reviewing some unfinished song ideas, looking through books of lyrics for possible titles . . . anything. You never know what long-discarded scrap of an idea might be just the spark you're looking for.

Meanwhile my sister Maureen, who was a huge Kenny Loggins fan, came over—purportedly to help clean up my bachelor-filthy house (which she did, bless her heart), but she "just happened" to have handy her Loggins and Messina records and a Sharpie. Seemed like a possible win-win deal all around.

So while Mo was engaged in some frantic housecleaning, I sat at the piano and bounced off her some musical ideas I might present to Kenny. I remembered that syncopated piano motif and found the envelope with what few lyrics I had. Thinking this one might be a bit of a stretch, I ran it past my sister, whose polite smile and shrug only further moved the needle on my insecurity, and I wondered if this was even worth showing to Kenny.

At that exact moment the doorbell rang, and I opened the door to find Kenny Loggins, struggling with his guitar and a shoulder bag filled with lyric notebooks, legal pads, and pencils—a small cassette recorder slipping out of his hand. The first words out of his mouth: "What was that you were just playing? Is that something new?"

I readily assured Kenny that it was as of yet totally unfinished and something I wondered if we might work on together. His response: "Perfect, let's jump into that one first."

I already had the opening bit—"She came from somewhere back in his long ago / Sentimental fool don't see / Trying hard to recreate what had yet to be created . . ." And Kenny, just from hearing that much on the other side of the door, had already come up with the next melodic bit, which soon became: "She . . . had a place in his life . . . / He . . . never made her think twice."

Kenny is one of the best songwriters I've ever worked with. His instincts with melody and chord progressions, lyrics and song structure, were pretty sophisticated. The strength of his melodies would often dictate the chord progression, even without an instrument, which greatly impressed me.

By way of a key change, the next day we found that lift into the chorus—"What a fool believes . . . he sees . . ." We wrote that part over the phone, me sitting at the piano, and so, over the course of two days, we finished our first song together. Piece of cake. Albeit a cake that took almost a year to bake—starting with some words scribbled on an envelope. (That envelope, by the way, with a few lyrics and some silly doodles scribbled on it, happened to be lying among some miscellaneous scraps of paper on my piano over a year later, after the song was a huge hit. David Gest, visiting one day, saw it and casually asked, "Hey, can I have this?" Sure. Next time I saw it, it was beautifully framed and prominently displayed on the wall next to the men's room in the Philadelphia Hard Rock Cafe.)

Kenny actually released the first version of "What a Fool Believes" on his album *Nightwatch*, before the Doobies even got around to cutting our version, if memory serves. (Just as "Minute by Minute" was originally cut by the Memphis Horns about a year before the Doobies' version.)

What I do remember very clearly, though, is that the Doobies' recording of the song involved a torturously long day of working on that one song, trying to get *the* take. We had done take after take after take, a small mountain of two-inch master tapes piling up on the control room floor, each reel containing three takes of that one friggin' song, and all of us getting more and more frustrated and less and less clear on what was missing . . . when Ted suggested we take a break. "I know we've got it somewhere in that pile of tapes."

So the band headed out for a smoke or whatever it was we needed, while Ted and engineer Donn Landee then meticulously—and miraculously—spliced together one complete take, sifting through the gazillion or so completed takes we'd recorded that morning. It seems that while we were continuing to swing and miss, unable to find that perfect start-to-finish take, Ted had been quietly making mental notes: "Reel four, take one, intro through first verse . . . Reel two, take two, first chorus . . . Reel three, take two, second verse and chorus out . . ." Right then and there, Ted and Donn created the hero take, physically razor-blading the actual two-inch masters themselves (this was before digital editing made it much easier).

Now, truth be told, any one of those completed performances was most likely more than good enough. But that just speaks to how neurotic and nitpicky we'd become with regard to our tracking sessions. And I was, I'm sorry to say, probably the worst offender.

—

CUTTING WHAT BECAME THE TITLE TRACK, "MINUTE BY MINUTE," A SONG I WROTE WITH Lester Abrams, was not much easier. When we wrote the song, I had in mind a certain kind of hypnotic feel; I don't want to say "precise," but a very *distinct* clocklike 6/8 meter that I didn't know how to quite articulate. Kind of a jazz shuffle, but with very little swing, if you will. Sort of a gospel syncopation to it, but . . . Like I said, I didn't know how to explain it.

And I tortured everyone over that song. It's a testament to these guys' patience and forgiving nature that they would still even speak to me after that session. When the band was trying to play it, we were giving it our best jazz/blues shuffle; it just didn't have that almost *mechanical* feel I was looking for. Once again, it was Ted who stepped in to suggest a way forward.

"Look, Mike, why don't you and Keith just go in there . . . You play piano, let Keith listen to you . . . and we'll get a drum track, and then build from there."

Which is what we did. In a departure from the usual approach—everyone playing "live" to tape together—this time everyone except Keith and me headed into the control room. I stayed put at my Fender Rhodes, and Keith hung in there on drums till we achieved that elusive, linear groove as best we could. I think I browbeat poor Keith to death to get the track we used. And he probably played it right every time; I was just so locked in and neurotic about wanting the song to have no noticeable swing.

In hindsight, by laying down that isolated rhythm track first, I think we were unknowingly poking at something that would later be much more simply and efficiently achieved with drum machines, that strict meter that spawned the neo-soul, techno funk music of the '80s and '90s.

I then wanted to go in and redo my keyboard part with a slightly different sound on the Rhodes. Ironically, none of my subsequent takes felt quite as good as the "original" I had just done with Keith. So we kept what we had. In the end, you always have to go with the "feel." When we finally got a track that seemed to work, at that point the guys came back in and overdubbed bass and guitar, and I later put on my lead and background vocals.

We finished recording the rest of the album in different personnel configurations, depending on the song's arrangement, hitting it pretty much daily, with interruptions here and there to jump out to do some live dates.

There was much to feel confident about on the *Minute by Minute* album: Pat's songs—"Don't Stop to Watch the Wheels," "Steamer Lane Breakdown," "You Never Change," and "Dependin' On You"—were solid Doobie Brothers tracks. Once again, however, I was feeling unsure of my contributions, but then with the overdubs by Bill Payne, John McFee, Rosemary Butler, Andrew Love, Norton Buffalo . . . I could feel those tracks starting to come to life. So many wonderful people lent their talent to the making of this record, starting with the band and, of course, Ted Templeman and Donn Landee. Did it take a bit longer than previous albums? Well . . . maybe a little.

Eventually we reached the final mix stage, and I was anxious to play the record for someone whose opinion I trusted, who I thought could listen with fresh objectivity. Friends and family, I feared, would likely frame their reaction in the most positive light, even if they hated it. I needed someone brutally honest. Someone who wouldn't hesitate to tell me if they thought it stunk. I needed David Gest.

—

AS I'VE MENTIONED, DAVID WAS AN ECCENTRIC GUY. NEUROTIC AS HELL, BUT NEVER LESS than entertaining. The whole band—Pat and I probably more than the others—even hung out with him beyond our professional relationship. David was enchanted by my dysfunctional family; his nickname for my mom was "Rhoda" (no idea why), and she was like a second mother to him. Of the two of us, he might have even been her favorite. And both my sisters worked for David at different times—just for the pure entertainment value of being on hand for the shit show that was his life. He seemed to always be embroiled in some full-blown drama, like being banned from the Chinese deli downstairs from his office for reasons that he never quite shared. (Next time I went in, I was actually thrown out too, just because the owner realized I knew David.)

Anyway, in spite of his penchant for calamity, the one thing you could always count on David for was an unvarnished, brutally honest opinion—on anything. Plus, since he had worked with so many of my favorite artists—Al Green, Ann Peebles, Carla and Rufus Thomas, Petula Clark—I trusted and respected his musical opinion.

So when I got my hands on the final mixes of *Minute by Minute*, I met David in the parking lot of some mall in the Valley (he liked to shop a lot), and we sat in his car and listened to every song—the whole album, all the way through.

After the final song faded out, he sat for a moment, stared straight ahead pensively, and gave a deep exhale before finally turning to tell me, "This is a total piece of shit."

Yeah, so okay, see, I was afraid of that. His critique totally stirred all my inner demons!

—

AS IT TURNED OUT, WE WERE NOT THE ONLY ONES TO SHARE THAT CONCERN. WHEN TED presented the finished record to Warner Bros.' entire A&R and promotion staff, the unanimous opinion apparently was a hearty thumbs-down. The consensus at the label was: "It's over for these guys."

Which might help explain the sacrificial mid-December release, basically a Bermuda Triangle of release dates. And it wouldn't be too long before *Rolling Stone* magazine chimed in with its two cents in the form of a scathing review. (Not being a glutton for punishment, I normally wouldn't read reviews, but being that this was *Rolling Stone*, I couldn't help myself—though it only took a couple of sentences for me to regret that.)

Fortunately, I was at that point unaware of the negative industry response. But still, I spent the next couple of weeks with my characteristic nagging self-doubt now blossoming into a full-blown cloud of despair. With the exception of a few recording sessions and a short run of some already booked dates, I was home, determined to lurk under the radar.

I didn't leave my house too often. I pretty much stayed in my bathrobe, waking up around two p.m. and spending the rest of the day into the wee hours smoking lots of pot, eating lots of cold delivery pizza, occasionally diddling at the piano. If I got too bored, I'd roll a couple of joints and head over to the little three-par golf course down the street and knock some balls around with my pal Larry.

A word about Larry, if I may.

Okay. So, on one of our tours, Doobies drummer John Hartman worked up an elaborate theatrical routine in our show in which he would swing a flaming mallet and bang that huge Chinese gong, part of a whole medieval-esque, gothic-rock carnival thing involving a company of actors—little people dressed as druids who would come onstage, cavort around, and then carry John away. (In retrospect, not quite as offensive as "midget bowling," but certainly up there.)

Well, my friend Larry was among this troupe of actors—impressive all-round athletes, we would come to learn, who at least on one occasion demonstrated their athletic prowess far beyond doing stunts onstage at a rock and roll show.

On one of our days off on that tour, the band was challenged to participate in a charity basketball game arranged by the big Top Forty radio station in that area, playing against the local fire or police department. Clearly, better judgment prevailing, we would normally decline.

However, as a result of Larry's encouragement, we accepted. Larry and a few of his colleagues in the troupe, along with a couple ringers we flew in for the game, were members of a little people's basketball league.

We knew the Doobies were pathetically no match for this much more disciplined local team. However . . . our second-string team was made up of Larry and his six actor colleagues, and they were waiting ever at the ready on the bench, eager to turn the tide. Picture a shorter version of the Harlem Globetrotters, moving up and down the court with lightning speed, going through the other team's legs, making three-point shots standing on each other's shoulders . . . These guys obviously put in some hours of practice on their play strategy and choreography.

So when the Doobies trailed dramatically in the first half by double digits, Larry and his gang took over and proceeded to wipe the court with the opposing team, all the while putting on quite a show.

Over the course of that tour, Larry and I became good friends, having mastered the art of the late-night hang: enjoying each other's company while doing a whole lot of nothing, which is precisely how we spent a lot of evenings back home after finishing *Minute by Minute*: Larry and his wife, Lydia (also a little person), and myself, hanging out at my house in the Valley, just the three of us on the couch, me in my uniform of ratty bathrobe, boxers, and terry cloth slippers . . . eating more delivery pizza and watching a lot of mind-numbing late-night TV . . . all while Larry and I smoked a lot of pot.

Lydia, on the other hand, didn't approve of drugs, so she would sit there mildly annoyed with both of us till she convinced Larry it was time to go home. And so it would end, on more than a few nights, with me still sitting alone in my bathrobe and slippers, staring at that TV for hours, sitting through endless repeats of the same Cal Worthington used-cars commercial and that jingle that poisoned my mind for years to come—"If you need a car or truck, go see Cal!"—until the end-of-broadcast sign-off, which was (mercifully) the great Ray Charles singing "America the Beautiful," immediately followed by the harsh reality of white noise and black-and-white static. This was my cue to drag myself to bed.

Such was life at Casa McDonald at the end of 1978.

—

MOST OF THE DATES WE PLAYED AROUND THAT TIME WERE IN SECONDARY AND TERTIARY markets: cities ninety miles or more away from the more major markets—places most bands wouldn't normally play if they were trying to promote a new record. But these dates were booked after the lukewarm response to *Livin' on the Fault Line* and were considered, in the eyes of our agents and the local promoters, to be safer bets.

Initially we viewed these shows as just obligatory—prior commitments we had to fulfill before we really got down to the business of seriously promoting any new release. We didn't yet realize their eventual impact. The audiences in these smaller cities were particularly receptive and appreciative; their towns were often overlooked on major tours, and the groundswell of support we garnered just by showing up there first was, I believe, a big part of why *Minute by Minute* started to take off.

At the time, we were caught up in the frenzied day-to-day routine of touring and didn't have any real perspective on what was going on with the record. It wasn't until we got home that any real details started to trickle down to us. I remember getting a phone call from Doobies management in early January '79 saying that the album had sold some thirty thousand units in the first week and was showing signs of climbing. I was shocked. I actually considered the possibility that I might've dozed off and dreamed that.

It was starting to look like the choice of the no-man's-land release date was, if only accidentally, kind of brilliant. Records were rarely released in late December, January, or February because everyone aimed to have their records in stores well before that big Christmas sales season, or they were held until the April/May slot, in hope of being one of the big summer releases. So this window of opportunity chosen by the Warners promotion team turned out to give us a clear shot at radio with little or no competition. Radio was hungry for any new release by any band of note during this typically dark period, and that was likely the main reason we actually made some noise on the airwaves.

In fact, the initially negative response of the Warners A&R and promotion team to this album seemed to be, in the end, the very thing that helped to make it a success. People just love a comeback story. And while Warners most likely picked this release date so as to not unduly expend precious resources on our behalf during their peak marketing months, to their credit they jumped on this surprising momentum and put their collective shoulder into it. Russ Thyret and the Warner Bros. promo staff at the time deserve much credit for the record's ultimate success, selling more than three million records.

And the *Rolling Stone* review? Well, ultimately it didn't hurt us too bad. Soon we were on the cover of the September 1979 issue, and the magazine even listed the album as one of its top year-end picks. So go figure.

But for now, we hit the road—and hard.

CHAPTER 18

DON'T STOP TO WATCH THE WHEELS COME OFF

With little or no rest for the wicked, we'd kick off 1979 with a monthlong run of dates on the other side of the planet. Japan to this day remains one of my favorite places to visit, for so many reasons: its natural rural beauty, the rich culture in its distinctive major cities, and, above all, the courteous and discreet demeanor of the people. But notwithstanding their fascination with rock and roll music and our culture in general, I don't know that as a demographic, traveling US rock musicians have done much to enhance the image of Americans in the eyes of the Japanese.

One of the problems for us was Japan's strict drug laws and disposition toward illegal substances in general, which made street drugs all but nonexistent there in the '70s and '80s. So while there, a few of us were suffering a bit from withdrawal, and all of us were a bit crankier than usual.

As with any tour, some shows are better than others. But when you're running ragged and dog-tired, little things can loom large, as we learned after a particularly frustrating night in Osaka, the last show of our Asian tour.

Being a band with two drummers was always fertile ground for tension between them. We also had three guitarists, but any disagreement in that area didn't seem as critical to the overall performance as what might be happening in the drum section. The drumming was ground zero and the foundation for the rest of the arrangement, and on any given night, one of them might feel the other was rushing or playing too many fills . . . or whatever it was. And normally that disagreement was contained between the two of them—Keith Knudsen and John Hartman. But on this particular night the argument spread to the whole band, with everyone taking sides. Three of the members wanted John Hartman's head and thought he should be fired, and the other two felt that was a little harsh—and unfair, as John was one of the founding members of the band. In the end, the only unanimous agreement we could come to was: "Fuck it! That's it. We're done!" So we decided to officially break up.

One slight hitch: unbeknownst to us, we just happened to have a single and album both about to reach number one on the *Billboard* charts. That's a problem that doesn't present itself too often. But . . . too late. "We don't care. We're done!"

Meanwhile, back in LA, the execs were pulling their hair out. "What are you doing?! We've counted this band out a hundred times before. If you guys are gonna break up, why now, for Chrissakes?!"

We all left Japan on different flights, without much real communication between us. Keith and John had their issues, Jeff Baxter and I were butting heads more frequently, and even Pat, I sensed, was starting to be increasingly demoralized with the overall direction of the organization; it was growing further and further away from its original roots. Whereas we used to rehearse up in the Bay Area at Winterland or take the short drive down the coast to the band's house in Half Moon Bay, now it seemed we were conducting our business more and more in LA. By this point, we even had our own individual accountants in Beverly Hills.

—

ON THE WAY BACK FROM JAPAN, KEITH AND I DECIDED AT THE LAST MINUTE TO STOP OFF in Maui for some much-needed R&R. (Maui also being the shortest distance between Japan and marijuana.) Day after day, we did pretty much nothing but smoke, eat, play golf, hit the beach, and carouse around Lahaina.

At some point during that week on Maui, Keith and I received a call from Pat to talk in earnest about this idea of breaking up the band. It was, after all, really Pat's decision to make; none of the rest of us really held that card in our hand. As one of the founding members, he was in many ways the conscience of the band, which the rest of us all followed. So when he expressed his desire to keep it going, we took it to heart and did ultimately agree to keep the band going—for a while anyway.

But I had some conditions—changes I felt had to be made before we could move forward. At the top of that list: I felt there wasn't enough room in the band anymore for me and Jeff Baxter to coexist. That's right: the guy but for whom I wouldn't have even been given this opportunity in the first place had, in my mind, become a thorn in my side. I'm not sure what that says about me exactly (other than perhaps I'm more than capable of being an asshole), but at the time, I felt if we were to continue, it was necessary for the band to re-emerge as a different and cohesive entity. We needed a chance to move forward with some kind of musical solidarity. It seemed like we'd become too creatively fractured. I know that as a writer, I felt I was constantly having to make too many concessions as to how the songs would be arranged, and Jeff and I were, at this point, on such different pages so much of the time.

I was grateful that Jeff ultimately didn't take it personally, and from my perspective it wasn't personal either. It's not that these changes don't hurt people's feelings. They do. But we'd all been around long enough in this profession to know that divorce is a natural consequence of creativity. It's often just the reality of any musical entity that hopes to stand the test of time. You're called upon to evolve. And with that come the tough choices—decisions that you perceive to be, or at least hope will be, in the best interest of the music you'll make in the future. I would fall prey to that same type of decision myself years later, when the band decided to re-form once again, this time without me. But most important, Jeff Baxter and I have remained friends after all these years.

However, back in 1979, from that crossroad moment, the band would go forward with a new lineup: Pat Simmons; Keith Knudsen; bass player Tiran Porter; new drummer Chet McCracken (whom I recommended when John Hartman decided to leave for his own reasons); saxophonist/keyboardist Cornelius Bumpus, who was an old friend of Pat's; guitarist John McFee,* who was a friend of Keith's; and percussionist Bobby LaKind, who, while he was working on the lighting crew handling pyrotechnics, we came to learn was a terrific conga player.

And with that team, we once again hit the road—with a vengeance, heading back out into the more major markets like LA, New York, Chicago, Detroit, Miami, and Atlanta.

—

IT WASN'T LONG UNTIL WE WERE ONCE AGAIN ALL A BIT FRAYED. WE WERE NOW LOOKING at sold-out, multiple-night engagements at large venues like Pine Knob Music Theatre (Detroit area), Alpine Valley Music Theatre (Lake Geneva, outside Milwaukee), and Universal Amphitheatre (Los Angeles). Our typical run might be six or seven days on and one day off. As the tour was mostly one-night stands, these multiple-night gigs here and there were actually a godsend—especially for the crew—because we could catch our breath by not having to travel for a couple days. But there was no sign of things letting up in the near future.

It's not surprising that some tour managers have notably short careers; the all-consuming task of keeping a machine like this and all

* John McFee had played with the band Clover, the original rhythm section on Elvis Costello's debut album, before some of them went on to become Huey Lewis and the News.

its moving parts up and running is an utterly demanding responsibility, executed at a brutally frenetic pace. (This would be made sadly evident by the loss of our good friend and all-time great Doobies road manager Phil Basile. Few are the guys who leave that gig unscathed.)

We just kept swinging away with our heads down, along the way dutifully sitting for local press and radio interviews. I would learn that certain subject matters were irresistible catnip to journalists. An innocuous comment like "Sometimes it can get a little boring on the road" could end up in print as "McDonald, grappling with his own demons and depressions while touring . . ."

Occasionally there were journalists from outlets with a wider reach; *Rolling Stone* sent out an up-and-coming young journalist named Cameron Crowe to travel with the band for a few days, and if you ever saw the film *Almost Famous*, Cameron's terrific homage to '70s rock and roll and life on the road, you've got a pretty good image of life with the Doobie Brothers back then. (Though I'd suggest also watching the film *This Is Spinal Tap*, as reality was somewhere between the two.)

We ended our year of relatively nonstop touring in October '79 in Houston at the Summit. No doubt, some of the sixteen thousand people in attendance saw us only ten months earlier in smaller towns like Corpus Christi and Odessa. After that last show, we were greeted backstage by the crew armed with fire extinguishers filled with chocolate pudding, which would be the last time I wore those clothes. It was a typically dreaded end-of-tour gag.

Still, what I remember most about that night is that eerie yet familiar wave of anxiety at the thought of returning home alone, without all these faces I'd grown accustomed to seeing every day: truck drivers, pilots and flight attendants, light and sound crew, drum techs, guitar and keyboard techs, road managers . . . the traveling entourage who miraculously functioned like a well-oiled machine for the last six months. There was the unsettling feeling of not having someone to tell me where to be and when to be there, and the fear of suddenly living in a stationary, momentum-less "normal"—an existence I wasn't sure I remembered how to manage. I was beginning to gain a deeper understanding of my dad's constant restlessness.

—

MANY TIMES, COMING HOME TO THE QUIET AND SOLITUDE OF MY OWN HOUSE WAS NOT THE restorative experience I was hoping for. Though I had bought a house for my mother and sister near me, my mother liked my house better. So I'd sometimes return home dead tired from months on the road, counting the seconds till I could climb and crater into my own bed . . . only to find my mother and a small congregation of her friends from back home enjoying margaritas and Manhattans in their sleepover attire of pajamas and muumuus. My mother would immediately declare, "Ya know, Bill and Dorothy wanted to stay in a hotel, but I told them, 'Nope—Mike won't have it! He wants you to stay with him!'" At that point I would make my best effort to confirm my mom's declaration so no one would feel they were imposing in any way, and then head off to sleep in the guest room (since my mom always insisted her friends take the master bedroom). The final nail in the coffin would be when I opened the guest room closet to put my luggage away only to find it completely filled with more muumuus.

After any long stretch on the road, there comes a point at which a traveling band and crew start to become a sort of human collective, in which you can lose your singular identity. Ironically, that was precisely the allure when I was young. Still, in my earliest band experiences, we had to at least depend on our own wits with regard to the daily logistics, and therefore remained grounded in reality to some degree. But when the only thing you have to do is find your way to an elevator and get down to the hotel lobby while someone else wrangles your luggage and handles all the little details of life in between, that all changes. You give up a certain amount of responsibility and self-reliance, ostensibly to "the greater good." And as a result, when it's all over, the simple thought of how to reintegrate or pick up your life when you finally get home can be mildly terrifying. On the road, my purpose and sole focus were so specific and well defined, it was like being a worker bee—and there's a reason worker bees don't take vacations; they'd probably end up in a bathrobe with bed hair, a joint in their mouth, and a salad bowl full of Lucky Charms on their chest.

Over the years, I've tried to reconcile with that reality by keeping my hand in some kind of project independent of the band, something I could stay connected to while out on tour and look forward to keeping me occupied when I got back. It served to keep me a bit more grounded, less likely to lose total touch with reality while out there for long stretches.

Still, even to this day, each time we climb on the bus to leave, I have to consciously surrender, at least in some part, to this all-consuming lifestyle that is The Road, where the whole point and focus are those couple of hours each night where it all makes sense.

—

THE BREAK AFTER THIS PARTICULAR TOUR WAS OUR FIRST REAL STRETCH AT HOME IN A while, so I was able to finally make some headway with Amy Holland's album. Patrick Henderson and I cut more tracks with her, including "How Do I Survive," written by a young British songwriter named Paul Bliss, whom Jeff Baxter had discovered and produced in England earlier that year. Jeff had asked me to sing background vocals on Paul's original version of the song, and I suggested it to Amy as a track that might suit her well. We later released it as a single that would eventually reach the top twenty on the *Billboard* chart—a very gratifying moment for me as a rookie A&R guy.

Inspirations for song choices can come from the oddest places. Another track for that album was an old song my father used to sing called "Forgetting You," which he discovered, believe it or not, in a *Three Stooges* episode. While they performed it in an up-tempo, three-part swing harmony arrangement, my dad saw the potential of the song more as a touching torch ballad, and it was actually one of his more popular numbers when he performed in the saloons. (And with all due respect to Moe, Larry, and Curly, the arrangement Amy and I came up with was more in line with my dad's vision of the song.)

For Amy and me, keeping our relationship platonic was proving challenging. Even though we were at this point both dating other people, we were spending more and more time with each other, and the pull became harder to ignore. Still, I was reluctant to give in to my growing attraction, as common sense told me that we had an already overdue and over-budget album to finish and turn in to Capitol Records. So now would not be the time to further complicate things . . . right?

Well, one night after working late, I walked Amy outside to her car as I always did (the studio being in a rough part of town, after hours and all), and there, our typically innocent goodbye hug somehow turned into a long good-night kiss that completely knocked me off base. I remember having the instantaneous realization as we kissed that I was gonna marry this woman—an incongruous thought for a guy whose ardent conviction since childhood had been to never marry anyone . . . ever.

If I wasn't already emotionally confused enough, there was also the whirlwind of activity that had ensued days earlier when, to our great surprise, the Doobies were nominated in multiple categories for the 1980 Grammy Awards, a huge, televised event to which I'd already invited someone else, a lovely woman named Paula whom I had been dating for a while. So much for not further complicating things.

For the time being, Amy and I made a determined effort to keep our focus on the album and to keep our relationship strictly professional; neither one of us wanted to cause the other any unnecessary grief. She continued to see her boyfriend (even spent the holidays with him and his parents), and I continued to see Paula, who was not shy about voicing her concerns with my being overly distracted by all things Amy. Paula seemed to know better than I just how serious my feelings for Amy were becoming.

And while I did feel guilty about being less than forthright with Paula, in some other part of my psyche I began to convince myself that possibly fate had, through the years, robbed Amy and me of something special, and this might be that last, fleeting second chance to make up for precious time lost.

—

AS USUAL, IN TIMES OF CONFUSION LIKE THIS, I FELT THE OLD FAMILIAR URGE TO BE somewhere else. So I took my friend (and accountant) Bernie up on his offer to take a drive into the mountains. And in my guilt for being inattentive of late, I invited Paula to come along. Just a short day trip to the small, picturesque town of Idyllwild, California, in the mountains above the desert. Up until that trip, I'd never heard of the place.

That evening, before heading down the mountain on our way home, we made a quick stop at a small general store, and there, in the parking lot, we bumped into, of all people, Amy—and her boyfriend, Jim. What are the chances of that? A gazillion to one? Never mind the absurdity of us both independently choosing to visit the same small town on the same day. But that we would cross paths at exactly this moment, me leaving town just as she was arriving? We could have so easily passed like ships in the night, but we didn't. So this must be a sign of . . . something, right?

Now, a true romantic might have read this as clear, cosmic proof that Amy and I were meant to be together. But my brain took me in the opposite direction; seeing her there—with her boyfriend, presumably to spend the weekend together—felt, in that moment, more like a wake-up call. This growing obsession with Amy that I was nursing of late, this baseless belief that destiny was somehow the reason we kept crossing paths throughout the years, suddenly seemed pretty foolish. Clearly, she was not home pining for me since our last kiss, and as awkward as this moment was, it might be the perfect opportunity for me to just finally snap out of it.

And I tried. I really did. I went to the Grammy Awards with Paula as planned. It was my first time at one of these things, and I will admit it was pretty exciting. We had rehearsed earlier in the day for our performance of "What a Fool Believes," and that night we did the red-carpet ritual before being finally escorted to our assigned seats. What a trip to see the likes of Barbra Streisand, Neil Diamond, Billy Joel . . . all the luminaries assembled for this event. My family was there too, including my grandmother Genevieve, who'd bought me that Silvertone electric guitar for Christmas back in 1964.

It was a thrilling, almost overwhelming night, with the Doobies winding up with four Grammys. *Minute by Minute* won Best Pop Vocal Performance by a Duo, Group or Chorus, and "What a Fool Believes" won Best Arrangement Accompanying Vocals, Song of the Year, and Record of the Year! I vaguely recall walking onstage together with Kenny Loggins to accept our award as songwriters and each saying a few words, but it was all a blur after that. I have no idea who I thanked over the course of the evening, but as anyone who's ever accepted an award at one of these things can tell you, we're condemned to live with the memory of those we forgot to thank.

—

FOLLOWING THE WARNER BROS. AFTER-PARTY AT THE LEGENDARY CHASEN'S restaurant—watching Paula Abdul and John Stamos disco-dance the night away alongside Cher and Gregg Allman, the "it couple" of the moment—Paula and I got back in the limo I'd rented for the evening, owned and driven by a guy who happened to be a neighbor of mine. Not quite ready to face the ominous quiet of my house in the hills, I asked him to head up Pacific Coast Highway for a bit; I just felt the need to keep moving for a while that night.

I lit up a joint and passed it around, and our driver, after a couple of tokes, became extremely chatty, which started to annoy Paula, who had already felt a bit neglected throughout the evening and, as she had previously made clear, maybe a little underappreciated overall lately. So with delicate apologies to our driver, I awkwardly raised the torturously slow-rising partition, his bewildered disappointment more than evident in the rearview mirror.

Now finally "alone," Paula and I recapped the events of the exciting evening now behind us, but it felt as though we were both doing our best to avoid the real subject at hand: the growing void she'd been feeling between us. At some point she laid her head on my shoulder, and we both fell silent, fixating on the moon's reflection over the Pacific. On that long ride home, and for some weeks after, we did our best to conceal from each other the lack of confidence we shared about our future going forward.

—

SOMEWHERE IN THOSE WEEKS, AMY LET IT BE KNOWN THAT SHE AND JIM HAD BROKEN UP, which caught me by surprise. Maybe fate was again trying to tell me something, albeit the opposite of what I thought it was telling me last time. (Hey, I'm nothing if not flexible.) But if that was the case, I feared I might be facing a limited window of opportunity if I didn't make a move and make my feelings known.

I languished for a couple days, trying to imagine how best to tell Paula what was already painfully obvious to both of us. For her part, Paula, wondering why I hadn't returned her calls, was done languishing and simply drove to my house and knocked on my door. This was a no-nonsense girl from Providence, Rhode Island; she was more likely to put a fist in my eye than to collapse into a puddle of tears.

I felt ashamed that my procrastination had put her through this painfully slow and awkward demise, that I hadn't been more forthright about my feelings for Amy sooner. But frankly it was all so confusing to me. At that point in my life, navigating an intimate relationship with a woman with honesty as a priority was not in my wheelhouse. And while I had occasionally been properly called out on my bullshit, in general, over the years, I still maintained a fairly healthy sense of denial with regard to the collateral damage I left behind. There's a saying, the gist of which is that the pain we never transform, we will surely transmit to others. Over the years, I had found that to be sadly true.

A few months down the road, I ran into Paula, and I was much relieved to find her upbeat and friendly. She seemed to have transcended the experience somehow and come to forgive, even being kind enough to ask how Amy and I were doing. I made my best attempt at another belated, stumbling apology for how it all went down, and when I asked her how she was doing, she said, "Look, I'm finally okay with it. It took a while, but . . . I can let go now."

CHAPTER 19

AMY

In the months to come, Amy and I became almost inseparable. Though we officially maintained our separate residences for a short while, we were almost always together at one of them. I wasn't running to the altar, mind you, but it was becoming evident even to me that this was something different, that we were, on some level, soulmates, and probably stuck with each other.

On a jaunt up to Santa Barbara one weekend, we stayed in a small resort on the beach in Montecito, a charming little community I used to pass through in the early '70s on the way to play the lounge at the Hotel Mar Monte. Back then, I remember fantasizing about what it must be like to live in this beautiful little hamlet in one of those lovely old estates. Now, almost a decade later, driving up with Amy, I had been given the number of a real estate agent, a well-connected local who was reported to have the inside track on which homeowners were thinking of selling before they officially listed. Word was that after the appropriate amount of cocktails (and juicy local gossip), he might share some of those pocket listings he was saving for "just the right client."

So out we went, and the second house we saw was a charming French country bungalow with beautiful older landscaping on a little less than an acre. As we entered the house, I was struck with the sense that generations of people had been happy there. Don't ask me where a feeling like that comes from, but it was almost like I heard the faint sound of children's laughter resonating in the walls. From halfway up the stairs I turned and looked back down and felt a kind of serene contentment, again like some otherworldly message from the past. What I couldn't have known then was that this was where, in two short years, I would propose to Amy; we would get married at the church around the corner and soon have two beautiful children of our own.

Professionally speaking, producing Amy's album introduced me to a whole new perspective on working in the studio and interacting with label execs that was beyond what I was used to. As an artist you're generally insulated from the real politics surrounding your projects by management and . . . well, your producer. In this other stratum of the music business, you needed to protect your flank at all times. And I was in for an education on how artists are viewed and talked about behind closed doors.

Case in point: there was a hugely talented, veteran female artist who, after several years off the radar, delivered the master tapes of her latest project to her label. The response was strikingly dismissive. It was, after all, the '80s; new-wave sensations were all the rage. And to their way of thinking, what could some "old-school" R&B artist who'd not had a bona fide hit since the '60s possibly have to offer? And now this? A collection of songs recorded overseas, written and produced by largely unknown British composers? I heard that her manager had to growl and bark a bit to force the label to give the album a proper release. Of course it wasn't long before those same execs would be all smiles while posing with Tina Turner and her framed multiplatinum plaque for *Private Dancer*—after selling six million copies.

The appeal of producing, for me, was all about wanting to see an artist's dream materialize and the creative endeavor of presenting them with some possible options to that end. I found no great joy in being responsible for the recording budget or dealing with everyone surrounding the artist, those who, in their expert opinion, had something to say about everything from the final mixes to the sequence of the tracks to whether they heard a hit single in there or not. The strongest opinions invariably came from people who'd never actually made a record in their life.

Escorting Amy to the Grammy ceremony—held that year in New York—where she was nominated in the category of Best New Artist, was the culmination of what it was all about for me. Of course, my best thinking told me that a wonderful experience like this could only be made better by a little cocaine, which led to getting embarrassingly inebriated in front of her parents and ending the evening with a grand mal seizure back at the hotel, only to wake up to see a company of New York firefighters standing at the foot of my bed, once again asking me what year it was. (What is it with all these people needing *me* to remind *them* what year it is?)

At some point around this time, during a brief period of relative calm in the Doobies' schedule, I was invited to join Randy Newman for a brief tour he was doing on the heels of the surprise success of his single "Short People," a perfectly Randy Newman–esque sideways satire of racism and bigotry (which ironically some people didn't quite get, criticizing the song—and Randy—for actually promoting bigotry).

Over the years, Randy had all but perfected the art of performing solo. However, in the attempt to capitalize on the success of "Short People," the label had coerced him into this experiment of touring with a band to promote the record. And the band they put together was an impressive group of musicians, all from the Warners stable: Andy Newmark from Roxy Music on drums, Fred Tackett on guitar and Bill Payne on keyboards and B-3 organ (both from Little Feat), and from the Doobies we had Willie Weeks on bass, Bobby LaKind on percussion, and me playing a Fender Rhodes and doing background vocals. And as unofficial music director (and occasional percussionist), we had Ted Templeman on board too.

As excited as we all were to play with Randy, I'm not sure it was a comfortable transition for him. In fact, the running joke on the tour between Randy and all of us was trying to quantify just how much he hated the band. (And in case it was unclear, he would board the tour bus every night after the show, shaking his fist in mock outrage at all of us while crying out, "You've ruined my life!")

—

I WAS INVOLVED IN SOME OTHER GREAT COLLABORATIONS AROUND THIS TIME, ARTISTIC pairings that I could not have seen coming—like finding myself in the studio with Burt Bacharach and Paul Anka.

I had actually met Burt a few years earlier when he was doing the soundtrack for the movie *Lost Horizon* and I was invited to come in and audition to sing one of the tracks. I remember that meeting as feeling very old-school—Burt at the piano, and the room filled with all these cigar-smoking publishing/movie execs. I sang a few verses, and while he had some complimentary things to say, he ultimately felt I wasn't right for that particular song.

But a few years later, Burt invited me to record a song he had written with Paul Anka called "I've Got My Mind Made Up" for the film *Together?*, starring Jacqueline Bisset. And thus began a friendship and ongoing collaboration for me, in the years to come, with these two major talents.

A quick note about Paul Anka: as talented, prolific, and successful as he's been as a recording artist and songwriter, all that almost takes a back seat to his phenomenal business acumen. One day he came into the studio carrying a beautifully ornate, exotic-looking tin of candy, some rare caramel/taffy concoction, reportedly from some remote mountain village in Turkey.

"Hey, try one of these."

I popped one in my mouth, and my instantaneous reaction was "Oh. My. God! This is the most delicious thing I've ever tasted!"

He smiled and nonchalantly said, "I know, right? I just bought the company."

Buying a Turkish candy company—not exactly an everyday occurrence for most songwriters.

Getting to know and work with Burt Bacharach was an invaluable education for me. I came to learn and appreciate how differently people can approach their writing. A classically trained musician who not only composed but had for years been an arranger and musical director for some of the biggest names in entertainment, Burt had an incredible ability to orchestrate melody in a way that was so heartfelt and beautiful. Not surprisingly, his process was nothing like my own.

The first day I went over to his house to try our hand at writing together, I sat down at the piano to play him some ideas I had in my head, and he said, "Ah . . . that's nice. Tell you what—put it on my cassette player." I recorded it on his small cassette player, and he said, "Lemme write this out tonight, and we'll work on it when we get together tomorrow." That was pretty much the extent of our first day's effort.

I came back the next day, and sure enough, that vague melody that had started only in my head was now improved and written out on this big sheet of score paper. He might have sketched out a rudimentary bass line underneath, but it was seeing the melody written out that concerned him most. Not the bass line, not the chord progression—just: "What's that melody doing, and how would I build the larger harmonic landscape around it?" I believe Burt was already orchestrating his songs as he was writing them.

By contrast, I wouldn't say my writing has ever been particularly melody-centric. For me, the melody has always been a bit malleable, as in the blues tradition, and open to improvisation. It's always more about chord progressions and the rhythmic feel of the song and the track. From listening to composers like Burt and Teddy Randazzo ("Goin' Out of My Head," "Hurt So Bad"), I discovered that by way of modal shifts and key changes throughout a song structure, you can sometimes get the emotional lift you're looking for—especially helpful when searching for that ever-elusive killer chorus.

Key changes, harmonic tension, unexpected passing chords between sections—that's the part of the writing process I love: the experimenting, allowing yourself to take chances, drawing outside the lines. "What if instead of there, we go here!" In most cases, I don't have the musical knowledge to know what's gonna ultimately work, or sound horrifically wrong, until I try it. (Once again: if I actually knew what I was doing, I might never have even gone there.) But to me, flying blind is where the fun and the magic are found.

—

BURT WAS DEFINITELY A HERO OF MINE, AND WHILE THEY SAY WE'RE SOMETIMES BETTER off never meeting our heroes because we're bound to be disappointed, I've not found that to be exactly true. Surprised sometimes? Sure. But never disappointed. I find anyone's humanity in whatever form intriguing. Case in point:

I had idolized Ray Charles since I could barely see over the dashboard of my dad's Ford Fairlane. Listening to that voice coming over our old Delco car radio was a feeling like no other.

Well, I finally got to meet Ray when I was invited to take part in a tribute show for him held in Pasadena. My buddy Al Kooper was working in the orchestra, and like myself and literally every musician I'd grown up with, Al worshipped Ray Charles. But when I showed up for the rehearsal, Al seemed a little beat up; apparently Ray had been pretty tough on the musicians and the audio crew earlier in the day. Ray's sometimes cantankerous demands on those who worked with him were the stuff of legend. I myself got off unscathed that evening; I had the honor of performing his iconic "I Got a Woman," and our only interaction was a brief hello during my rehearsal slot.

I wouldn't be so lucky next time.

A few years later, I got to work with Ray again, ironically enough at a Yamaha tribute that featured *my* music. He came down the day before the show for rehearsals with me and the house band. As we ran through the tunes scheduled for the show, we jammed on a couple of my favorite Ray Charles classics and struck up, I thought, a friendship of sorts.

I made a point to express to him just how much it meant to me to have him participate in the evening and just how much his music had meant to me growing up. I also wanted to reassure him that the proceeds of the event were going to a worthy cause—the NAMM Music Education Fund. I'd presumed he was already aware of the charity aspect of our event, and I took for granted that like all the other performers, he had agreed to waive any official compensation so that all revenues would go directly to the cause.

Well, it seems Ray hadn't gotten that memo. On the day of the show, in a scene straight out of a gangster movie, his road manager, an imposing figure with his silk suit and walking stick, came up to me and said, "The boss wants to talk to you."

So I went into Ray's trailer and there he was, in his bathrobe. My first thought was: "Man, if my buddies back in Ferguson could see me now! Sitting here shooting the breeze with Ray Charles in his trailer!"

Rocking gently back and forth in that unmistakable Ray Charles way, he said, "Yeah . . . Michael, man, I just wanna say, I love getting to sing your song 'Hey Girl'! When did you write that one?"

Okay, first of all, I didn't. It was hard for me to believe that Ray wasn't aware of the original Freddie King version, but when he asked, I readily explained, "Uh, no . . . Actually, that's a Carole King–Gerry Goffin song. I didn't write that." And right there in that moment I could sense a good measure of whatever respect he might have had for me evaporate. And it went downhill from there.

"Well, hey, uh, no matter. I'm certainly glad to be here, Michael, ah . . . But man, you got to give me something."

I was pretty sure I knew what he was getting at, but I didn't want to presume, so I said, "Well, Ray, what can I do for you? What do you need? Everything all right as far as the accommodations backstage?"

"No, man, what I'm sayin' is you *gotta give* me somethin'! There's been a grave misunderstanding here, son! I can't be doing this shit for free!"

In Ray's defense, he came from the old school, where promoters were notoriously slick and you could bet the deal was in flux right up until downbeat. In case there was any possible misunderstanding, he then spelled it out: he needed a bit of extra incentive—in cash—before he would go onstage that night.

Now getting the message loud and clear, I said, "Ray. Believe me, I would gladly come up with whatever you think you need in a heartbeat! Out of my own pocket! But here's my problem: I've made a rather solemn promise to everyone on the show that all monies would go to the foundation, and in the interest of keeping it simple, we all agreed none of us would take any compensation. That was the arrangement. So, for me to go and pay anyone, even out of my own pocket, I'd be breaking my promise to everyone else on the show, and I can't really do that."

With that, he kind of stopped rocking for a moment, turned in my direction, and in a slightly elevated pitch explained, "I don't give a fuck about your arrangement! I'm an old man, goddamn it! I don't got time for this shit!"

Once again, I thought, "Man, if my buddies back in Ferguson could see me now—sitting here with Ray Charles, getting my ass chewed out!"

It truly pained me to not give this man, my musical idol since childhood, whatever he needed to feel respected, to feel good about the night's performance. But I felt my hands were tied, that I was only as good as my word to all the others.

In the end, he did go on, but he wouldn't allow us to use the footage of his performance in what would ultimately be a film of the concert. I wouldn't get to document working with my all-time hero. Was I disappointed? Sure. But I honestly felt worse about the idea that he was angry with me. Feeling I'd let him down seemed to trigger old feelings of disapproval I'd felt long ago from my dad. That sense of disappointing someone I loved and respected always cut deep for me.

—

A FEW YEARS LATER, I GOT WORD THAT RAY WANTED ME TO JOIN HIM ON HIS DUETS album, *Genius Loves Company*, to sing "Hey Girl" again with him, and that meant the world to me—not just to get to work with him again, but to know that if he was upset with me, I'd been forgiven, that there was no lingering ill will.

On the day of the recording it was, of course, good to see him, and again we had some laughs, but I could tell he wasn't feeling all that well. As it turns out, Ray was very sick and would pass away shortly afterward, which only makes me all the more grateful that he took the time and made the effort under the circumstances to reach out to me.

That afternoon, as I stood at the mic next to my idol, on a soundstage surrounded by a forty-piece orchestra, I could almost believe this was a dream, that I might wake up still a kid back in my room in Ferguson. But any doubt soon gave way, once again, to the thought, "Man, if my buddies could see me now!"

CHAPTER 20

IF THAT'S WHAT IT TAKES

In 1981, the Doobies were in LA, off and running, working on our next album, and I would also find myself putting together songs for a solo album that, frankly, I hadn't really planned on.

Notwithstanding the fact that at eighteen I jumped on a plane the minute someone dangled the prospect of making my own record, the truth was by this time I no longer saw myself as a solo artist. I wasn't a guy who felt he could write twelve songs, a whole album's worth of really good songs. I was a guy who could write a *couple* of good songs, and with the help of six or seven other guys who were writing too, we might make a pretty decent album.

In my heart, I've always been a "band guy." That was my comfort zone. I didn't really feel I had that personality for live performance. I'd like to think I've gotten better at it, but from the earliest time, I never truly thought of myself as a front man, the guy whom the audience is looking at the whole time, who has to come up with something interesting to say between songs. I was always more comfortable being the keyboard-playing singer getting to sing lead on a couple of songs.

However, there had apparently been some discussion between Warner Bros. and Doobies management about signing me to a solo deal. I wasn't even involved in those discussions until they presented it to me as simply an opportunity to pick up a nice advance and explore some other musical avenues, to be delivered at my own pace. "No pressure."

But I came to find out it was somewhat more complicated, and perhaps not entirely altruistic on their part. A bit more light was cast on the situation by my old friend Irving Azoff. Irving and I had kept in touch over the years, and he had, by this point, become hugely successful. He had always given me great insight since we met back in the '60s. On this occasion, he had two points to make clear to me: First, that this was definitely the time to make such a deal. With the success and momentum from "What a Fool Believes" and the *Minute by Minute* album, this was the strike-while-the-iron-is-hot moment. And second, I was in a very powerful negotiating position since contractually, I was a free agent. In other words, the Doobies were signed to Warner Bros., but I wasn't. My agreement was strictly with Doobro Entertainment Corporation, the band's corporate entity. So this offer from the label to record my own album wasn't so much about the A&R department encouraging me to expand my creative efforts by way of a solo career as, I suspect, it was simply an effort by the legal arm of the label to get my John Hancock on some paper as quickly and cheaply as possible. I hadn't realized any of that.

So I asked Irving to represent me as manager and negotiate the deal with Warners—probably one of my better cognitive moments, as he got me a *much* larger advance than was originally offered.

—

GOING ON A YEAR LATER, I WAS ALREADY LATE DELIVERING MY SOLO ALBUM, BUT Warners was willing to overlook that, as it seemed to be in everyone's best interest at that point to keep the momentum up for the Doobies. The band was fine with me doing a solo album, and it was never perceived as any kind of conflict of interest. In fact, Pat was already in the process of negotiating his own solo deal.

Personally, I wasn't viewing the solo record as any kind of jumping-off point or new career direction. The Doobies were still my first priority. Nonetheless, I did owe Warners that solo record now, so in good faith, even before we started work on the Doobies' next album, I went in and recorded the first couple of tracks for my album, one of which was a song I wrote with Patrick Henderson called "Real Love," an upbeat but lyrically mournful resignation as far as love is concerned—"Darlin', I know I'm just another head on your pillow / If only just tonight, girl, let me hear you lie just a little."

I felt it was the best song I had at the time and would have been a terrific addition to my solo album. But my allegiance to the band was such that I believed I owed my best effort to them first. So I re-recorded it with the Doobie Brothers for the album that became *One Step Closer*, and "Real Love" ultimately turned out to be a hit for the album, reaching No. 5 on the *Billboard* singles chart.

After that first solo tracking date, I put my solo album project on hold for the time being, figuring I'd have plenty of time to come up with a viable replacement for that track later. I was committed to the Doobies for as long as they stayed together—or until I got myself bounced.

One Step Closer had some memorable highlights for us as a band. Legendary British singer Chris Thompson ("Blinded by the Light," Manfred Mann's Earth Band), one of rock and roll's truly great voices and a talented composer as well, joined us for some of the writing and vocalizing on this record. Singers Nicolette Larson and Rosemary Butler lent their talent on several tracks as well.

The title track was a great tune written by Carlene Carter, John McFee, and Keith Knudsen. New member Cornelius Bumpus brought a new power to the band's sound by way of his B-3 organ and sax playing and stepped in on occasion to handle lead vocals. He also wrote the song "Thank You Love," probably our most traditional Latin jazz arrangement.

And in one last personnel change, original Doobie bassist Tiran Porter, who played on all the tracks of the album, decided he just wasn't up for another tour. So it was around this juncture that Willie

Weeks joined us, and it wouldn't be long before he became a principal member of the Doobie Brothers. (It's Willie who appears with us in the cover photo.)

For me, *One Step Closer* was one of the most fun projects we'd done since *Takin' It to the Streets*. I didn't realize then that it would be the last studio album I'd record with the Doobies for thirty-four years.

As 1981 rolled into 1982, the band was still pushing, and I was no doubt reaching a crisis stage health-wise. To this day, looking at the album cover of *One Step Closer*, that beautiful photo by Norman Seeff of us on a Malibu beach at twilight, I can't help but see the toll that alcohol and drugs had taken on me by then. That photo, and a passport photo I took around that time, still looks to me like I had recently been beaten about the face with two-by-fours. The blackouts, the seizures, and the strained personal relationships—all of it was somehow still not enough to get me to admit that my life was becoming increasingly unmanageable.

—

AMY AND I WERE BY THAT POINT STILL HAPPILY LIVING UP IN SANTA BARBARA, BUT THE year started out with a painful loss for me: my grandmother Genevieve, the woman who had raised us during the toughest times and for whom I had such affection. Her passing was something I hoped I'd never have to witness. Throughout her battle, she stayed brave, loving, and strong in her religious faith. Although at one point, during her last hours, in a rare conscious moment, she looked at me and said, "I understand that it's my time, but why would God let me suffer like this?" I wished I had a comforting answer to offer, but for the life of me I didn't. As much as I never wanted this day to come, still I was glad to have been there to hold her hand and say a proper goodbye.

It was while I was at the hospital keeping vigil over my grandmother that I received a message to call Pat Simmons, and when I stepped out to use the pay phone in the hall outside my grandmother's room, I learned, in the course of a particularly heartfelt conversation with Pat, that he had decided to leave the group. I was aware of how profound this decision was for him. To his credit, he wanted everyone in the band to know first and to hear it from him personally.

Pat and I had always communicated easily and had no problem being honest with each other, whether it was in casual conversation or while, on rare occasion, throwing furniture at each other in the dressing room. But now, given how much had changed since he started this band years earlier, his frustrations had reached a point of no return.

I totally understood where he was coming from, and I'd like to think I took the opportunity to express my gratitude for the generosity he'd shown me over the years and how much I valued his friendship. Collectively, in different evolutions, we'd all made it around the horn a couple times, as individuals and as a band. I believe, in one way or another, we'd all paid our dues to get there. But Pat was one of the founding members—and to think of all that had been achieved since the early Winnebago days: the platinum albums, years of sold-out arena gigs, Grammys, prestigious TV appearances on *Saturday Night Live* and *The Midnight Special* . . . And hey, the friggin' cover of *Rolling Stone*! Now that he was leaving, I think most of us wondered how this thing could possibly still work without him. Pat, after all, was the last remaining "keeper of the flame," the one we all depended on to represent that distilled, collective conscience of the band.

We did play one performance that spring without him: just a couple of songs at Radio City Music Hall in New York for an event (that David Gest would not let us out of) called "Night of a Hundred Stars." The actual taping was long enough, but coupled with an all-day rehearsal—and the monumental effort of the promoters to control the alcohol and drug consumption backstage with that many entertainers—it was a grueling seven-hour ordeal.

There were some upbeat moments during this otherwise torturously long affair. I did get to meet Lauren Bacall and Elizabeth Taylor. Correction: I was actually *summoned* to meet them, and the short walk down to their dressing room was all the time I needed to convince myself that these two stunning Hollywood legends must be Doobie Brothers fans. What else could it be?

When their assistant introduced us, Liz (as I like to call Elizabeth Taylor) motioned for me to lean in closer. Be still my heart! As I bent down, she whispered in my ear, "I understand you're the guy to talk to about finding us some booze." Okay, so my ego took a slight kidney punch, but in a strange way I felt kind of validated, even a little notorious.

—

UPON RETURNING TO CALIFORNIA, WE ASSEMBLED TO REHEARSE FOR SOME SHOWS WITH the remaining lineup minus Pat; I guess the thinking was that we might still, at some point, tour. But from the first song we played down, the elephant in the room loomed large: the lack of any original members at all.

When Tom Johnston had left a few years earlier, as integral as he was to the group's success and ongoing legacy, it didn't seem unreasonable that the band could go on in his absence—as long as enough original guys remained, especially Pat, who'd also written a good share of the songs and played this music from the beginning. John Hartman and Tiran, more than any of us "new guys," had also earned the right to carry the name forward. The thought of taking the stage as "the Doobie Brothers" with literally none of the original guys seemed, more than anything, unfair to the audience. Those of us who remained just didn't seem to add up to the Doobie Brothers anymore.

It was a solemn moment that none of us wanted to face—because we weren't pulling the plug on just the band members; there was a whole organization of twenty-five to thirty good folks, and for many of them the Doobie Brothers really was their whole livelihood. This was a huge blow for a lot of people.

Still, I felt like the prospect that we had reached the end of the road had to at least be discussed. And as soon as it was put out there, it was hard to rationalize away; it seemed we all had come in that day thinking the same thing. I was just the one who didn't have the sense to not bring it up.

I couldn't tell if some of the guys were mad at me for broaching the subject, and I'd have understood if they felt like I was trying to make some unilateral decision for everyone. But I wasn't. I was just trying to articulate what I saw as the truth in that moment: that I didn't feel any more prepared than anyone else on that stage to step up to fill Pat's shoes as the leader of the Doobie Brothers.

Needless to say, rehearsal was over for the day.

—

IN THE EARLY PART OF '82, I FINALLY FINISHED MY SOLO ALBUM *IF THAT'S WHAT IT TAKES*, a project that was memorable for me for so many reasons. For one thing, the fact that details of the arrangements didn't have to be subject to group consensus was liberating—and scary. For better or worse, those decisions were mine to make, though I would always consider any suggestions by the producers, and I was in particularly capable hands with my old mentor Ted Templeman, who coproduced the record with Lenny Waronker, whom I was working with in the studio for the first time. Together they helped me make a more unabashed R&B record. With so many remarkable players—guitarists Steve Lukather, Dean Parks, and Robben Ford; keyboardists Greg Phillinganes, Michael Boddicker, and Michael Omartian; bassists Louis Johnson, Mike Porcaro, and Willie Weeks; drummers Jeff Porcaro and Steve Gadd; percussionists Lenny Castro and Paulinho da Costa; and saxophonists Tom Scott and Edgar Winter—the album had a more sophisticated rhythmic texture, which seemed like the logical next step for me at the time.

I'd also had the privilege of writing for this album with some truly great songwriters: Ed Sanford of the Sanford-Townsend Band, Kenny Loggins, Randy Goodrum, Grady Walker, Harry Garfield, and Jackie DeShannon, who wrote the title song with me (and shared some great stories from having toured the States with the Beatles).

It was also thanks to Ted and Lenny's brilliant A&R instincts that I was given one of the most memorable experiences of my career: working with the great maestro Marty Paich, who wrote and conducted the orchestration for "I Can Let Go Now."

Singer-songwriters often talk about writing as a welcome, cathartic venting of their troubled emotional inner life. Song as a running diary, as confession; song as therapy. "Turn that heartbreak into a great song!" That's never been me. I wish I could do that more, but I've always had a hard time writing about myself in the first person. For me the worst question you could ask is "How do you feel about that?" I've never been good at getting in touch with my innermost feelings about anything—let alone talking about them. I'm more likely to get irritated by the question than I am to try to get in touch with how I actually feel about whatever it was that made you ask me that in the first place. I've always felt more comfortable writing in the third person, as if I'm telling someone else's story—observing human nature from afar.

But "I Can Let Go Now" is a notable exception. With lines like "It was so right, it was so wrong / Almost at the same time," it was a pretty personal, raw, and honest song. While it was actually inspired by the words of the woman who was finally free of the pain I'd caused her, still, it seemed to speak to my own confusion about love, loss, and healing.

I like to think that, as I've gotten older and with some effort, I've gotten better at digging a little deeper, writing from a more vulnerable and honest place—though perhaps not enough to make any credible therapist say, "Great, Mike. I think our work is done here."

There were some steep learning curves on this album, especially on the technical side. The studio was at the time transitioning from analog to digital recording, which was still a somewhat new technology, so there were some hiccups.

We discovered that the new digital tape machines had an issue in the transport motor (and please feel free to skip ahead if this gets a little too techno-tedious). It seemed that when the take-up reel got too heavy, it would cause the tape speed to gradually slow down ever so slightly, resulting in pitch and tempo fluctuations throughout the recording stage that weren't evident till later, in playback. Fortunately Donn Landee, in his genius, devised some kind of magical device that regulated the speed of the take-up reel motor. But the whole episode was good for a mild panic attack, because for a minute there, we thought we might have to scrap the whole project and start over.

Recording that album was also my opportunity to work with Jeff Porcaro in the studio for a second time. We had played live together and worked on some of the same Steely Dan tracks throughout the '70s, but never in the studio at the same time, not until we recorded the original version of "Real Love." And now I got to further experience the magic Jeff brought to a live tracking date, the way he would build his distinctive drum patterns over the different sections of the songs, and his grooves were legendarily unfaltering—even on the rare misstep.

On one track, after we finished the first take, Ted called us all up to the control booth, presumably, we thought, to offer some direction for the next take. Instead, he assured us that we had it. This was the take.

That's when Jeff spoke up: "Um . . . if you don't mind, I'd like to do another, 'cause . . . I actually dropped a stick on the vamp-out." We thought he was kidding. So we played back that region of the track, where, he explained to us, his hi-hat stick had started to splinter, catching on the cymbals and flying out of his hand. And apparently, without missing a beat (pardon the pun), he had bent down, snatched the stick up from the floor, and finished the song. He swore he could hear his hi-hat pattern change as he was leaning over to retrieve his stick. Literally no one else in the room could hear anything disconcerting, and we unanimously voted to go with that take because it was just so good.

And that was the one and only take of "I Keep Forgettin'," which was the only hit single off that album. The track took on a kind of hypnotic, soulful feel by way of Louis Johnson's killer bass line and Jeff Porcaro's infectious groove, but everyone on the floor that day—including Steve Lukather on guitar and Greg Phillinganes on clavinet—contributed something musically unique that caused the stars to align on that track. (And just so you know, the alluring female background vocal on that track was my little sister, Maureen.)*

—

WHILE I WAS FINISHING MY ALBUM, PAT SIMMONS CONTINUED TO WORK ON HIS OWN solo project, *Arcade*, and I was thrilled when he invited me to play keyboards and sing backgrounds on a few tracks, including a tune we had written together called "Why You Givin' Up."

I've heard from more than a few people over the years that trying to pin down the exact arc of the Doobie Brothers story can be a tad confusing. There's a reason for that: it *is* confusing. After all, we did change personnel and start and stop more than once. And no sooner had we come to terms with this last, bittersweet, seemingly final wind-down of the band's operation than Pat floated the idea

---

* Once, after sampling Maureen's voice on an emulator, we found that when we played it an octave down, she sounded just like me. It must be in the DNA.

that maybe we should do one last farewell tour to show our appreciation to the loyal fans who'd been there for us all those years. He even suggested we record some of the shows to release as a live album. We were all down for that.

While the initial appeal was simply a nice opportunity to get back together and make music one more time, the additional excitement was that after a long and restorative period, health-wise, Tom Johnston had agreed to come join us for these recordings. I, on the other hand, was moving rapidly in the other direction, my health being at its most compromised. Due to my excessive drinking I was having problems just paying attention and struggling to develop my parts on multiple keyboards while singing at the same time. Ted Templeman, thank God, was there on hand to help with new arrangements and the flow and sequence of the final two shows, which would be recorded. Knowing this would now culminate in a finite, one-off experience, and having become such a consistent part of one another's lives over the years, we all came to this endeavor with a renewed gratitude for what we had shared, and this was shaping up to be something special.

—

OUR OFFICIAL, PUBLICLY ANNOUNCED FAREWELL TOUR STARTED IN JULY 1982, AND IN every city where we performed, our appreciation of and unique connection to those places seemed deeper than ever. It was truly a heartfelt farewell to all the loyal fans who had collectively become more like old friends over the years.

One night that stands out to me is ChicagoFest at Navy Pier, where we played to something like fifty thousand fans. I remember at one point in the evening looking out over this vast sea of humanity, fist-pumping in perfect unison, the deep connection between band and audience undeniable, and thinking, "Really? We're really just gonna walk away from this?"

In anticipation of the big crowds that ChicagoFest usually drew, we had decided to work up one track each from Pat's and my respective upcoming solo albums to play that night. I was up first, and I remember with some embarrassment the polite but somewhat tepid response to "I Keep Forgettin'"—the first time all night that the audience seemed to actually calm down. I decided, "It's probably just that they haven't heard this song before. Yeah . . . that must be it."

The very next song was Pat's brand-new tune "Out on the Streets," and about two bars into it, here we go again with the fist-pumping. The crowd just ate it up. I remember thinking, "This doesn't bode well for my first solo single release." My song did ultimately go on to be a bit of a hit, but on that particular night? Not so much.

We played just about every night through August and into September of that year, closing things out at the Greek Theatre in Berkeley, California, where Tom Johnston, Tiran Porter, and John Hartman joined us for our final two shows. Those were the shows we recorded for the Doobies' *Farewell Tour* live album, which was deftly overseen, produced, and mixed by Ted Templeman and engineer Jim Isaacson. Along with Donn Landee and Ted Templeman, Jim's audio engineering genius was such a big part of the Doobie Brothers' signature sound and sustained radio success. Sadly Jim, at the height of his career, would pass away soon after.

If it had to end, that tour and the live album that came of it sure seemed like a good way to go out. We had always looked forward to every touring season for the longest time as if we thought it would never end.

Notwithstanding our personal struggles and somewhat different histories, this had been our life for most of our early adult years.

And now, it was time for whatever was to come next.

CHAPTER 21

OUR LOVE

Well, one thing that came next was: I asked Amy to marry me.

During the Christmas holidays of 1982, Amy's parents were visiting us in LA, and they were wonderful folks. Her dad, Harry Boersma, was born in New York to Dutch immigrant parents (hence Amy's choice of "Holland" as a professional name) and worked as a mastering engineer in New York City for Mercury Records. Working out of their facilities above the Russian Tea Room and Carnegie Hall in midtown Manhattan, he oversaw the mastering of many hit singles from the '60s—records like "Walk Away Renée" by the Left Banke, and some early hits by Lesley Gore, Dusty Springfield, and the Four Seasons—even some Sarah Vaughan classics.

Amy's mom, Verna, grew up in Memphis and was a wonderful musician/vocalist who had a career of some renown in radio from the '30s through the early '50s as hillbilly persona Esmereldy. (Little piece of trivia: Amy's mom was also the voice of Possum Pearl on some of the early *Popeye the Sailor* cartoon shorts.) She had a few hit records on the Musicraft label with novelty tunes such as "My Bucket's Got a Hole in It" and "Slap Her Down Again Pa" (a title you might want to think twice about using today) featuring her impressive yodeling skills—a vocal characteristic that Amy inherited and subtly incorporated in her singing style that so pulled me in from the get-go. Verna even had her own radio show on WABC in New York City, which was where she and Harry first met.

It was in the glow of familial warmth we were all feeling during their holiday visit that I proposed to Amy. Her dad was over the moon; he and Amy were so close, and the thought of walking his youngest daughter down the aisle gave him something wonderful to look forward to in the New Year.

Sadly, this was not to be. Only days after returning to New York, Amy's dad passed suddenly of a massive coronary. Though it was a tragic shock to us all, I know that it was a blow that Amy will never completely reconcile. We postponed the wedding and went back east to help her mom make arrangements for her dad's funeral.

At the wake, it was clear to me that for Amy and her sister, Sherry, the proceedings were sadly surreal; this was all new to them. For me, however, having grown up Irish Catholic, I'd been imbued with a strong sense of mortality. Our family went to wakes almost as often as we did the grocery store, so the only thing that seemed strange to me about this service was how solemn the whole affair was. The people in attendance were so quiet, walking up to view Harry as he lay in state, then quietly returning to their seats, hardly a word spoken the whole time.

Until . . . Aunt Anne (Harry's sister) burst through the door with more than a couple already under her belt. She walked straight up to the casket and bellowed, "He looks terrible! I'm goin' for a beer! Anyone else comin'?"

I thought, "Well, chalk one up for the Dutch." I, for one, was suddenly feeling more comfortable.

—

BY THE TIME WE RETURNED TO LA, WE FOUND, TO MY SURPRISE, THAT "I KEEP FORGETTIN'" seemed to be making some noise on radio, thanks to the Warner Bros. promotion team—specifically its R&B department. Normally, my album would likely have been assigned to the adult contemporary radio team, the AOR (album-oriented radio) people, or perhaps the rock radio teams that historically handled the Doobie Brothers' albums. But it was the enthusiasm shown by Warners' R&B team—and the *lack* of enthusiasm for the album by the other departments—that ultimately gave us a story to tell. Their initial interest was actually piqued by the positive response from the immediate staff in their office. We artists are always indebted to the record company secretarial pools, because, in my opinion, they're the ones who do the best job of picking the next singles.

Truth be known, the success of this track was in fact a culmination of the largely unrecognized Black audience support that had always been there for the Doobie Brothers over the years. Ernie Singleton, head of Warners' R&B promotion team at the time, said, "We've always dug the band—I'm just glad they finally let us run with the ball." And Ernie worked hard to build a platform for "I Keep Forgettin'" through his relationships with privately owned, independent R&B stations, of which there are far fewer today.

In many cases, the station's owner / manager / program director (who was often the main on-air personality as well) was passionate about the music; the business of owning a radio station was in their blood. They were typically on-site just about 24/7, and in many cases this meant that if you just showed up to say hello, they might sit you down on-air for an interview and play your whole album from start to finish, and the decision to add your single into rotation could be made before you even said goodbye.

In those days, an enthusiastic DJ at a regional station could make all the difference; they could single-handedly jump-start a hit record. If it took off in that region, word would get out, and it might then spread across the country. This happened all the time. When I was a kid, Roy Head's big hit "Treat Her Right" broke out because of one station in Texas. Legend has it that Billy Joel's career launched because of one station in Philadelphia that put into heavy rotation a recording of "Captain Jack" from one of his live shows. Even the Doobies' first No. 1 record, "Black Water," was actually the B-side of a single that had come out a year earlier—but one station in Roanoke, Virginia, took a shine to the song, and . . . boom.

Radio, like the music industry itself, is an ever-evolving beast. When I started really listening to records in the late '50s and early '60s, the stuff I loved on the smaller, independent labels like Stax, Motown, Volt, Chess, Bang, and Smash grew in popularity as a backlash to the few major labels who, up to then, were more or less dictating the music that people were most likely to hear. And later, FM stations were a similar response to the restrictive Top Forty formats prevalent in national AM radio.

Today, unfortunately, radio stations have, yet again, largely syndicated into a uniform, nationwide format that basically predetermines what the masses will hear, and that yin-yang dynamic seems to always be in motion. For every effort made by the corporate mainstream to control the market, you can bet there will always be that counteraction by the public at large to widen the artistic playing field. Today, Spotify, iTunes, and the like have vastly expanded access to music that might not otherwise be heard. (But in the process, they've arbitrarily rewritten the regulations that would give any fair compensation to the artists and songwriters who provide this content. Hopefully a more equitable arrangement is in the near future.)

But back then, prior to the release of my solo album, these independent stations and more adventurous program directors were still going strong. So toward the end of the Doobies' Farewell Tour the previous summer, you can bet that Ernie Singleton would have his regional promotion person pick me up at the hotel to swing by these small, local popular R&B stations. And that was how "I Keep Forgettin'"—the song that had markedly underwhelmed the ChicagoFest audience only a few months earlier—eventually reached No. 5 on the *Billboard* Hot 100 chart and set me up to tour in the summer and even perform on *Soul Train* and *Saturday Night Live*.

—

IN A FURTHER EFFORT TO FIND MY WAY INTO THIS NEW PHASE OF MY LIFE AS A SOLO artist, I proceeded to outfit my personal studio. While our home was still up in Santa Barbara, I had earlier bought a house on Dilling Street in North Hollywood that had a little studio attached. It wasn't much—just a little demo studio in the back—but I was having a blast doing a reno/build-out, outfitting the space with a bit more professional-grade gear I'd purchased from Amigo (Warners) Studios in North Hollywood: an API console, a 3M twenty-four-track, and an Ampex half-inch stereo tape machine that had actually been first owned by Lamont Dozier. The good mojo and sweet happenstance of working on equipment passed down from one of the giants responsible for so many of the Motown classic songs that had rocked my world was not lost on me. Soon, both the studio and the control room were filled with a drum kit, keyboards, and all sorts of other gear—limiters, outboard mic pre-amps, and a slew of cool vintage microphones . . . I was a kid in a candy shop. All I had to do now was learn how to work this stuff.

As the equipment was very much used and had been in storage for quite a while after that, there was a lot of time spent chasing gremlins in the system and working around certain faders and sporadically noisy modules. So while engineer Jim Pace worked tirelessly at maintaining and further tuning the room, I was hanging around pretending to be of any help whatsoever setting up this new workstation layout, but really just trying to avoid the feverish frenzy of wedding planning going on in the house.

The wedding itself was in May '83, and for the week leading up to it, it seemed half the city of St. Louis had migrated west to attend. My house was filled with Amy's family and my old bandmates, and the overflow—my dad coming out from Florida, some of my folks' friends going back to their high school days—were camped out in the San Fernando Valley at (what had by now become) my mom's house.

I'll never forget how beautiful Amy was on our wedding day in Montecito, held at the little mission-style church down the street from our house, followed by a reception around the corner at our friends Irving and Shelli Azoff's home.

For the music at the reception we spared no expense, hiring the Harry James Orchestra, but for the same money, unbeknownst to us, ended up with Buddy Something-or-Other and *his* big band. Our friend David Pack, lead singer of Ambrosia, knowing it was Amy's and my favorite song, went up and performed his most recent hit, "Biggest Part of Me," after which the entertainment morphed into an extended jam session involving all the musicians there—my old St. Louis pals and groomsmen Chuck Sabatino, Steve Scorfina, and Pat Molloy joining Edgar Winter, assorted Doobies . . . even my father took the stage and belted out a few.

As much as this day was a sad reminder that Amy's dad wasn't there to share it with us, remembering how happy he was just anticipating it served to remind us that this was still a joyous occasion to be shared with all the people who came to celebrate with us: family and friends, some folks we'd known forever and some we'd never laid eyes on in our lives—like the five bikers in leather chaps, shirtless but for the denim vests bearing some club insignia. They were standing in the reception line behind a group of nuns whom we also didn't know from Adam. (As a survivor of Catholic grade school, I wasn't sure which group to be more afraid of.)

After that we had a short honeymoon in the Cayman Islands and Jamaica, which was apparently more like an extended blackout, according to some photos we had developed after we returned home—like the one of my wife, feeling no pain, at the beach, atop a human pyramid of the US Navy's Seventh Fleet.

The Jamaican excursion could have gone terribly wrong before it even got started. On the way from the airport to the hotel, I chose to make a stop in downtown Kingston, where I decided it would be a good idea to leave my new wife alone in a running taxi with a total stranger driving, while I jumped out at a crowded open-air marketplace—a promising location to find some ganja, a notoriously potent form of Jamaican cannabis. Once again—what could possibly go wrong? As I stood there perusing the crowd, looking conspicuously like the

Dumbass Tourist in Search of Drugs, I turned and literally bumped into a Jamaican fella with long dreadlocks, a man of few words, who said simply, "I'm Rasta Charley. I know what you want. Follow me."

Thanks to Rasta Charley, I managed to score some pot and not get arrested—or killed. Amy and I made it to our hotel, where the first order of business was, of course, to get high, thus beginning the more "chilled" version of our honeymoon. Or so we thought.

Clearly, I'd smoked a lot of weed in my time, but ganja is a whole other animal, with a much more intense psychotropic effect. By the time we took a few hits, I for one was seeing things in my peripheral vision that simply weren't there. Feeling extremely paranoid and conspicuous, we somehow managed to walk through the hotel lobby and make it down to the beach, only to discover it was being patrolled by a vigilant group of uniformed hotel security with hard-to-miss automatic weapons slung over their shoulders, giving us the sense that this was no average day at the beach. We immediately did an about-face and went back to our room, where, after a few days holed up smoking more ganja, paranoia got the better of us and we decided it was time to go home.

—

WE SETTLED INTO MARRIED LIFE THAT SUMMER, SPENDING OUR WEEKDAYS IN LA AT OUR Dilling Street studio while I wrestled writer's block to the floor in hopes of coming up with songs for my next album. At this point I was feeling the pressure to up my game. I felt like I needed that home run this time—at least platinum status, which would put me on the map as a solo artist—but I wasn't exactly sure how that would be accomplished.

Enter Quincy Jones into the picture.

I had been a huge fan of Quincy's work with Michael Jackson, Patti Austin, and James Ingram, and his own solo records were some of my favorites, as they always showcased not only his brilliant production and arrangement skills but also some phenomenal vocalists and songwriters. He and I had met for the first time at the Grammy Awards, and he later reached out to me after hearing my first solo album—which he personally thought "should have been better." Quincy, or Q, as he was known to all his friends, said, "You need to do your next one with me. We'll do the record you need to do."

Well, who wouldn't be thrilled to hear that from Quincy Jones? I'd always admired how his records seemed to infuse undeniable musical sophistication with funky energy. His records spoke to my musical heart; I'd always seen myself moving toward more of a pop R&B genre and liked the idea of putting myself in the hands of someone who had the musical command that I lacked. Having Quincy Jones on board as producer would be not only hugely prestigious, a great validating seal of approval, but also a sure guarantee of doing it right. So I felt like this might be a godsend—an opportunity for me to make a whole different kind of solo album.

Step one: Q instructed me to go home and write some "real songs," while suggesting I also try writing with some new partners: Rod Temperton, a founding member of the British group Heatwave, whom I was a big fan of (Rod cowrote Michael Jackson's "Thriller" and "Rock with You," among countless other monster hits), and James Ingram, whose debut solo album Quincy was in the midst of producing. At Q's urging I met with James to write something for his solo project, and we instantly became great friends.

James was a joy to work with. For that matter, it hardly seemed like work. First of all, he had *that voice*, the natural, soulful voice we all aspired to, and timbre-wise, our voices seemed to work well together. Second, he was a fountain of creative energy. He'd come over to my studio, and we'd crank my new big playback speakers, program some drum patterns, and just kind of explore a few different keyboard and bass jams until we found one that we thought might want to be a song.

After several at bats, James and I finally came up with a song that Quincy was pleased with. If memory serves, it was built on a bass line and beat that Quincy sang to James, to which we added the chord progression, melody, and lyrics—and a very strange working title. Q, of course, had some more suggestions musically, resulting in Rod, James, and me composing a bridge right there on the date, at which point engineer extraordinaire Bruce Swedien magically turned our demo into something much more sonically inspired.

Quincy then suggested that James and I record it as a duet. I couldn't believe my good fortune! I was flabbergasted at the generous offer. Oh, and surprisingly he had no problem with our working title, so we kept it. Now we just had to figure out what the hell "Yah Mo B There" actually meant.

"Yah Mo B There" heralded a direction that I hoped to go in with Quincy on this next solo project. It had that energetic, soulful funk and sophistication that was a hallmark of Quincy's production. It raised my hopes for the future.

The single would go on to be a bit of a hit in Europe and the United States, and as I had already planned a tour of sorts with my band around the time of the song's release (December '83) the momentum of that single certainly helped.

The "tour," such as it was—the first with my newly assembled Michael McDonald band—actually started with a week of shows at Harrah's up in Lake Tahoe. It was a good way to iron out the kinks before my broader summer tour of '84, which would take us to Japan, opening for Joe Walsh and Boz Scaggs—all three of us being in a bit of a transitional period; Joe had left the James Gang, made his foray into production with Dan Fogelberg's first album, and just released his solo album *But Seriously, Folks . . .* , while the *Silk Degrees* album was the latest evolution and a whole new level of success for Boz Scaggs.

And my band even played some US dates as headliner, ending at the Universal Amphitheatre in LA. The band was a stellar lineup: George Perilli on drums, Willie Weeks on bass, Robben Ford on guitar, Brian Mann on keyboards, and the incomparable Edgar Winter on keys, sax, vocals, and percussion. I was completely blessed to take the stage with these guys as a first-time solo artist. I had this world-class ensemble that would always make it worth the audience's while, my myriad shortcomings as a front man notwithstanding.

There were other kinks to be ironed out regarding the operational aspects of my touring. Around this time, my mom was our travel agent. She had only recently reinvented herself in this new career and had already built a solid reputation for finding the best deals for her mostly showbiz clientele.

But I was her son, and in what seemed at times like an almost passive-aggressive exercise, she was gonna save me money no matter how miserable my life became as a result. Booking flights for the band was a particular area of contention. Though I was happy to fly coach with everyone in the spirit of solidarity, it didn't do much to endear me to the band and crew, since apparently my mom just couldn't resist the further cost-saving measure of booking us all in middle seats. I sensed that the guys might've been approaching the end of their patience when, on one particular flight, as I crawled over someone to take my assigned middle seat, I looked back to see that every middle seat in coach, all the way to the last row, was filled by someone in my organization—each of them at that moment making direct eye contact with me. It was Chuck Sabatino who, speaking for the group, called out, "Hey, Mike, on the next flight maybe your mom could hire a dentist to come along and drill our teeth."

Back home after that tour, I continued writing and hoped to pick up the conversation with Quincy about the pending album. But when we met to listen to some rough demos of song ideas I'd come up with, Quincy explained that he was unfortunately going to be tied up with other projects for the foreseeable future and it would be a while before he could give it his proper attention. That wasn't surprising; this was one of the busiest men in town, at that moment riding a particularly spectacular hot streak and a skyrocketing trajectory into movie production and the management of his new record label, Qwest.

However, he insisted he still wanted to do my next album with me—if I could be patient. I said, "Sure," and asked if he'd like to hear what I had come up with so far. He listened politely but then suggested I keep writing in the meantime. I didn't get the feeling he was all that impressed.

I had learned from James Ingram that you had to work hard to "ring Q's bell" with a song. He was only looking for home runs. No demure album cuts for Q. Any album that he was gonna put his energy into had to be loaded for bear, song-wise, and that was okay with me. I figured it would only raise the bar overall for the project. So I put my shoulder into the work and for the next several months kept myself busy writing, but in all honesty, he didn't seem too crazy about any of the songs I was sending him.

—

IT WAS ABOUT THIS TIME THAT I STARTED TO FEEL A BIT OUT OF SYNC WITH THE RECORD business. For one, I got the sense that no one wanted to hear another Michael McDonald background vocal—I had dipped into that well perhaps once too often, somewhere between fifty and a thousand times. I also remember one of my writing partners around this time pointing out that my keyboard style was "too '70s" and that I needed to try to be "more '80s." I had no idea what that meant, but it didn't sound good. I was starting to feel like my mojo was definitely on the blink. Looking back now, I realize I was better off sticking to what was organic to *me*—my peculiar but unique style of piano playing and harmonic sensibility. There was also the issue of my love/hate relationship with synthesizers in general, which unfortunately were all the rage in the '80s. I just never had a natural affinity for them; I was always more drawn to piano, organ, and clavinet, as I felt those were the keyboards God had originally intended . . . I'm pretty sure.

Now, at this juncture, in the early half of the '80s, Quincy Jones seemed to only get busier, pushing any hope of starting a project further into '85, at best. Meanwhile, Warners execs were anxiously wondering when I might deliver my next record, as it was now going on three years since my previous album was released. On a conference call with my managers and Warners VPs Ted Templeman and Lenny Waronker, I could only offer the excuse that scheduling had been difficult because Quincy was so busy, and I wasn't sure at this point when he'd be available or, frankly, if he was even still interested.

Ted and Lenny had another idea. Unlike Quincy, these guys seemed genuinely enthusiastic about the demos I was coming up with. (Out of habit, I'd copied Ted on the songs I was working on, since he had long been a reliable sounding board for me, always offering insightful feedback.) He and Lenny felt these raw, somewhat primitive demos had a charm of sorts, and, with some reworking and added production value, they might in fact be the record to release in the meantime, and simply push back my plan to do a record with Q until he was more available. My fear, of course, was that Quincy might lose interest and I might miss the opportunity to work with him altogether.

But the more we discussed it, the more it seemed like putting out this interim album might actually be the solution to everyone's problem: Warners would get its long-overdue album from me, and Quincy would have one less immediate obligation to worry about on his obviously overflowing plate.

I expressed my concern as to how to appropriately present the idea to Quincy, as I didn't want to appear to be pressing for some renewed commitment from him. It was then suggested by someone that maybe Warner CEO Mo Ostin should be the one to talk to Q since they were so close; they'd known each other since their shared Sinatra days in the '50s. The danger was, of course, that I'd be counting on someone else to reiterate my desire to still work with Quincy in the future. Then again, I rationalized that if Q really was having second thoughts about working with me at this point, he would probably be more comfortable confiding that to Mo. Hindsight bringing its perspective as it surely does, I realize it was a conversation that only I should've had with Quincy. I think I knew that then, but, simply put, I fucked up.

And so the unanimous consensus was that Mo would present the idea to Quincy, with the assumption being that, given the situation, he would most likely agree it was a good strategy.

Unfortunately, that's not the way it played out. None of it sat well with Quincy. He expressed to me later that it was more the way it was handled than anything else. So much seemed to have gotten lost in translation. Not that Mo said anything wrong or handled it poorly in any way (as a matter of fact, I can't say for sure that it was actually Mo who ultimately talked to Q about it), but the fact that I hadn't called Quincy personally to explain the situation made him feel, I believe, like he'd been unceremoniously relieved of our planned project. It all just seemed woefully inelegant and frankly, for Q, insulting. Quincy Jones deserved better from me.

I felt terrible. When Quincy and I finally talked, I apologized for not having spoken to him myself. But this was one of those things in life where once it's done, there's no undoing it. He made it clear to me that I had disappointed him as a friend. And I certainly can't criticize anyone else's handling of what was clearly my responsibility to begin with. I feel bad about it all to this day, but I remain grateful to Quincy—not just for the opportunity he gave me to record with James, but for his honesty about his feelings and for giving me the chance to apologize.

Our project, unfortunately, would never come to be, but I'd like to think our friendship survived all this, as I've had the pleasure of working with him at his request several times in the years since.

But for the time being, I still owed Warner Bros. an album, and making that record would prove to be a profound transformation for me.

CHAPTER 22

SOUNDTRACKS, DUETS, AND PIGEONS

Having my Dilling Street studio was a new era of sorts for me as a songwriter; not only did it provide me with a personal warehouse for all my instruments and gear, but it was also a creative sandbox of sorts—a space where, absent the pressure of expensive studio time and rented storage space, I was free to take my time and experiment more. And not being obligated to confer with anyone else was a nice change.

This was a scaled-down operation—just me and an engineer. And it was probably a good thing that I at least had an engineer showing up, because my drinking and drugging at this stage was such that if I didn't, I would have more than likely blown the day off just getting high.

But the big plus of this smaller operation was that I was able to get the songs down quickly, guerrilla style; they were a little rough around the edges—certainly not as pristine sounding as what the Doobies had done with Donn and Ted—but the tracks had a certain sonic personality, a lo-fi quality that felt more like a deliberate stylistic element I was starting to like. A guitar may have sounded too compressed or "squashed," a vocal may have been a bit distorted . . . I would think, "I'll come back to that track later and get a better sound." But upon returning, after hearing it a few times, I often grew to prefer the character of the original track, as lo-fi as it was.

I'd head into the studio most weekdays, usually kick off around noon and start working on a tune, normally playing all the instruments myself at first, and if we were on a roll, we'd just order in some dinner and often continue on till midnight. In my previous recording experiences, we'd bring in a relatively finished composition with only a vague image in our heads of what the track might eventually sound like. Before actually tracking anything, we'd often work for hours to get a live drum kit to sound "inspiring"—finding the right place in the room to set up the kit, the right mics at the right distance, using sound baffle placement to minimize any leakage onto other tracks . . .

But the LinnDrum machine introduced in the early '80s was a game changer. A far cry from the earlier incarnations of beatboxes that sounded conspicuously synthetic with limited, preprogrammed drum patterns, the LinnDrum machine had more state-of-the-art drum samples at your disposal, and being more programmable, it worked as a writing tool in helping to lay down a groove in the earlier stages of a song's development.

As I continued to work on my long-overdue follow-up album, the end result was becoming something different and accidentally positive. In what was an entirely new process for me, these raw demos started to become the actual tracks for the album.

I had essentially been producing the tracks myself, but when Ted jumped on board, we had the chance—and budget—to upgrade the elements we felt were needed. We started looking at the overdubs we might want to add and whose talents we might employ to help bring these tracks up to speed and make them worthy of being released as an album. Jeff Porcaro and Willie Weeks would do some drum and bass overdubs. Joe Walsh came by to add some great guitar work, as did David Pack and Robben Ford. These guitar sessions mostly took place in the evenings and did a good job of rattling the less-than-soundproofed exterior walls. My neighbors could pretty much hear whatever we were doing, which some of them enjoyed less than you might think.

Just next door to us lived a rather large guy who worked in security at the Universal complex. One night while we were recording, he came out to see what the racket was and, ostensibly, to make sure no one was trying to break into my studio. His real concern, of course, was the volume. It was, after all, getting late. So when he showed up at the fence, I could tell he was determined to make an impression, and the Dirty Harry .357 Magnum revolver he was holding surely did the trick for me. We were, thankfully, able to civilly negotiate some reasonable parameters—curfews on the loud stuff and such—but our relationship was later further strained by the fact that my dogs kept killing off his prize roosters when they jumped our fence. To his credit, he didn't blame me or the dogs necessarily, but his affection for us wasn't exactly growing by leaps and bounds either.

He passed away later that year, and I think it's possible he exacted some revenge from the afterlife when his widow set his twenty or so homing pigeons free right after his funeral. They didn't go too far; they proceeded to sit on my roof and shit all over my house and driveway for about six months. I'd chase them off with loud noises, then watch them fly out over the Valley and circle back in a tight formation like some kind of Squab Squadron, making a beeline back to my roof.

Such was life in our quirky Studio City neighborhood, where a whole bunch of creative types—iconic rock and roll photographer Henry Diltz, songwriting partners of mine like Randy Goodrum and Peter Leinheiser, actors like Angela Cartwright and Dick Wilson of Charmin tissue fame (who was just as fastidious about anyone touching his lawn as he was about people "squeezing the Charmin" in his famous TV commercial)—all lived in a lovely few square blocks of architecturally diverse and charming bungalows built in the '40s, '50s, and early '60s. In fact, the house three doors down from us was used in the exterior shots of the TV series *The Brady Bunch*.

—

THE *NO LOOKIN' BACK* ALBUM, ALL TOLD, TOOK ABOUT A YEAR TO COMPLETE AND DID fairly well on the *Billboard* album chart, even producing three chart singles: the title track, written with Kenny Loggins; "Lost in the Parade," written with Grady Walker; and a song I wrote alone called "Bad Times," which featured Joe Walsh's brilliant slide guitar. (I think his solo was actually better than the song.)

This experimental period also brought with it some terrific surprises and new collaborations. I got a call from friend and composer Carole Bayer Sager, whom I had written with a few years earlier and who was by this point married to Burt Bacharach. She and Burt were producing a track for Patti LaBelle's forthcoming album, on which I would now have the good fortune to record a duet with her called "On My Own."

Patti and I hadn't met and didn't sing it together in the studio, as she was in New York performing on Broadway at the time. Her vocal was recorded first, so I was an overdub, which I actually preferred, as Patti had already nailed her performance and it allowed me to shape my performance around her vocal.

In fact, we didn't do the video together either. We shot our individual scenes on two separate coasts: Patti in New York, and me on the beach in Malibu. (Fortunately, the footage of me on the cliff doesn't quite reveal the terror I experienced as the helicopter film crew passed only yards from my forehead. Even after numerous takes, it was all I could do not to hit the dirt every time they whipped around me up there.)

Patti and I wouldn't actually meet until the night before we were to perform the song together for the very first time on *The Tonight Show*. I found Patti to be lovely and gracious, and finally getting to meet her was the best part of the whole experience.

I also got the fortuitous opportunity, before the year was up, to work with Rod Temperton once more, when he asked me to sing the lead on a tune for the soundtrack he was composing for the 1986 film *Running Scared*, starring Gregory Hines and Billy Crystal. It became the hit single "Sweet Freedom," written expressly for the movie by Rod and Dick Rudolph.*

The sound of that recording was quintessentially '80s, with all its sequenced, digital drums and synthesizer sounds, which was a leap forward for me at the time. I made the conscious decision to defer to Rod Temperton's technical skills as a composer, keyboardist, and producer and enjoyed the luxury of not having to figure that all out for myself for once.

After the release of the *Running Scared* soundtrack, my album *No Lookin' Back* was remastered and reissued with the track "Sweet Freedom" added, as well as a revised version of "Our Love" for single release. Producer/engineer Humberto Gatica successfully took it from a lilting African lullaby-feeling track, with not much more than kalimba and light percussion under the vocals, and turned it into a more powerful rock ballad, with the addition of Steve Lukather's soaring guitar track.

And we shot a video for "Sweet Freedom" in a small joint in Malibu, which was transformed into a mock tiki bar setting. The shoot did not start off particularly well; the dead goldfish floating on its side in the fishbowl prop next to my piano was a pretty accurate metaphor—until Gregory Hines and Billy Crystal showed up on set unannounced and pretty much took over the shoot with their totally improvised shenanigans. Even the goldfish might have come back to life. But for sure, those guys saved the day.

---

* Dick had been married to the wonderful singer/composer Minnie Riperton, and their marriage produced two talented offspring: Marc Rudolph, a brilliant recording engineer, and the terrific actress Maya Rudolph.

—

LANDING A SONG IN A FILM CAN BE A BIG DEAL; FILM AND TV SYNC LICENSES HAVE become the logical alternative to radio spins and video plays as those avenues have narrowed. So I was excited, a few years down the road, in 2000, to share the news with my friend Jim Photoglo that the song we wrote together, "The Meaning of Love," was getting placed in a movie! "How perfect is this," I thought. "We're releasing this song as a single, so if the movie is a big summer release, it could really boost the album sales!"

Jim had the "audacity" to suggest we might want to see the scene it was being used in before we gave our consent. My attitude was "Hey, this is a Mike Nichols film! What difference does it make what the movie is about?! I'm sure, given the lyric content, it's gonna be used in a tender love scene of some sort."

Well, no. The movie, *What Planet Are You From?*, written by and starring Garry Shandling, was, in fact, about an alien android who comes to Earth retrofitted with a mechanical penis, employed specifically to impregnate female Earthlings. And the scene our song was used in was one such sexual encounter, with the song barely audible in the background—when not completely drowned out by the buzzing mechanical penis. (Did I mention the penis also had a headlight?)

So the moral here is: A film sync license isn't necessarily everything you hope for. Sometimes, though, it is.

Like *The 40-Year-Old Virgin*. In this 2005 Judd Apatow smash hit, Steve Carell and Paul Rudd work in an appliance store whose giant showroom wall of TV monitors simultaneously—and endlessly—all play a live video performance of mine. The manager of the store, played by the terrifically funny Jane Lynch, is a pathetically fervent Michael McDonald fan and will not allow anyone to play anything else. The running joke is that it drives Paul Rudd crazy; at one point he says, "If I hear 'Yah Mo B There' one more time, I'm gonna *yah mo* burn this place to the ground!"

1. My dad (Corporal Robert James McDonald, USMC) singing with Bob Crosby and the Bobcats in 1943.

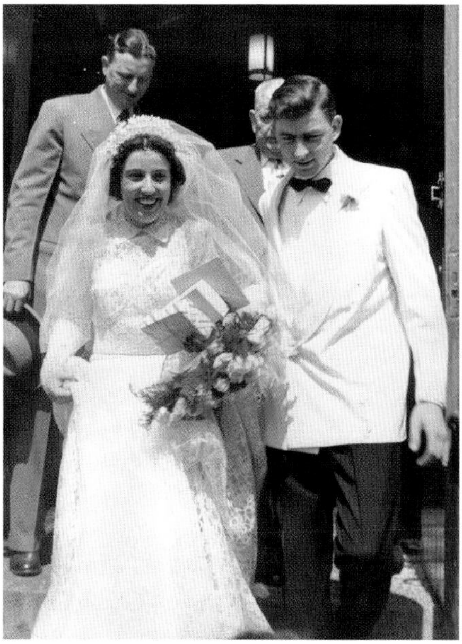

2. Robert and Mary Jane on their wedding day in 1948.

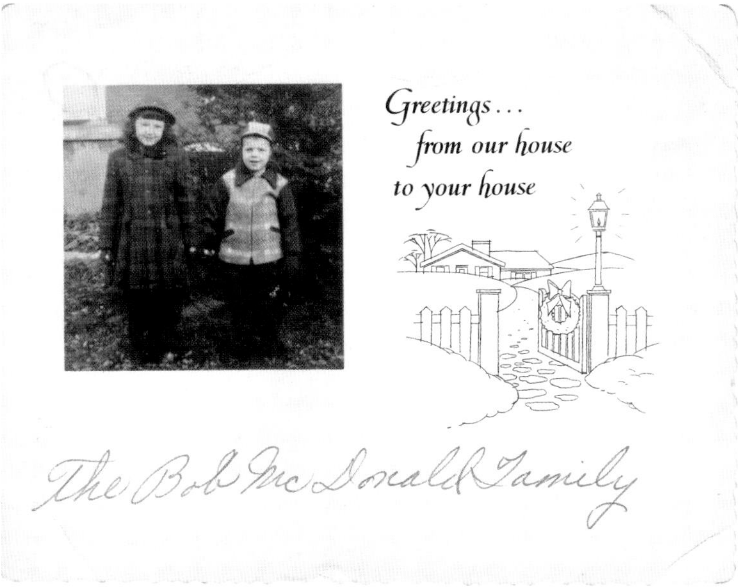

Greetings...
from our house
to your house
The Bob McDonald Family

3. My sister Kathy and me on Maryville Avenue in downtown St. Louis in 1955.

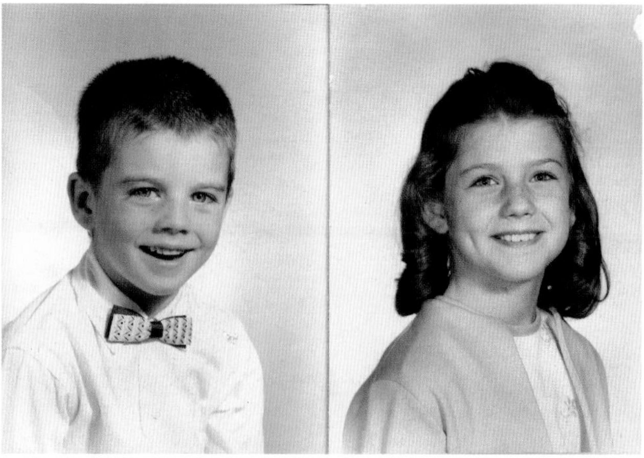

4. My sister Maureen and me.

5. The Majestics at Howard Johnson Motel in 1965, playing poolside. I was the youngest. *Left to right*: me, thirteen; Steve Scorfina, fifteen; Bob Bortz, fourteen; and Pat Molloy, fourteen.

6. Documenting my demotion: our business cards started with "Mike and the Majestics," then became just "the Majestics," 1964–65.

7. The Sheratons in 1967, upon winning the regional competition and Vox endorsement, running up to the final show in New York City, the Vox Battle of the Bands.

8. Club Imperial owner George Edick and his son, Greg, pose with members of Ike Turner's band in the late 1960s.

9. The Sheratons, boarding the flight to New York. At the bottom of the stairs: Irv Satanovsky (*left*) and manager Joe Pokorney (*right*).

10. Blytham Ltd. personnel and artists in 1969. Managers and agents: Bob Nutt, Irving Azoff, John Baruck. Bands: One Eyed Jacks, REO Speedwagon, Blue, the Guild, the Finchley Boys, etc.

11. Blue, 1968. *Left to right*: me, Russ Bono, Bob Bortz, and Pat Molloy.

12. Arch Records (a subsidiary of Stax/Volt Records): the Delrays (featuring the Memphis Horns), "(There's) Always Something There to Remind Me," 1968. Producers: Nick Charles and Steve Cropper.

13. RCA Records: Mike McDonald, "God Knows," 1971. Producer: Rick Jarrard.

14. The Guild, 1970. *Left to right*: Rich Lang, Terry Dugger, me, Jim Lang, Bill Ulkus, and Denny Henson.

15. Steely Dan (live), 1974. *Left to right*: me, Royce Jones, and Donald Fagen.

16. Steely Dan (live), 1974. *Left to right*: Donald Fagen (mid-flight), me, and Royce Jones.

17. Steely Dan (live in studio), 1975. *Left to right*: Donald Fagen, Walter Becker, me, and Denny Dias.

18. The Doobie Brothers' photo shoot at the San Francisco Botanical Garden, 1975.

19. The Doobie Brothers' Christmas card for A&R departments and radio stations, 1975.

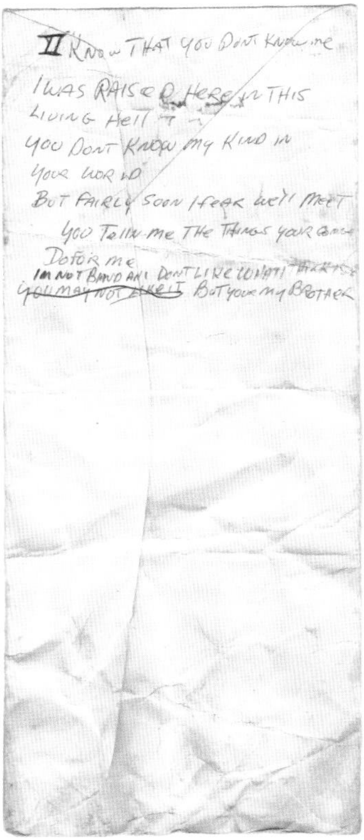
II Know that you dont know me
I was raised here in this
living hell
you dont know my kind in
your world
But fairly soon I fear we'll meet
you tellin me the things your gonna
Do for me
Im not blind an I dont like what I
~~You may not like it~~ But your my Brother

20. Early draft of lyrics to "Takin' It to the Streets," 1975.

21. Rehearsal at SIR Studios, 1975—hard at work as usual.

22. The *Doobie-liner*, with family, 1975.

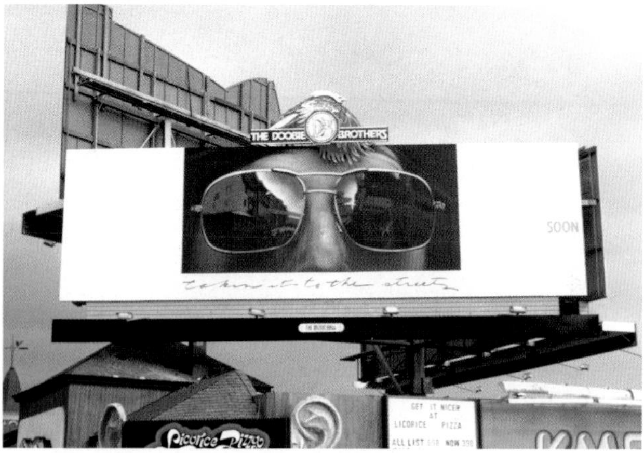

23. The *Takin' It to the Streets* billboard on Sunset Boulevard, 1976.

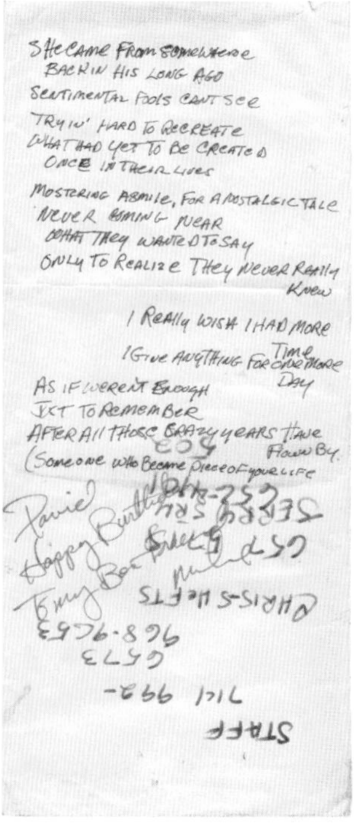
SHE CAME FROM SOMEWHERE
BACK IN HIS LONG AGO
SENTIMENTAL FOOLS CANT SEE
TRYIN' HARD TO RECREATE
WHAT HAD YET TO BE CREATED
ONCE IN THEIR LIVES
MUSTERING A SMILE, FOR A NOSTALGIC TALE
NEVER COMING NEAR
WHAT THEY WANTED TO SAY
ONLY TO REALIZE THEY NEVER REALLY KNEW

I REALLY WISH I HAD MORE TIME
I GIVE ANYTHING FOR ONE MORE DAY

AS IF WERENT ENOUGH
JUST TO REMEMBER
AFTER ALL THOSE CRAZY YEARS HAVE FLOWN BY
(SOMEONE WHO BECAME PIECE OF YOUR LIFE

David
Happy Birthday

STAFF

24. Original draft of lyrics to "What a Fool Believes," 1978.

25. The cover of *Rolling Stone* magazine, September 1979.

26. At a Randy Newman tour rehearsal, 1977. *Seated, front*: Randy Newman. *Standing, left to right*: me, Bobby LaKind, and Ted Templeman.

27. Backstage at the *No Nukes* MUSE concert in New York City, 1979. *Standing, left to right*: David Crosby, Stephen Stills, Jackson Browne, Graham Nash, Jesse Colin Young, John Hall, and Phoebe Snow. *Seated, left to right*: Carly Simon, me, James Taylor, and Bonnie Raitt.

28. Day on the Green in Oakland, 1975–76. Elton had come backstage to say hello and graciously agreed to join the Doobies onstage for the encore. The audience erupted!

29. Photo shoot for the *Together?* film soundtrack, 1979. *Left to right*: Burt Bacharach, Jackie DeShannon, me, Paul Anka, and Libby Titus.

30. The Doobie Brothers and Kenny Loggins at the Grammy Awards, 1980. Song: "What a Fool Believes."

31. My Warner Bros. Records publicity photo, 1982.

32. Amy and me in the studio, 1983.

33. Amy Holland's Capitol Records publicity photo (hubba-hubba), 1980.

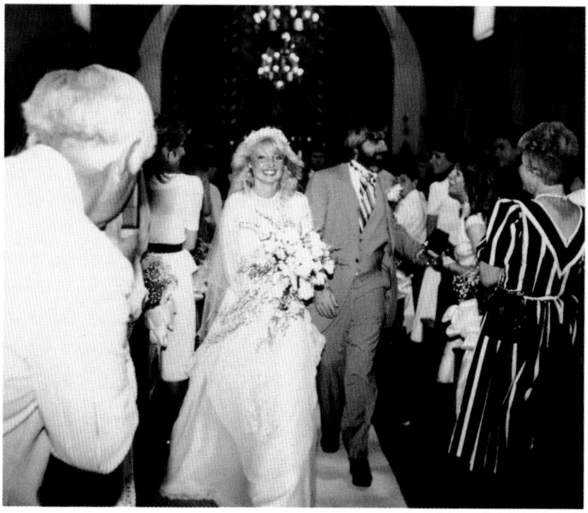

34. Our wedding in Santa Barbara, 1983.

35. James Ingram and me at the Grammy Awards, 1985. Song: "Yah Mo B There."

36. On *The Tonight Show Starring Johnny Carson*, 1990—such an honor. (Johnny had just asked me what I thought of his drumming. I told him to hang on to his day job.)

37. Patti LaBelle and me at the B'nai B'rith Honor Gala. One of the many times I enjoyed performing with Patti over the years.

38. *Left to right:* me, David Pack, and James Ingram after performing "I Just Can't Let Go" at the Music Tennis Benefit for the American Cancer Society.

39. Valerie Simpson, Nickolas Ashford, and me at WhyHunger's 2005 awards dinner. It was such an honor to have two of the greatest composers ever present me with ASCAP's Harry Chapin Humanitarian Award.

40. Christopher Cross and I performing with the "Yacht Rockin' Roots" on *Late Night with Jimmy Fallon*, 2009.

41. My band in Hamburg, Germany, in 1983, sitting on the *very* stage that the Beatles performed on before their international success and notoriety. *Kneeling, left to right*: Charles Frichtel and Bernie Chiaravalle. *Seated, left to right*: George Perilli, me, Chuck Sabatino, and Vince Denham.

42. At the Yamaha tribute show rehearsal at the Shrine Auditorium with Ray Charles, 2000. Apparently, I'd said something funny. Alan Koslowsky was filming.

43. Sitting in with Steely Dan at the New Orleans Jazz and Heritage Festival, 2016. It was the last time I saw Walter.

44. My band and crew in Boulder, Colorado, 2019.

45. The Doobies during the Fiftieth Anniversary Tour, in Ottawa, Canada, 2023.

46. Amy and the kids and me on Maui, 2018.

As it happens, my friend and writing partner Harry Garfield was one of Universal Studios' music consultants on the film and would alert me to whatever new and increasingly pointed comment was thrown at the song—and me. His concern was that I might be offended. I wasn't. It was hilarious stuff.

And in the end, the film even boosted our summer ticket sales. So, there you go.

—

BUT GOING BACK TO THAT SUMMER OF '86, I WAS SURPRISED TO FIND MYSELF ON A LITTLE bit of a hot streak for a minute: a new album, a couple of hit singles, videos in constant rotation . . . Life was good. But even with all that, there's never a shortage of forces aligning to "keep it real." For example: my mother.

Growing up, I learned early on that when enough family members are gathered together, all bets are off and some kind of shit show is not far behind. And what better setting for such a display than the old hometown gig.

I had just finished a sold-out show in LA, and typically, friends, family, and some business associates would congregate backstage to say hello and celebrate the end of a (hopefully) successful night. However, this particular venue, the decades-old Wiltern theater, didn't have a whole lot of room backstage. So I asked my road manager at the time, Joe Wilson (who is also my cousin), to book us a private room at one of our favorite restaurants nearby where our guests and family could visit more comfortably.

My mom, convinced that being shuffled off to an entirely different location was some sort of second-class treatment, pitched a fit, tearing into poor cousin Joe, bringing a slight pall over the proceedings, to the point that I felt the need to confront her about it later—in private.

So the next day, my mom and I were both braced for this inevitable showdown. It felt like a couple of sumo wrestlers circling each other in the ring, each of us poised to engage. I politely asked her if she'd like me to make her a cup of coffee, to which, with barely concealed pique, she answered, "No thank you." Then, as noncombatively as I could, I tried to explain how needlessly unpleasant she had made the situation the night before in her constant need to rewrite the fucking script all the time. I kind of knew I was leading with my chin at this point, and then came her earth-scorching opening attack:

"Well, I hate like hell to put you out, big shot! Maybe from now on, I shouldn't bother coming to your shows at all!" (Slight pause.) "Yeah, don't worry about me. I'll just wait to come see you when you're playin' the supermarket parking lots again." Boom! There I stood, rendered speechless, neatly dispatched by my sweet little red-headed Irish mother.

But it turns out there was an even bigger piece of humble pie waiting for me just around the corner.

CHAPTER 23

THE MILLION-DOLLAR QUESTION

All the good fortune I was enjoying in my career and personal life only served to distract me from the insidious ticking time bomb that was always waiting to blow it all to smithereens.

For the longest time, I had thought all I needed was to have some success in the music business and I would be happy. Yet even now, as fortunate in my career as I had ever dreamed of being, with a beautiful wife whom I loved more than anyone and who, in spite of my flaws, I knew down deep in my heart loved me—here I was, somehow still wallowing in the depths of despair.

No amount of awards or hit records or associations with stellar talent and dear friends was gonna ever fill that bottomless hole. I was always running neck and neck with my fear that I didn't deserve any of this. I felt I was out of my league and it was just a matter of time before everybody else realized that.

Even the newfound sense of peace I gained from my relationship with Amy wasn't enough to bring me to grips with my growing problem with alcohol and drugs. The hours I spent not under the influence had, for the most part, shrunk to zero. I remember feeling I had become a guy who was no damn good after six p.m.; if you gave me a simple form to fill out my personal information, I wouldn't have been able to do it.

The first thing I looked for every morning, before my feet even hit the floor, was that tray of pot next to my bed. Then after a good dose of some potent THC, followed by a stiff cup of coffee and a cigarette, I'd roll a couple joints for the day's proceedings before making the arduous journey to the studio . . . all of ten feet away in my backyard.

If we actually went out for a dinner break, I'd likely add some wine or a couple of margaritas to the mix. Cocaine at this point was done less discreetly. My attitude was: coke should be reserved for a special occasion. But as time went on, I managed to christen more and more occasions as "special."

It definitely impacted my songwriting. In my endless pursuit of inspiration, I had long believed that I couldn't really write a good song unless I was high, but the reality becoming harder to ignore was that my ever more frequent bouts of writer's block were in fact a product of that growing substance abuse.

One notable exception: I was scheduled to write with Jesse Colin Young, an artist I've always admired. But unfortunately—and not uncharacteristically at this point—I had totally forgotten about our plan to get together . . . until the morning he showed up at my house. On top of that, having not yet been to sleep and totally exhausted from an extended coke binge the night before, I was barely able to keep my eyes open. Still, I couldn't very well cancel now. So I sat at my piano and we got to work . . . Well, except for my nodding out repeatedly and practically going backward off the piano stool several times. Finally, for my own safety, I suggested we move over to the couch to focus on the lyrics. Truth was, I was just thinking that if I did ultimately nod off completely, at least I wouldn't break my neck.

Once on the couch, I kept drifting in and out of consciousness, till at one point, with my head cocked back, my mouth open and incoherently muttering, I heard Jesse's voice in my half-conscious state: "You got something, man?"

Snatching myself back from the abyss, scrambling, I sat straight up, pretending I had indeed simply been lost in deep, creative thought, and I started blabbering some hallucinogenic nonsense. "Yeah, man, I was just thinking . . . Like, there's fire, and ya know, it's out on the water. So, it probably can't last *too* long, ya know. Being surrounded by water and all . . ."

I fully expected him to just write me off and pack it up at this point, but after a short silence that, for me, felt like an eternity, he said, "I like it!" And that's how the song "Fire on the Water" came into being.

I don't doubt that Jesse was being generously patient with me that day, though that kind of sheer luck was becoming increasingly rare during this darkening period of my life. I started to isolate more. I'd regularly retreat to my studio after dinner, under the guise of "working," but I really just wanted to be free to use, out of the view of others, my wife included. It's not like Amy was unaware of my problem; she was just trusting my assertion that I had it under control.

But in fact, my life had already become an endless cycle of substance abuse, morning to night, day in, day out—just to maintain. There *were* people in my life who expressed concern for my overindulgence. I remember my sister Maureen admonishing one of my cocaine coconspirators, even flushing his bindle of coke down the toilet right in front of his eyes, to his utter disbelief.

I, on the other hand, would always react with that old righteous indignation to anyone sticking their nose into my business. One exception, interestingly enough, was when my dog Luke, a big old black Lab, laid his head in my lap and stared up at me with a furrowed brow, his big brown eyes seemingly full of concern, and I thought, "Now I really feel bad. Even my dog's worried about me."

And my overindulgence had come to play a part in my relationship with Amy too. Not just as recreation anymore, but as a quick Band-Aid remedy for any bump in the road. I came from a family where no one ever said "I'm sorry." That just wasn't in our vocabulary. Growing up, emotions would just erupt, and then sometime later in the evening, someone would say, "Hey, you want a baloney sandwich or something?" and you'd soldier on. There was always so much left unsaid.

So I had no skill in that area, no ability to reasonably sort through and respectfully resolve conflict. Neither did Amy; her family's specialty was the silent treatment. But one recreational pastime we did have in common was we liked to drink. And smoke pot. (Okay, so that's two.) So that was always the great resolver; we'd have a fight, then later in the day we'd smoke a joint and forget about it. We'd even maybe start laughing about it.

But ultimately the remedy can become the problem. At some point, Amy began to show signs of fatigue from trying to keep up with what had developed into my not-so-recreational drug use, and in time, she hit her breaking point.

I got the call in the middle of a recording session.

"Mike, I can't do this anymore."

She told me she had decided to admit herself into a thirty-day drug and alcohol treatment facility.

My initial response was something like, "I think you're just taking all this way too seriously." Yeah, that was me, Mr. Empathy.

But something in Amy's voice told me I needed to get home to her. I explained to the producer of the session that I had a family emergency. He wasn't thrilled. I'd never walked out of a session before in my life (though it's possible I might have forgotten to show up for one or two due to drunkenness).

I went home to find Amy already packed and ready to go to treatment; our family physician had set it up for us to go straight to the hospital and start the admitting process. By that evening, after a lengthy orientation, including discussion of the seemingly important—though not mandatory—family participation, I returned home to a house that felt suddenly and painfully empty. It was just me and the dogs.

The next day, determined to be a responsible participant in Amy's recovery, I proceeded to the hospital—already somewhat late—for the first of the family counseling sessions. I could tell Amy was anxious about my ability (and even my willingness) to participate like all the other patients' family members. And I've got to admit, as eager as I was to get back to her that morning, this place, with all its references to "the *disease* of alcoholism," gave me the creeps big-time.

We were scheduled to break for dinner around 5:30, and rather than eat there with Amy, I told her that I needed to run home and quickly check on the dogs—which was not quite true; I'd already made arrangements to have my sister go by and check on them. The truth was I just needed to get the fuck out of that place for a couple minutes and down a couple drinks across the street to brace my resolve to go back and be supportive.

I usually was able to hold my liquor when I needed to. After all, I had always been the caretaker in our relationship. On a typical outing, when I decided *she'd* had enough to drink, I'd usually suggest it was time to go home, always mindful of keeping it together enough to drive. Now I found myself barely able to walk the short distance back from the restaurant to the hospital.

I made it back for the last family group session of the evening, and showing up late for the second time on that very first day must've been a glaring red flag. I thought I was pulling it off pretty well, but Amy's obvious rising anxiety told a different story.

—

THE NEXT DAY I MIGHT'VE BEEN HUNGOVER, BUT THAT WAS NORMAL. MOSTLY, THOUGH, I was consumed with guilt knowing that I was adding to Amy's anxiety and, at the same time, dreading the idea of spending the whole day ahead at the treatment facility. Not that I didn't already miss Amy and want to be there to support her, but the endless program rhetoric and therapy sessions had me pretty much crawling out of my skin. I actually had considered the idea that once Amy came out of treatment, I'd likely have to get clean myself to truly support her. Then again, I rationalized, this was *her* choice, not mine, right? Maybe I'd just not do it in front of her. As if that could actually work. I couldn't even "just not do it" in front of an entire treatment facility staff!

I thought for the time being, I should probably go smoke a fat one before I stepped foot in that place again, but that program-filled day still seemed like a grueling belly-crawl up to dinner break.

Amy had asked me to make arrangements to have dinner with her there that night, but I lied again and told her I couldn't find anyone, that I needed to go home to feed the dogs. (I didn't; I had already taken care of that.) I just knew I'd have to escape from there for just a few minutes by dinner break. This time, though, I had decided I'd have only *one* drink with dinner, so as to keep it together a little better when I returned for the evening's final family sessions. And this time I'd make it a point to be on time!

The restaurant across the road was crowded, so I gave my name to the hostess and went to the bar for a drink. Just one, mind you. One little Jack and Coke. (One that happened to be a double shot of Jack, but who's counting.) As I finished my drink, a nice couple visiting LA who were Doobie fans sent over another drink, and it seemed the polite thing to do to go over and thank them personally, so I did, and they invited me to sit and chat. Well, after some pleasant conversation, it seemed only common courtesy that I reciprocate and buy the next round. So we chatted and drank some more—and after that, I lost count.

I soon realized, to my embarrassment, that I was having trouble with my diction and that I'd apparently missed my name being called repeatedly by the hostess, not even registering this couple's numerous attempts to bring it to my attention. All of that eventually gave way to several minutes of awkward silence . . . and lo and behold, I was once again late for family group therapy.

At this point I wasn't even sure I could actually stand up. So, struggling to my feet, I practically knocked over the table and at least one of the drinks landed in someone's lap. Barely able to feel my legs, I could only smile awkwardly and wave goodbye, bouncing off a few more people on my way out.

—

HARD AS IT MAY BE TO BELIEVE, SHOWING UP DRUNK TO A REHAB SUPPORT GROUP—TWO days in a row—is generally frowned upon. Having witnessed my behavior to this point, the head counselor had apparently asked the admitting desk clerk to notify him the minute I signed in downstairs. So as I came off the elevator on the seventh floor, he was there waiting to intercept and inform me that hospital procedure dictated I not be allowed up on the floor anymore until I could show up sober.

It was in that moment of clarity that I realized something I'd been in denial of for years: I simply wasn't capable of doing that. It was virtually impossible for me to not drink long enough to show up *anywhere* sober.

He asked me point-blank, "What are you gonna do?"

Now, this wasn't my first time in this situation; I'd dropped off a few friends over the years at places just like this, and they'd always ask the same million-dollar question: "What are you gonna do?" In the past I'd always bristled at that question. However, this time, with so much at stake, I felt the need to mention that I was already somewhat familiar with the program, having gone to a couple of meetings years ago, and I even had a sponsor of sorts, my probation officer. "But that was at least fifteen years ago, and I haven't seen the guy since then. I don't know if he even still lives in LA."

It was at that very moment that I glanced over at the nurses' station, and seeing a familiar face, I said, very matter-of-factly, "Actually, I think that's him right there."

The poor counselor must've thought I was losing my shit altogether, but fortunately Ray Paul noticed me, came over, and said, "Hey! Long time no see!"

What makes this synchronistic moment even more implausible is that Ray didn't work there. He'd never stepped foot in this place in his life until that night. He happened to be on a list of possible substitutes for guest speakers missing in action—and he wasn't even the first call! The *first four subs* they tried were all unavailable that day, so Ray got the call. And that was the only reason he was standing in front of me at that exact moment, on that very evening, just as I was recalling our friendship—for the first time in years—to a total stranger.

"What are you doing here?" he asked.

"Well," I said, "I think I'm being thrown out. But oddly enough, I was just talking about you to my friend here."

I can still see the look on that counselor's face. I was in no less total disbelief myself. As we stood there, I suddenly heard a clear and distinct voice in my head, though not my own, saying, "The jig is up!" My very next thought was: "'The jig is up'?! Who the fuck says that? Some private eye from the '40s, maybe."

Then, just as clearly, another thought came to me—this time my own inner voice:

"Hey, dumbass, the bus is leaving. And if you don't get on this time, you might not be here when it comes back."

We stood there in awkward silence for a moment, until finally Ray asked, "So . . . what are you gonna do?"

Okay. So maybe I just needed to hear that question one more time. Because this time, instead of getting indignant and looking for the nearest exit, I just surrendered and said, "I don't know." I felt completely defeated, totally powerless, and here I was, once again being thrown a lifeline by a guy I hadn't seen in years. This could be no coincidence. The only question now was: Did I finally have the courage—and enough strength left—to grab hold of it?

He then asked me, "Do you want to go to a meeting?"

And it was as if I were hearing someone else's voice when I heard myself say, "Yeah . . . Yeah, I do."

That was the first step. The critical one. Ray then suggested I not drink anymore that night and told me to meet him the next morning at nine a.m. at the Lodge, a halfway house that held meetings. Miraculously, I didn't drink anymore that night. That alone was proof that something had changed. Something that had been utterly impossible for me to get a handle on was all of a sudden as easy as "breathe in and breathe out—and don't take a drink in between breaths." There were none of the cold sweats, shattered nerves, or abject fear that usually accompanied any attempt I made before this to quit using. For a long time, I swore every morning, "I'm not going to drink today," and never made it past ten a.m.

Only months earlier, I had tried to quit on my own willpower. I was off the road for a week, home in Santa Barbara, and already out of drugs. Determined not to leave Amy to drive all the way down to LA, wake up my dealer at two in the morning, and then drive all the way home with drugs on me, I sat there desperately gripping the arms of a chair, completely broken, thinking, "If this is sobriety, I'd truly rather die using."

—

FROM THAT DAY ON AND THROUGH TO TODAY, I FEEL LIKE I ENTERED A WORLD OF NO coincidences. I experienced a profound spiritual shift of sorts, unrelated to any religious upbringing I had experienced to date. Certainly Catholic school training didn't provide much, if any, comfort or support for me in that regard. If anything, my concept of "God" was largely my fear of a moral reckoning that I did my level best to keep at arm's length for as long as possible. And the whole idea that "God" was predetermined to have a certain appearance, gender, history, birthplace, code of conduct . . . never sat well with me either. It seemed like a form of conditional love, man's attempt to create a god in his own image.

Instead, I've come to find this trust in a higher power, mostly through fellowship with people who know my story by way of their own experience. That connection, that human bond, to me is the most prominent clue to the existence of this higher power. Now, it's as if anything anyone says to me is really part of an ongoing conversation with a "god of my understanding"—and to be honest, probably most of the time in that conversation, I'm not even listening. But when this power greater than myself makes a point to get my attention, I'm reminded that I can trust it with the outcome of everything that happens to me from now on, like it or not.

Which was, frankly, a relief. After all, it's not like my own best thinking was bringing about any desirable results for me. In fact, at the lowest depths of my alcoholism and addiction, I remember saying things to myself in the mirror that I've never said to another human being—because I've never loathed or resented anyone else that much. Looking at myself knowing that the night before I had once again drunk myself into a stupor, I felt disgusted for being so weak and pathetic. I felt less than worthless.

There are things in my past for which I've yet to fully make amends or reparations, and, in some cases, may never be able to. But if each day, just for the next twenty-four hours, I can manage to do the next right thing, make the "living amends" going forward, I just might, in the process, be reminded to forgive that poor bastard in the mirror. The only thing I'm pretty certain of is that if I ever get in the ring alone with my disease again, I'm gonna get my ass kicked.

Early in sobriety, I remember venting to Ray some of my frustrations with and long-standing resentments of other people, and this obsession with them seemed all-consuming—the kind of things I used to drink at but was now having to deal with sober. Ray gave me some sage advice that I try to follow to this day: "If I were you, whatever your best thinking is telling you to do in the moment, I'd do the exact opposite." He was half kidding, but I was so desperate and confused at that time that I actually took his advice to heart—and remarkably, it worked like a charm!

—

THE "MAKING AMENDS" THING CAN BE A BIT COMPLEX. THOUGH IT'S EASY ENOUGH TO SEE where you might have wronged others, it may take a while to remember it clearly and to then—without procrastinating too much—evaluate and gather the courage to make the appropriate amends.

It gets a little trickier when we consider those situations where we feel *we've* been wronged by individuals who we're pretty sure are fully deserving of our wrath. What I've learned from taking this kind of personal inventory is usually enlightening, though at times, again, counterintuitive.

Case in point: There was a guy who years earlier had royally screwed me over in a business deal. I think it's safe to say I had some "resentment." Ray, being familiar with the story, suggested I call this guy up and apologize.

"Me? Why the hell should I apologize?! I didn't steal anything from him!"

Ray calmly responded, "You should apologize for resenting the shit out of him for twenty years. And besides, you're not doing it for him. You're doing it for yourself."

"Yeah, but . . ."

"And by the way, in the meantime I suggest you pray for the son of a bitch to get everything in life that you would want for yourself and those you love most."

What?!

See, that's where the counterintuitive part comes in. But Ray was someone whose opinion on these matters I'd learned to trust. So I followed his suggestion and called this guy for what would prove to be an eye-opening phone conversation.

The guy answered the phone, somewhat surprised to hear from me at all, and certainly not expecting what came out of my mouth next.

"Yeah . . . Hi. So . . . the reason I'm calling is . . . I just wanted to . . . apologize."

No response. I plowed ahead.

"I'm just calling to say . . . I'm sorry for resenting you all these years."

More awkward silence.

"And I want you to know I'm not looking for any response from you. I just . . . This is something I just need to do for myself. For my sobriety. You see, resentments of this nature are very often exactly the kind of things that alcoholics in recovery—like myself—start drinking over again. So . . . I just want you to know that whatever happened between you and me, I'm apologizing for my part in it. Specifically my ongoing resentment, because I need to move on."

After an even longer and considerably more awkward pause, he finally said, "Uh . . . Mike . . . what exactly are we talking about here?"

And that's when it hit me: This guy didn't even remember the incident. He hadn't lost a minute's sleep over what I'd stayed awake grinding my teeth over for twenty years. I'd given this guy rent-free space in my head this whole time! For years, at more than a few stoplights, I'd sit there going, "That *motherfucker*!" And think of all the potentially carefree moments I might have enjoyed had I not spent them going through this bullshit resentment and taking it from the top one more time (of course responding ever more cleverly each time, if only in my imagination).

Per Ray's advice, I refrained from laying any blame or listing any of his transgressions (that was a struggle, believe me) and tried as best I could to focus only on my side of the street, as they say.

After more honest evaluation, the harder pill to swallow was realizing that I probably had as much or more to do with creating the situation in the first place, and was ultimately as much or more to blame than anyone else. My fingerprints were all over this one. I was the king of giving other people too much control and then reveling in my resentment of them for years afterward. And while there were more than enough lessons to learn from this one conversation, that first realization alone—that for years I had been "drinking the poison hoping someone else would die"—made that phone call more than worthwhile.

And adding insult to irony, the deeper revelation for me was recognizing that some of the people I'd resented most over the years were in fact the very ones who had opened the door to some of my biggest opportunities and defining moments. Yeah, they might have had their hands a little too deep in my pocket, but in some way they also made an important contribution to the career I'm grateful for today.

CHAPTER 24

IN THE BLINK OF AN EYE

From that day on, by the grace of God, I've never had another drink. But that's not to say it was a cakewalk. I still had to learn to navigate life sober.

For instance: in those first few months, going out to dinner to celebrate our anniversary. A celebration with no alcohol? I mean, what's the point?

I have vivid memories of that night, trying to reassure Amy that not only were we having a good time, but in the absence of alcohol, we might even remember it. She wasn't especially impressed with my feeble attempts at cheerleading, and as the conversation waned into awkward silence, I found my attention drifting to the next table, where an obviously dysfunctional family was struggling to communicate: the father was trying to get the waiter's attention to replenish his martini, and the mother desperately tried to steer a discussion about her son and his fiancée's impending wedding, while trying to engage her husband through his drunken indifference.

Then, turning my attention to the next table, I watched two couples—evidently a brother and sister and their respective spouses—attempting reconciliation of what appeared to be a long-standing rift, culminating with the two women jumping to their feet in a heated screaming match. "*See?! She always does that!*" In short order they were all asked to take it somewhere else, whereupon the family feud continued out on the sidewalk.

Watching both of these scenes play out in real time was once again like God trying to tell me something, because all of this behavior was painfully familiar. That was me, many times in the past. But now, even only a few months sober, I was able to see it more clearly.

They say for the first year or so of sobriety you should refrain from making any important life decisions, like moving, getting married, or extensive traveling. Well, Amy and I had already made most of those decisions while we were still drinking, so of course in our first sober year, why wouldn't we go ahead and tour Europe and get pregnant while we're at it!

Funny how things work out. It was actually almost a year into our sobriety that we were in Amsterdam and took a beautiful sightseeing/dinner cruise on one of those long canal boats, and to be honest, we suffered a bit of melancholy once more when we saw the wine flowing and people around us having a great time drinking. But it was still a wonderful experience, watching evening fall on this picturesque city while floating down the canal—an experience we likely would have not even fully registered, much less remembered, had we still been drinking.

Later on, while we were in Venice, Amy and a friend discovered a striking, somewhat dilapidated old palazzo where a group of women of all ages were creating and selling handmade Venetian lace. With little or no ventilation in the place, Amy suddenly got dizzy and almost fainted. One of the older women got her some water and uttered something in Italian that made the other ladies react with smiles and joyous laughter. Thankfully, one of the younger women translated: it seems they were speculating that Amy was pregnant.

I think at that moment Amy knew they were right, for all the reasons a woman knows such things. She later shared the news with me, and while I was thrilled to think it might be true, I was also secretly worried. We had been trying for a while and had sadly suffered a couple of miscarriages over the previous few years, and we still had a long way to go before we'd be back home in California. But I kept my fears, for the most part, to myself, and we had a wonderful time in Europe—grateful for this exciting possibility, grateful for being sober, and grateful for the fact that we didn't die driving on the wrong side of the road in Ireland.

On our way back to the States, we stopped in my ancestral homeland, where we evidently had some guardian angels looking over us—one of whom manifested as a little redheaded Irish girl with pigtails, overalls, and rubber boots, sitting alone on a stone bridge. She was too cute not to notice, and as we passed, she was staring so intently at us with the most inquisitive expression that I turned to my wife and said, "You know, we must just look like foreigners. Did you see the way that little girl was staring at us?" And in that instant, it hit me: I brought my attention back to the road, to the blind curve just a few yards ahead on this two-lane highway, and immediately whipped the car into the opposite lane just as a semitruck rounding the curve laid on the horn, barely missing us. Sweet Jesus!

That little girl's expression as she watched us pass was the only reason I even realized it. If it had come to me a split second later, we'd have surely been in a head-on collision. Stranger still, it was just about twilight when we passed her, all but dark, and to this day I'm still haunted by thoughts of that moment. What was a little kid like that doing out on the highway, all alone at that time in the evening? If only for my own benefit, I'm all but convinced she was some kind of heavenly messenger sent to save us on that road. (But then that might just be the Irish in me talking.)

—

AFTER RETURNING HOME, AMY AND I WOULD SPEND MORE TIME IN SANTA BARBARA, THE idea being we'd be closer to her doctors and would enjoy the slower pace of life during her pregnancy. I could cut back my schedule but still work up there, writing songs and making demos. More important, I had promised myself that I'd make an effort to be on hand to focus on Amy and our soon-to-be arrival. I mused about giving Amy foot massages, playing classical music for the baby in the womb . . . keeping things all calm and tranquil. Somehow that morphed into the decision to totally renovate our house. "Calm and tranquil" went right out the window.

As anyone who's gone through these life-changing events knows, construction always takes months longer than you think, whereas pregnancy usually does not. So it was that in December 1987, well before our remodel was finished, our son, Dylan Michael McDonald, came into the world and spent his first days after leaving the hospital with us in a hotel villa, away from the construction chaos.

There was one magical moment in particular I recall from that first week, when I took Dylan outside onto the patio and his attention was drawn to a bird singing in a tree above us. As his eyes widened and he looked around for the source of that mysterious sound, I realized: "This is the first bird he's ever heard in his life." And I was there for it! I was witnessing his awakening awareness of the world around him, and I think that memory will stay as vivid in my heart and mind as the moment it happened, till the second I leave this world.

After a couple weeks, the three of us moved into our guesthouse, a small space with a kitchenette and a sleeping loft, where we spent some of our happiest days to date waiting for the house to be finished.

—

WHEN YOU'RE A FIRST-TIME PARENT, EVERYONE TELLS YOU EXACTLY WHAT TO EXPECT, yet it's still inevitably all kinds of unique and surprising. Looking back to the morning after Dylan was born, I remember driving home from the hospital to check on the house and get some things for Amy. As I was driving, looking out over the hood of the car, I can remember suddenly being mildly terrified, thinking, "Oh my God—I'm a father!" It wasn't till that moment that the reality actually hit me—along with the accompanying mixed bag of emotions. I knew I wanted to be more present for my son than my father had been for me, but at the same time I was feeling the re-welling shame of knowing I'd already failed miserably at that when I was fourteen, with Diane. I had tried over the years to come to peace with that memory, rationalizing, "Hey, you were only a kid. Give yourself a break." But that never quite reconciled it for me.

While becoming a father is by any measure a profoundly transformative experience, I brought to it a certain amount of extra baggage, knowing that given the work I'd chosen (and my penchant for being so consumed with it), I'd likely be away from home a big chunk of the time.

My own traumatic experience of watching my dad leave without explanation, wondering if he'd ever come back, caused me to lean hard in the other direction; I became somewhat obsessive about reassuring my toddler son that "Dad is always coming back and is never gonna be out of reach." This was, of course, years before he could've possibly understood what I was talking about. That was just my own neurosis, and hopefully I wasn't transferring on to him my own pain and fear of abandonment.

As a kid—and even later as an adult—I measured everything I did, consciously or not, against what I believed my father might think, especially with regard to persevering through bad times. If I ever hit a rough patch in my career and caught myself thinking it might be wise to give up and try something else, I'd invariably find myself, before too long, pressing forward with renewed conviction, driven in no small part by my need to prove to my father, as much as to myself, that I could in fact stick with it and not have him see me yet again fall short and just quit.

Now, years later, as a new father, I'd have to reconcile this 24/7, single-minded pursuit of a career with the realities of marriage and raising a kid, the irony being that I found I was more like my dad than I had thought; I'd grown comfortable with being in perpetual motion. That kind of obsessive pursuit felt normal to me.

—

AS FATE WOULD HAVE IT, FOR THE FIRST FEW YEARS OF DYLAN'S LIFE, THERE WAS TO BE a lot less motion. We had toured Europe a couple years earlier, in '85, and found the audiences surprisingly enthusiastic. But upon returning to the United States, we struggled for the next two years with radio play, and the disinterest of agents and concert promoters in the States was palpable. I won't lie; it was worrisome. My fear was that I had lost my momentum and unwittingly lowered my trajectory. I felt like I was disappointing everyone who had helped me to this point.

Now I look back on that time as a blessing in disguise, for so many reasons, but especially because it gave me some precious time at home with Dylan and Amy that I might have otherwise missed. After all, had the gigs been there, I would've surely jumped at the opportunity to tour. With my solo career just starting up, had there been any momentum at all, the pressure would have been there to capitalize on it.

Also, being in early sobriety, it seemed like fate was helping me do what I couldn't yet do for myself: slow down. I didn't see it then, but just standing still and facing my demons would be the biggest challenge I'd have to face on my way to becoming a better parent.

I was relieved to discover that I was totally comfortable holding Dylan and bonding with him; showing physical affection wasn't a problem for me. Nonetheless, I was flying kind of blind in that department. Neither my dad nor my mom, for that matter, was terribly affectionate. Did we love each other? Sure we did. Did we ever say it? Not a chance! So I had no real example to draw from there. Now, as a father, I felt like I had to consciously remind myself to be more affectionately demonstrative.

There were other instances, however, where my father's example really helped me. When Dylan was around ten months old he got a bad flu—high fever, terrible coughing and congestion—and it absolutely terrorized me to see my little one suffer like that. But in the midst of it all, I had a visceral memory of my dad driving me to the hospital to get stitches when I was about four or five, after I'd fallen off the back porch and hit my head on a sharp rock. What came so vividly to mind was the comfort I felt as a child sensing my father's cool, calm composure. I could still see him looking over at me in the car, talking me through how to keep pressing the cold towel on the wound, and I remember thinking, as I bled all the way to the hospital, "I'm gonna be okay. Dad's not worried, he's got this." I wanted my son to feel that same confidence in me. (And for the record, as much as little Dylan hated that little turkey baster / suction thing up the nose, it was worse for me, but I got pretty good at it.)

—

NOTWITHSTANDING THE FLURRY OF TIME-CONSUMING PARENTAL DUTIES, I WAS ALSO managing to chip away at the next album, though at this point in my career, I wasn't entirely sure of my relevance in the musical landscape. It's ironic that my popularity as a solo recording artist was arguably at its highest point during the '80s, considering how increasingly out of step I felt with so much of the trending musical styles—not to mention the advent of MTV and the music video. I knew that world was not for me. I had no desire to be a face on the silver screen. I didn't even look great in Polaroids.

To be sure, there were music-oriented film clips going back as far as the '30s—soundies, as they were called, promoting new record releases before the main features in movie theaters. And there's plenty of documented footage from the '50s, '60s, and '70s of bands playing their music, either captured live or lip-synched performances on TV shows.

But it wasn't until 1981, when MTV introduced the twenty-four-hour cycle of music videos, that the world of music marketing shifted. Suddenly it was video plays more than radio that determined the success of a record.

I personally felt there was a danger that people might start *watching* music instead of listening to it—much the same way, I'm sure, folks must have felt when radio gave way to television, or silent film actors probably felt when sound was added to their medium. Both radically changed the preexisting art forms.

To be clear, I'd always loved the classic operas and Broadway musicals, written by great composers as vehicles for their wonderful music. However, it felt to me a bit disingenuous and forced when MTV started to present the latest rock and roll or R&B release with something more akin to one of the big, choreographed numbers from *Guys and Dolls* or *Oklahoma!* It reminded me of that queasy feeling I had as a kid when, after the thrill of sneaking into my sister's room to listen to her Elvis records, I found myself in some drive-in movie with my whole family, feeling sorry for the King of Rock and Roll having to act his way through *Clambake*, wondering, "How could God let this happen?"

I much preferred listening to music without the visuals, being transported by way of my own imagination to some epic live performance in a smoke-filled nightclub or harshly lit recording studio, where the musicians and everyone else on hand suddenly realize they are witnessing magic. (I should also admit that since these daydreams were of my own creation, I usually placed myself in the rhythm section to further enhance the fantasy.)

On a more personal note, when making my own videos, there was the added humiliation of the label always insisting I dye my hair before each shoot, because being in a rock video with gray highlights was pretty much taboo. (Both my parents grayed early, although in the case of my mom, to quote the old commercial, "only her hairdresser knows for sure.") As a money-saving measure, my first attempt at dyeing my hair was done at home over the sink, my wife applying some store-bought hair dye—Chocolate Kiss was my shade of choice—and no matter how expensive the stuff was, it still looked like shoe polish and made my head smell like a rented tuxedo.

—

FOR THIS NEXT ALBUM, EVENTUALLY TITLED *TAKE IT TO HEART*, IT WAS SUGGESTED BY THE label that I work with more contemporary producers, even trying my hand in the then emerging sound of hip-hop. I ended up working with several producers on various tracks—all talented guys for sure, but not all a perfect fit for me. But then Don Was came on board.

Don, at that point, already had a string of successes under his belt producing his own band, Was (Not Was), and the B-52s, among others, but this was just before the breakthrough success of his multiple-Grammy-winning *Nick of Time* album with Bonnie Raitt. He later went on to produce everyone from the Stones to Willie Nelson, Elton John, Ringo Starr, John Mayer . . . you name it. But it was clear, even back then, that there was something special about Don's skills, personality, and process that made him such a brilliant producer. What jumped out at me most was his positive, easygoing, and supportive nature.

As he listened to the tracks I had already cut, he remarked, "This all sounds great, but I don't think anyone's gonna bother to cross the street to hear Michael McDonald do hip-hop. We should go with what you do." Which was such a comforting thing to hear. It didn't feel like he was discouraging me from experimenting, but rather encouraging me to feel good about what it is that I might do more naturally—to embrace that rather than turn away from it.

Don's natural instinct to be instantly supportive almost took me by surprise. I would play him a couple of songs, and he'd say, "Yeah, man, that's great. They're great." And based solely on my previous experiences, I'd respond, "Really? Don't you wanna kick it around a little bit?" To which he'd say simply, "No, man, they're great. Let's go with those two."

I also loved his openness when it came to choosing musicians best suited for the gig, even if they weren't necessarily the most in-demand session players. By contrast, most producers of solo artists were always hyperconscious of who were considered the newest and best "A-listers."

After the Doobies, my band, in its many incarnations, was always made up of great musicians who were, nonetheless, not the guys who typically played on my records. I usually deferred to the producer to make those choices. In my experience up till then, I had always considered it to be part of a producer's coveted domain. So when I asked Don whom he'd like to use and he said, "Well, what about *your* band?" that took me by surprise. I told him, "Well, they're great, but . . ." To which he responded, "Great, so let's use them."

It seemed like such an easy, logical way forward. The simple truth was that these guys were world-class musicians, and we had a unique rapport that we brought to that experience, and fortunately Don understood that.

Working with Don was such a formula shift for me, I was almost suspicious of how easy and creatively spontaneous it all was.

—

IT WAS ALSO DON'S SUGGESTION THAT I TRY TEAMING UP WITH DIANE WARREN. DIANE had already written some of the decade's most commercially successful songs and was a consummate professional composer. Not that the other writers I'd worked with weren't professionals too, but Diane was supremely driven on a whole other level. She had a crystal-clear understanding of the commitment and daily discipline required to excel—more so than us hapless band members who'd occasionally write some songs for the next album.

Seriously dedicated composers like Diane, I came to learn, also had a level of engagement with the music business suits that could border on hand-to-hand combat. Whereas guys like me were for the most part oblivious to the politics and machinations involved in actually making a record a hit, writers of Diane's stature weren't shy about going toe-to-toe with any major label's head of promotion, any radio program director, or any industry publication they felt might not be pulling their weight or treating them fairly. This was the big leagues, and in their effort to make a record a hit, they left little or nothing to chance. They were in it to win.

Case in point: on the day Diane came to my house to write with me, she displayed a rather remarkable aptitude for multitasking. That particular week she had a shot at simultaneously having seven of her songs on *Billboard*'s Hot 100—a feat never before accomplished in *Billboard*'s history—and was, at that moment, only one song short. So throughout the day, she was in hot pursuit of any updates on the chart situation, while at the same time managing to stay completely focused on our writing session, as we had, in short order, come up with some chords, some lyrics, and a working title.

We were making good progress when she asked to take a break so she could get on a brief conference call to check on her *Billboard* status. I directed her upstairs to the loft bedroom phone. (Back then "landlines" were just called "phones.") It wasn't exactly the most private of situations, and while I tried to not eavesdrop, I couldn't help but overhear her spirited exchange with some poor soul on the other end.

I carried on at the piano downstairs, quietly fishing around for some chords to hopefully point the way to a chorus by the time she was done. Still just noodling, I hit on a chord progression while singing our title in my head . . . when I heard Diane yell down to me, "*Fuckin' A! That's it!*"

Frankly it startled me enough that I almost forgot whatever it was I'd just played. She told the parties on her conference call she'd get back to them and sprinted downstairs, proceeding to prompt me to review what I'd come up with.

I assumed that the chorus should end with the title. Diane felt otherwise.

"No! We *start* the chorus with it!"

So I sang the lyric "Take it to heart" over that first chord of our new chorus, as she "suggested." But it still wasn't right to her ear. She was convinced that that first note had to really grab you. She pointed into the air, telling me, "Needs to be higher."

So I went up a whole step: "Take it to heart!"

She kept pointing up. "Nope. Higher."

Okay. How about another whole step?

"No!"

She kept pointing. I went up another whole step, which was beginning to be a bit of a stretch for my vocal cords, but—bingo! We've got a chorus!

The "Take It to Heart" single would later go on to make it to No. 4 on the *Billboard* adult contemporary chart. (And, just for the record, Diane did end up getting those seven slots of the Hot 100 she was gunning for. Still not sure what the body count on that phone call was, but apparently they got the message.)

—

IT WAS GREAT TO HAVE A HIT SONG ON THE CHARTS AGAIN, BUT NOW I HAD A BIT OF A dilemma. On one hand, this seemed like the perfect opportunity to build on the momentum of the single by hitting the road, but in truth, I must admit I was really enjoying my time at home with Dylan and Amy.

Seeing it somewhat as my duty to all concerned, I entertained the idea of some touring. I thought it would be a good move to play Europe again, somewhat out of the spotlight of the US market, and if things went well, that would only enhance the interest of domestic promoters upon our return. I even suggested I go out as an opening act on someone else's tour. It would put me in front of larger audiences sooner, and also, frankly, I didn't mind not having to shoulder the pressures of headlining. That idea was initially met with a bit of skepticism by management. Aside from the expense, there was concern that being perceived as an opener would be detrimental to my career in the long run. I didn't care. Playing to bigger audiences with my name in small type was, to me, still much better than playing to *smaller* audiences just to have my name in *large* type. I just wanted to see what we could do on the big stages and hopefully come back to the States with a story to tell.

To their credit, my managers at the time, Craig Fruin and Howard Kaufman, put their shoulder into the effort and managed to bring me the opportunity of a lifetime: opening for Tina Turner's farewell tour in the UK.

Earlier that year, Warner Bros. UK had unexpectedly decided to release a *Best of Michael McDonald* CD, and it ended up going platinum in England. So on the heels of that, we had played a short tour of three-to-four-thousand-seat theaters in London, Manchester, Liverpool, Birmingham, Glasgow, and Newcastle, and apparently made enough noise with that tour that the promoters thought we'd be a good fit for Tina's tour—which was a whole new ball game for us.

It was my band's first experience playing to twenty thousand, thirty thousand, or more each night, and we got a quick education in what worked and, more important, what *didn't* work when playing to an audience that size, and in the first week of shows, we scrambled to get our footing.

Tina's band, on the other hand, was a finely tuned, stadium-ready, unrelenting musical machine, occupying a unique niche somewhere between rock and soul music, unlike anything I'd heard before or have heard since.

After all the ups and downs of a four-decade-long career, Tina would hold her audience spellbound every night, from the first downbeat to the last note of her performance. Her routine was executed with clockwork precision: she'd pull up to the venue literally minutes before she was to go onstage, emerging from the back of her Bentley already dressed for the performance, makeup and hair done to perfection, and then walk onstage and sing with astonishing power while dancing nonstop for nearly three hours—a performance that could no doubt kill a talent half her age.

Playing in my band at the time was my high school pal Chuck Sabatino, and little could we have imagined when we were teenagers, paying to see Ike and Tina at the Club Imperial in St. Louis, that we'd be here, all these years later, opening for Tina in sold-out soccer stadiums. It was beyond surreal.

At the end of the show, Tina would immediately stride offstage into her already-running car and just go. Every show was an amazing experience. The enthusiasm and adoration of her European audience was something to behold. Her stage presence was so authentic; she was powerful and gracious all at once and remains to this day, I believe, unmatched as a performer.

Years later we would return to Europe, opening for Cher—another wonderful opportunity to tour with yet another legendary performer. Cher's audience, however, had a somewhat more fanatical, almost cultish feel.

As the opener, it's always good to bear in mind that the audience is there to see the headliner, not you. You never want to wear out your welcome up there. Yet I couldn't help but notice that a certain percentage of Cher's audience was clearly there to "more fully experience" the performance and maybe, if only in their mind, actually participate. In just about every other row there was some ardent fan—gal or dude—dressed like Cher, completely done up in one of her iconic costumes, no doubt counting the seconds until we got offstage and they could join the goddess herself in song, employing that most essential accessory: their blinged-out fake microphones.

Some nights, the audiences were crystal clear in voicing their discontent about waiting for Cher to hit the stage. The night we played Paris, we were one of three opening acts, and it seemed that, collectively, we did little more than try the patience of Cher's devoted fans. We watched the group that went on before us, a hip-hop act (a *lip-synching* hip-hop act, at that), and the crowd was not pleased. As I watched from offstage, I remember thinking, "This is not good." But we're professionals, and the show must go on, right?

When it was finally our turn to take the stage, from the very first song, aside from the palpable disinterest from the crowd, I kept hearing this strange, faint sound that I couldn't quite identify. "Is that feedback? Birds?" It kept getting louder and louder.

By the third song, I realized: it was whistling. It was the whole crowd whistling. Now, granted, there are all kinds of different whistles, and it could potentially have meant anything. Perhaps it was a "We love you!" whistle. Or "Cold beer here!" whistle. But no—this was a clear and uniquely French "Get the fuck off the stage!" whistle. There was no mistaking the hostility behind it. Generally speaking, when you see some guy all made up in a Cher wig and gown standing on a chair giving you the finger, it's time to go.

Making the executive decision to cut our losses, I turned to the band and made a gesture I'd never had to make before: a dramatic swipe across my throat. "We're leaving." The band looked at me oddly, thinking perhaps they'd misread the sign. Another big gesture across my throat. "Oh yeah, we're going."

We jumped to the last song of our set list, barreled through it, waved a polite good night, and got the hell offstage, prompting our first enthusiastic round of applause of the night (our only one, for that matter). Much like my very first gig as a twelve-year-old playing the PTA women's group in Ferguson, we had other songs prepared, but evidently the audience felt, "That won't be necessary."

Still, all in all, the tour was a profound experience. We would eventually return to Paris—on our own—a few more times in the coming years to play sold-out shows at the Casino de Paris and the Olympia. Though the venues were a bit smaller, the audiences were great, and it felt like a bit of redemption in Paris.

—

MY TAKE ON TOURING WAS EVOLVING. I STARTED TO REALLY APPRECIATE ITS IMPORTANCE for the longevity of a career. I noticed that the guys who stayed out there and were perennially touring—James Taylor, Randy Newman, and all the bands that went out every year like clockwork, like the Doobie Brothers—had over the years built for themselves an audience that would come out and see them time and time again, with or without a new record in release. And I wanted to be one of those guys. Playing Europe was an extension of that plan.

As the '80s rolled into the '90s, we continued to add more dates each year to our US summer touring schedule and returned a few more times to the UK, Europe, Scandinavia, and Japan, usually in late summer or early fall.

In 1993 I also had the pleasure of recording an album with producer Russ Titelman. It was an inspirational experience on so many levels, not the least of which was getting to know Russ's almost encyclopedic knowledge of popular music. We would sit and listen to all manner of recordings—Ry Cooder's *Paradise and Lunch* album, Miles Davis's *Sketches of Spain* (with Gil Evans's brilliant orchestrations), Ennio Morricone's *Cinema Paradiso* soundtrack . . . These impromptu listening parties at the studio and the musical impressions we gained from them seemed somehow to work their way into the fabric of the album that became *Blink of an Eye*. My old mentor Ted Templeman, upon hearing the final mix, remarked, "I think that's the record that Mike always wanted to make."

As much as I enjoyed working with Russ, recording in New York for the first time was also a new adventure for me. I seem to always search for my sense of balance when I'm there. The neighborhoods, though sometimes minutes apart from each other, always seemed like entirely self-contained and unique worlds. To me, it felt like people in New York were in a constant state of flux, living in one apartment but already thinking about where they'd be moving to next. There was a momentum there that appealed to me, but with my Midwestern sensibilities, I still couldn't help but feel a bit like an alien.

While I was working in New York, Amy and Dylan did come to visit several times, and I have wonderful memories of carrying Dylan on my shoulders as we walked through Central Park, trying my best to make up for the time I'd been away. But it wasn't until I finished the album and got home to Santa Barbara that I felt I could really make it up to him. And though I thoroughly enjoyed fatherhood, I found it to be a bit of a double-edged sword: one minute it's your greatest joy, and the next it's sheer terror.

And with Dylan, there was no shortage of sheer terror.

CHAPTER 25

ORIENTATION DAY

From the day he was born, Dylan hit the ground running, and it was up to the rest of us to keep up. He was such a happy infant at first, so we were blindsided when, at eighteen months, he started to exhibit some worrisome behavior. I remember the day it became apparent that something had changed: orientation day at preschool.

For what it's worth, I'm on record as having been against sending him to school that early; I worried that with my touring, preschool might be too much separation too soon. But friends of ours convinced us otherwise.

So we enrolled him at this well-regarded private preschool in Montecito and were immediately strangers in a strange land. We were suddenly tossed into a world where the other parents were passionately concerned about things like the school's accreditation status, securing a position on the board of directors—stuff that meant less than nothing to us. All we cared about was our son's ability to thrive and be happy.

Cut to: orientation day. Amy and I were getting the tour of the place, and while we were chatting with the school director, trying our best to present as more conservative, "responsible" parents, this guy came through the crowd, obviously pissed off and holding Dylan up in the air with one hand. He was a big guy too, an actor who in years past had been the muscle-man action hero of a popular TV show (and, it must be noted, was already notorious at the school for being a bit of an asshole).

In all fairness, on this occasion he had reason to be upset; it seems that out on the playground, our little Dylan had decided that his kid had been on the swing long enough, so just went over and grabbed him by the cheeks and pulled him off the swing and onto the ground. I'm sure had the situation been reversed, as a parent, I'd have been a little upset too. But this guy was incensed.

"Your kid was pummeling my child!"

I couldn't imagine a two-year-old pummeling anything, but when I saw his kid, I did feel bad; he had these big red finger marks on his cheeks. I apologized profusely and looked at Dylan, thinking, "What just happened here?" He had never done anything like that before. It was as if that was the day he decided to strike out at the world, as if he suddenly realized he was a little guy in a big world and he had to go on the offensive. We loved him beyond measure; he was such a bright little guy. But all of a sudden, he was not an easy kid.

At a very young age, Dylan already had a wicked sense of humor. He had an uncanny instinct for setting up any situation of importance or potential teaching moment with a trapdoor that I almost always stepped on and fell through. Though some adults would get his sense of humor, many would not, and it was the latter group he would deliberately target for his own amusement.

Like the outing to the grocery store (rarely, if ever, a positive experience) where, just before entering, he proclaimed aloud, "Dad, my dick itches." After a short discussion on the difference between acceptable and unacceptable words, we encountered a very nice older woman who, admiring my seemingly innocent little tyke, asked, "And what is your name, sweetie?" At which point he shot me an impish glance, turned back to her, and replied, "Dick."

Exhausted, I promised him one of his favorite chocolate chip cookies if he behaved himself at our next stop: a local coffee shop where Dad might find a strong hit of caffeine—just to keep pace.

Well, we made it as far as the checkout counter without incident, but as I paid the cashier, and Dylan took a bite out of his well-earned, ridiculously oversize cookie, I could just tell from the look in his eyes the wheels were turning. Time to get out of here. So I grabbed his little hand, and we were inches away from a clean exit when he announced, loud enough for all to hear, "Fucking lawyers! Now *there's* a bad word!"

With apologies to all the good and talented legal professionals who have so expertly advised me over the years, truth be known, I may have, once or twice, used that particular descriptive phrase. Of course Dylan heard it and banked it in the back of his brain, to be used at a later date on an occasion of his choosing.

By the time Dylan was four, Amy and I were convinced we must be the middle-aged parents from hell. Then we were blessed with the arrival of our little girl, Scarlett—an angel sent from above—which totally confused the hell out of us, because she soon proved to be the easiest child imaginable.

Now, obviously it wasn't because we were suddenly genius parents; she and Dylan were just naturally polar opposites. Whereas Dylan found his power by keeping the world on its heels, Scarlett just wanted everyone to be happy. In an effort to at least somewhat balance the scales here and provide a story or two of Scarlett's misdeeds, I must tell you in all honesty: I got nothing. I literally can't think of anything she ever did wrong. When she was still a little thing, I remember realizing not only that there is no other love like the kind a father has for his daughter, but that she'll likely never meet a person in this world who doesn't fall under her spell.

Impressively, she'd always hold her own with Dylan no matter what he dished out. She was no shrinking violet. Still, she loved everyone unconditionally, including her brother, and she became an increasingly calming influence for the anxiety that plagued Dylan throughout his adolescence.

—

MY DAD HAD COME OUT TO CALIFORNIA WHEN BOTH KIDS WERE BORN, AS HE DID FOR most every holiday. He and my mom were still the best of friends after all these years, and they both truly enjoyed his visits out west.

However, per my mother's intractable rules, my dad's second wife, Carol, to whom he'd been married, by this point, for years, was not allowed past the Rio Grande. How he worked it out with her to spend most holidays and special events with his ex-wife and kids, I have no idea.

Some of my fondest memories of my dad happened during those visits to California. We played some golf, fished out in the channel . . . To see my dad bond with Dylan—and later with Scarlett, with whom he shared a uniquely special connection—was truly gratifying. He actually made a point of telling me that he thought I was a good dad, even later taking the opportunity to write me a letter here and there to say as much. That meant the world to me.

But still, it was obvious to me that he didn't exactly feel in sync with the peace and quiet, nor the upscale lifestyle of Santa Barbara. One day, while buying supplies at the local gourmet deli, my dad stood alongside me watching the young cashier tally up the overly pricey items. When she rang up the small bag of imported coffee, he reached for it to double-check the price himself and exclaimed, "Jesus! You finish ringing the rest of this up, I'm gonna run home and put this in the safe!"

Part of the original appeal of Santa Barbara—speaking for myself—was the need to keep a little distance between myself and the LA contingent of my family. My mother, sisters, and I had always pooled our resources during lean times in the past, which in its own way set us up for a certain dysfunction and enmeshment that was, at least for me, not particularly healthy.

When they first came out to LA, we all had to pitch in for them to make it out there and ended up, at least for a while, all living under the same roof. In the following years I was able to help them meet most of their needs and still afford my own independence, but over time, I discovered that creating even a little more distance helped.

Santa Barbara, about a hundred miles north of LA, perfectly fit the bill and was certainly more idyllic, but I couldn't help but notice that whenever my friends from Ferguson came out, they would always comment that as beautiful as Montecito / Santa Barbara was, it just didn't "feel real." And I kinda knew what they meant. There was a sense that it was maybe a bit too picture-perfect, with its nonindigenous palm trees, pristinely manicured hedgerows and landscapes—and five-dollar cups of coffee. And now that we had children, Amy and I started to wonder ourselves if maybe in fact we needed to find a place where the kids could really thrive, someplace a bit more rural and "realistic."

Eventually we wound up moving to the Santa Ynez Valley, about two hours north of LA, living on a small ranch with two horses, two dogs, and a couple cats.

It was while we were living there that Dylan and I took a little "guy trip" to Disney World in Orlando to celebrate his fifth birthday. My dad even came down from St. Louis, where he was living at the time, to join us, and that alone made it a more than memorable occasion. The three of us had a great time, spending a whole day and night at the park, and then we hopped up to Nashville to visit my sister Kathy and her husband, Grady, who had settled there a couple years earlier. Kathy was starting to find her way in the music scene there and had always urged me to come check it out for myself.

I'd always loved Nashville. In my earliest band days back with Jerry Jay and the Sheratons, we'd make the drive down from Ferguson to visit my Aunt Dorothy Hogan, who lived just outside of Nashville in Gallatin, Tennessee. After sleeping on Aunt Dorothy's floor (all fourteen of us), we would—in our manager-approved wardrobe ensembles—excitedly bombard the different labels there, especially Monument Records, for which the Nashville office was world headquarters. Monument was keen on signing pop acts with novelty records; its walls were covered with gold records for hits like

Ray Stevens's "Gitarzan" and "Ahab the Arab" (another song title that wouldn't fly today).

—

I HAD ALWAYS THOUGHT THAT IF I HADN'T BECOME A PERFORMER OR SONGWRITER, I'D have been happy to work in publishing. Having inherited my dad's love of a good song, the idea of sifting through mountains of demos in search of the ideal pairing—the right song for the right artist—held a certain romance and seemed to me a rewarding and noble profession.

While Nashville had always been an exciting and welcoming town, it had by this point steadily grown into a more cosmopolitan city, and the music coming from there seemed to be also further evolving and expanding. Still, I was struck by how quiet and simple life seemed to be there, compared with life in Southern California. You could still buy a two-hundred-acre farm on beautiful rolling hills ten minutes out of downtown Nashville—for a fraction of what you'd pay in LA for a crappy house in a terrible location.

So this whole fantasy started building up in my mind: We'd move to Nashville, live on a farm, ride horses, raise cattle . . . live the gentrified farmer life. Kinda retire and just write songs with all these great musicians. I even spent the day with a real estate agent friend of my sister's to look at some properties, taking a whole bunch of pictures to bring back to show Amy.

Her reaction? "Why in the world would you want to move to Nashville? Your whole career is here in LA."

Well, that pretty much burst my bubble. I thought, "Yeah . . . she's probably right. It is crazy." All my musical and professional connections made in the last twenty years were in LA: the guys at Warners, all the musicians I'd come to know . . . But that argument didn't hold for long.

By the end of the following year, pretty much everyone I knew in the executive offices of Warner Bros. Records was gone. Ted Templeman, Lenny Waronker, Mo Ostin, Russ Titelman—all had moved on.

And the recording scene was also changing. Not only were we living further out of LA, making it harder to get into town, but the recording studios themselves were starting to go under too. Throughout the '70s, the large commercial studio complexes like A&M were always booked to capacity. But by the early '90s, I'd go in to record and sometimes be the only artist in the building.

I really missed the excitement of LA as I knew it when I first got out there. There was no telling who you'd run into out in the hall: Elton John, Joni Mitchell, Paul Williams, or any of the A-list musicians working on their sessions. I once bumped into Ringo Starr, and while we did meet again years later, at the time of that first encounter in the halls of A&M Studios, I was too dumbstruck to tell him how much those Beatles records meant to me. Turns out he was there visiting John Lennon and Harry Nilsson, who were recording across the hall with Phil Spector. So I made quite a few extra trips to the coffee machine in the hall that day, hoping for a "chance" encounter with them all.

Finally, before leaving for the day, I made one last attempt, only to find their studio now empty and several LAPD officers gathered around the receptionist's desk in what looked like some serious investigation. I didn't know what was going on, but figured it was best to not hang around.

Well, as I heard it explained later, it seems in the middle of John and Harry's session, Phil Spector had pulled out a gun and shot into the ceiling during an argument. The police were called, and everyone split before the cops got there.*

So I never did get to meet John Lennon.

---

* Interesting tidbit: it was later that same night that John and Harry famously got tossed out of the Troubadour for drunk and disorderly conduct. So it's possible it was the gunplay of that afternoon that later prompted some excessive recreational drinking.

—

BUT IN THE YEARS THAT FOLLOWED, THE BUSINESS OF PROFESSIONAL RECORDING MOVED from the large industrial complexes we were all familiar with to a more cottage industry feel, if you will, with private studios becoming more the norm. And by the early '90s, that buzz, that sense of close proximity, that central location that engendered so much collaboration and camaraderie, just didn't seem to be there anymore. LA had changed.

And so Nashville went from "out of the question" to looking more like the next logical step. Amy's thinking had started to change too. Though she grew up in New York, her mom was from Memphis, and Amy had fond memories of her childhood summers spent there with her aunts, uncles, and cousins. So she slowly warmed up to the idea of moving to Nashville. Once she started to read *Southern Living* magazine and imagined us with our two young kids in a big ol' house with a big ol' porch, living a slower, more subdued (and, yes, "realistic") southern-style life . . . I knew Tennessee was on the horizon.

But there was one more unforeseen incentive to leave California: my dad was dying.

CHAPTER 26

NASHVILLE

In 1964, when I was twelve and my father was not yet forty, I remember him lying on the couch on a Saturday morning, watching TV with his usual pack of Camel nonfilters and an ashtray in close proximity on a nearby tray table, when a special news report came on—and my best recollection is that it was Walter Cronkite, that most trusted authority we had—to announce the surgeon general had determined that cigarette smoking caused cancer. And in that moment, my father reached over, picked up his pack of cigarettes, crumpled it in his hand, and dropped it into the ashtray. And that was it. Once again, just as he did with alcohol, he white-knuckled it and never smoked another cigarette in his life.

Nonetheless, though not having smoked for nearly thirty years, my dad was diagnosed with stage four lung cancer, and as Nashville was a lot closer to St. Louis, the move allowed me to be within reach, to help him with his doctors and a treatment regimen that could hopefully grant him more time to spend with his grandchildren. I'd have given anything for his illness not to have been part of the decision, but there are always the silver linings.

I remember flying from California to St. Louis to hear his initial prognosis—and it was grim. "Large tumor in the pleura. Six months at most. Be sure your affairs are in order." That was pretty much it. The doctor then asked my dad how he felt about that, and with his typically dry humor he answered, "Well, frankly, I was feeling a lot better before this conversation."

We were all shocked by the seeming certainty of it all. I did my best to stay hopeful, for his sake. It wasn't till I was leaving for the airport to go back home that we both got emotional. I could hardly get out the words as I hugged him.

"I love you so much!"

At that moment, it was never clearer to me. Over the years, I'd become so guarded with respect to that kind of emotional vulnerability or verbal expression, especially with my dad. I'd spent a good deal of my life learning how to deal with missing him, but what we faced now would be so final.

As sad as the moment was, I'm forever grateful for that opportunity to say something that neither of us could remember ever having said to each other before. We soon started talking much more regularly and saying those words much more often. The fact that he wanted me there to walk this last mile with him meant everything to me. It was like that last streetcar ride so long ago; he now, once again, took the opportunity to give me the one thing I wanted most from him my whole life: to let me know I was important to him. All of a sudden, it seemed he was no longer in a hurry to be somewhere else. All this time, I'd thought my goal was to be that son he could be proud of by way of my accomplishments, because that seemed to be the only way I could get his attention. But all I really wanted, I now realized, was to feel he needed me in his life as much as I needed him in mine.

Leaving him that day to catch my flight home, I was torn. Sensing my ambivalence as I turned to him at the door, he just smiled and reassured me with the old familiar thumbs-up, as if to say, "It's gonna all be okay."

—

MY DAD DID LIVE LONG ENOUGH TO VISIT US IN OUR NEW HOME.

Having sold our ranch in California, we bought a big piece of land in Fairview, just outside of Nashville, and moved lock, stock, and barrel—cats, dogs, goats, horses, and kids—and started a new life in Tennessee.

We loved it. It was an easy transition in some ways because we had family and friends there already. Unlike California, the landscape in Tennessee changed dramatically with the seasons, as did our life in general. We had over a hundred acres! Mostly rolling pasture bordered by a large scenic creek on three sides, dotted with a couple of ponds, one of which we stocked with trout and smallmouth bass, which kept the kids busy fishing. We camped out down by the creek in summer and sledded down the hills in the occasional Tennessee snow. Life was good.

Above and beyond the lifestyle that Nashville afforded us as a family, there was, of course, the thriving music community that I'd always been enamored with and was now eager to be a part of. Nashville would present the opportunity to work with some of the most talented people I'd ever met. Even before I moved there, my longtime friend and writing partner Randy Goodrum had always encouraged me to get to Nashville as often as possible and get to know the community of writers there.

It had always been a mecca for singer-songwriters, from Hank Williams to Johnny Cash and June Carter, Roger Miller, Willie Nelson, Guy Clark, Steve Earle, Vince Gill, and Amy Grant—but now it was also drawing musicians from across the country. The early threads of California mainstream country/rock, from the Byrds to the Eagles, were reemerging in Nashville with bands like the Dixie Chicks (now the Chicks) and the Mavericks, heralding a new age of pop/country music. When I got there, there were countless opportunities to play live in much more intimate settings, such as writers' rounds or guitar pull gigs at small, iconic music venues like Green's Grocery and the Bluebird Cafe, or just sitting in with friends as part of a rhythm section at places like 3rd and Lindsley or the Exit/In downtown. The furthest distance you might drive in Nashville was still a rock's throw compared with the sprawl of LA. And of course there was the legendary Ryman Auditorium, the mothership of all Nashville venues, which over the last century had always welcomed with open arms any and all wandering minstrels who found their way to Music City, USA, a venerable old church building that will forever feel like home to me.

Aside from all the opportunities to play live music locally, it was the writing scene that, for me, was the real heart of this talented community. Writers of any kind—novelists, poets, screenwriters, songwriters—often develop a specific, idiosyncratic set of requirements to be at their best; they need to be at the right desk with the right chair, the right instrument, at the right time of day . . . They need the consistent setting. For me, it's almost been the opposite. Though we've all had that urge to "pull a geographic," thinking, "Man, if I could just live *there*, I'd be so happy!"—that never really works out, because when you get there, you've still brought yourself along. But for the more specific purpose of songwriting, I have found that a new environment really does help sometimes. The location itself isn't nearly as important as the *change* in location; going somewhere new has always helped charge my creative batteries and kick-start the creative process.

When I moved to Nashville, it was with an eye toward evolving more as a songwriter. I felt inspired again and started writing differently, looking to embrace the more storytelling style of the Nashville tradition. In LA, it often seemed that you were only as good as your last five minutes, whereas in Nashville there was an ingrained respect for the songwriter, regardless of how recent their success. Composers like Mickey Newbury, who wrote the iconic "Just Dropped In (To See What Condition My Condition Was In)," a career-launching hit for Kenny Rogers (then Kenny Rogers and the First Edition), and years later wrote "San Francisco Mabel Joy" and "An American Trilogy," and Harlan Howard, who wrote "I Fall to Pieces," "Too Many Rivers," and "Busted"—they were still considered at the top of their games, and everyone was eager to write with them. I was lucky enough to write with the likes of Alison Krauss and her brother, Viktor, Jim Photoglo, Jon Vezner, John Scott Sherrill, John Goodwin . . . and the legendary Brenda Lee.

I had been such a big fan of Brenda's ever since Aunt Bitsy introduced me to her records when I was a kid, and I even had a bit of a crush on her through some very formative years. (I also had some memorable dreams about the Lennon Sisters, but I digress.) Needless to say, I was more than a little thrilled to have been invited to Brenda Lee's home to try to write a song together.

She lived in the same beautiful Craftsman-style bungalow she bought early in her career, in a neighborhood that at the time was likely considered "out of town" but, following years of Nashville's increasing sprawl, was now properly "downtown."

Brenda was as charming and lovely as I had imagined her to be, all four feet nine inches of her, and I would find myself duly impressed with her songwriting skills. After a refreshing glass of sweet tea—the official favorite nonalcoholic beverage of the South—I sat down at her grand piano, which was ever so slightly out of tune. She sat on the couch with pen and paper; and, joined by her guitarist and friend Dave Powelson, the three of us began to formulate our song.

Atop the piano was a vast collection of little porcelain tchotchkes—souvenirs, I imagined, from every city she had ever played. There were so many of them grouped so close together that every time I'd hit a chord on the piano, the little figurines would jingle as they vibrated against one another—which was not a problem for me as much as it was for her little dog keeping vigil under the piano. As far as I could tell, the dog didn't like me much to begin with, and now, every time my piano playing made the figurines rattle, the dog would growl and bare its tiny teeth. This little drama was unfolding, I might add, uncomfortably close to my crotch. So as I played, of course as gently as possible, I kept one eye on the keyboard and one eye on the Yorkie.

I'm happy to report that I left there unharmed, and the collaboration did yield a song. And it turned out to be a collaboration in the broadest sense; it seems as though every person who passed through the living room that afternoon—her husband, her daughter dropping off groceries, her housekeeper, the landscaper there to install a new sprinkler—literally *everyone* was invited by Brenda to offer their two cents. And bless their hearts, every one of them had an opinion. "I think the chorus could be stronger." "It needs a bridge." "It feels a little long, I think." I started to wonder how many names were going to be listed on the writing credit.

Community consensus aside, our song, "The Kind of Fool Love Makes," went on to be recorded by a couple of iconic artists—first by Wynonna Judd, a recording session I actually got to play on, and later by Kenny Rogers.

Another artist I was blessed to work with while living there was the legendary Tony Joe White. Early in his career, as a dashingly handsome young rockabilly guitar slinger, he was being groomed as sort of the next Elvis Presley. But I think he proved himself to be too "authentic" to evolve into a pop icon persona, and ultimately, it could be argued, he was responsible for the advent of the genre now referred to as Americana. Tony was as funky as one man could possibly be all by himself. Performing with just a drummer, he would employ his unique guitar style, implying a kind of bass line on the lower two strings while he played some killer syncopated groove on the higher ones, and adding his moody baritone vocal, he'd somehow provide all the music and rhythm your heart and mind needed to hear.

But it was as a songwriter that he reached the pinnacles of his success, with compositions such as "Polk Salad Annie" and "Rainy Night in Georgia," as well as writing "Steamy Windows" and "Foreign Affair" for Tina Turner. I had the privilege of writing a couple songs with Tony, including one called "Where Would I Be Now," which was later covered by the great Joe Cocker.

—

MY FANTASY OF MYSELF AS A NASHVILLE SONGWRITER—LIVING ON HIS FARM, GOING down to Music Row once in a while and writing songs for other people to record and tour behind, while I stayed home and enjoyed a more sedentary lifestyle—was short-lived, as that's not exactly the way it worked out.

As much as I was enjoying life in Nashville, it wasn't like I was writing a lot of ASCAP Songs of the Year, and I was soon fielding that age-old question from my accountant: "Hey . . . you gonna be working anytime soon?"

So now, based out of Nashville, I once again found myself hitting the road pretty regularly with the same guys I had worked with from LA: drummer George Perilli, who had moved to Nashville not long before I did, and guitarist Bernie Chiaravalle. Bernie came to Nashville to write with me and ended up moving there himself. Some of the first recordings I did in Nashville were songs written with Bernie—"No Love to Be Found" (a duet with Wendy Moten) and "Someday You Will," which soon became the first tracks recorded for *Blue Obsession*, the first album I made while living down there. (Expertly produced by Tommy Sims.)

I will say touring as a dad was a new world for me. Ever since I started playing live shows again in earnest, I'd made a point to bring the kids and Amy out for part of each tour, because I really didn't want to be away from them any more than I had to. So we did a lot of traveling as a family in my mid-thirties, and I have vivid memories of the crew busting my chops as they watched me pack up strollers and haul diaper bags onto this rock and roll tour bus.

Though we had moved about as far from Santa Barbara as possible, the old adage "wherever you go, there you are" proved to be very much the case. Problems and challenges come right along with you that, in my case, could at times challenge my sobriety.

For example: Dylan and school.

Even in the new, more relaxed environment of Nashville, this was not a kid who was going to thrive in traditional school settings. When he was around nine or ten, I remember sometimes having to chase him out the front door and across the pasture and physically tackle him to get him back in the house, get his shoes on, and get him to school.

And that wouldn't be the end of it; even when he was dressed and in the truck headed for school, I would sometimes have to physically hold on to him, knowing full well that if I went too slowly down our long driveway, he'd try to jump out of the truck and run home.

On those same mornings, Scarlett, our angelic little fairy, would come out on the porch with her hair in perfect little pigtails, totally put together, her books neatly tucked under her arm, imploring me, "C'mon, Dad, we're gonna be late." I'd look at her while dragging Dylan back across the yard, thinking, "How do you reconcile these two kids being in the same family?"

Our attempts to keep Dylan in school lasted only so long. The last school he went to, I tried to impress upon the school staff, "If this is gonna work, you really have to hold on to this kid. I mean, like, physically hold him. Hang on to him at least till I get down the road, and even then, you're gonna have to convince him to stay in class and not go hide in the bathroom."

The final straw was one such day when I got him into school, waited to make sure he didn't sneak out of the building, then started out of the parking lot, driving slowly, just to be sure. A little bit down the road, I was convinced I'd successfully delivered him to the teacher's charge—until I glanced up at the rearview mirror to see Dylan running behind my truck, waving and yelling, "Dad, wait!" down the center of a friggin' rural highway.

Of course I immediately pulled over, and in that moment, I remember thinking, "Maybe he just knows better." As he climbed in my truck, I wasn't even upset with him. I was only grateful he hadn't gotten killed. I just said, "You're right. This isn't working." And I made up my mind right then that I was not gonna put either of us through this anymore.

—

FROM THAT POINT ON WE STARTED OUR ADVENTURES IN THE HOMESCHOOLING OF DYLAN and his sister, which ultimately turned out to be a huge step in the right direction. At first, I thought, "Oh my God—this is gonna be a nightmare!" But I have to say: it was fun. Admittedly the lion's share of responsibility fell on Amy's shoulders when I was away, but the big advantage was we could do this on the road and on our own schedule wherever we were; we could start whenever we wanted and end whenever we chose.

With the kids being homeschooled, I soon realized that beyond just being more involved in their classwork, we were suddenly more engaged in their daily experience outside of school too, in ways we never imagined. We went from the typical tired dinner talk—"What'd you do in school today?" "Nothing."—to even planning our family dinner around the lessons we studied earlier in the day. If, for example, we were reading about the Spanish missions along El Camino Real, we might plan and prepare our meals around traditional Mexican dishes, which piqued their interest, initiated conversation, and brought the experience to life for the kids.

We'd also sometimes plan our lessons around where I'd be touring. And that gave me a whole new insight into how Dylan's brain worked.

We happened to be touring the West Coast while studying California history and its Hispanic roots, so we decided that would be a good time to go visit some of those Spanish missions. Upon entering a restored mission near San Diego, we were given those little museum tape machines that describe the significance of what you're looking at. Well, this particular afternoon, Dylan was not having it. I tried reasoning with him.

"Look, this is our lesson for the day, then we're done! Yes, it's mandatory, so let's just get it done, and then we'll go for lunch afterward. Okay, buddy?"

His position: "This is bullshit!"

It was frustrating trying to keep his attention. I found myself constantly badgering him. "Are you listening to me? Do you hear what I'm saying?"

The field trip tour culminated with Dylan physically grabbing the tape machine out of my hand and ripping the cassette out, the two of us now literally wrestling over it in the courtyard of this old mission, me swearing like a sailor—all of this going down in front of a group of horrified nuns whose misfortune it was to visit the mission the same day as the McDonalds. (I'm starting to wonder if, in this lifetime, I'm destined to never be on good terms with nuns.)

As we got back in the car, I was irritated, to say the least, and exhausted, and convinced the day was one colossal failure. I remember saying to Amy, "This was a terrible idea! What were we thinking?"

Cut to: backstage at the gig later that night. One of the crew guys casually asked Dylan, "Hey, D—what'd you do today?" And then my son proceeded to give a detailed description of the impressive construction of the campanarios (the towers that housed the mission bells), elaborating on how the padres were tasked with building each mission going up the coast, each one situated no more than one day's ride from the last . . . He took it all in! Everything! Things I didn't remember hearing myself.

We came to understand that's how kids like Dylan learn, which, if I'm being honest, is not that different from how I learned everything. As a kid—and even as an adult—I've always tended to learn things in a kind of immersive way. I could never understand written instructions for the life of me, and if someone tried to teach me anything in a rudimentary way, I would immediately check out and just stop hearing their voice altogether. (I look back now with a lot more compassion and appreciation for my poor piano teacher Tom Hanlon.) And like Dylan, I tended to respond to being lectured by displaying a bit of a rebellious streak as a defense mechanism. Even with music, formal instruction was of little or no use to me. I had to learn it all in my own way.

More often than not, the things about Dylan that pushed my buttons the most were the very attributes that reminded me of myself. It was particularly frustrating for me because I always wanted it to be easier for him. Realizing that was a big step toward a better relationship with my son and a clearer understanding of my own character defects that compounded my frustration as a parent.

The Nashville chapter of our lives turned out to be formative and wonderful years. I even bought another property in neighboring Williamson County, a little tract house where the previous owner (another Hollywood transplant) had built a fairly sizable recording room and control room off the back end of it: a fully equipped, up-and-running studio that was in fact designed to emulate Sunset Sound in LA. I've done at least some part of all my subsequent recording projects there.

And it was there, for the first time, that I had my own personal central office of operations, run by my terrifically capable assistant, Lisa Patton Souther. Having previously managed the Orpheum Theatre in Memphis (home to everyone from Elvis to B. B. King), Lisa brought a wealth of experience and organizational skills that greatly enhanced my development as a solo artist.

It turns out the thriving musical environment in Nashville was good for Dylan and Scarlett too. When Dylan was ten or so, I taught him a few power chords on the guitar—simple I-and-V (one-and-five) chords manageable for small hands, and with that two-note voicing you've immediately got yourself a heavy metal version of almost any song. One important ingredient: a small amp from the closet with a blown speaker. Our favorite jam was an all-power-chord version of the Everly Brothers' "Wake Up Little Susie." And of course there was no stopping us when we jammed the Kinks' "You Really Got Me" and "All Day and All of the Night." We were building our repertoire and it was great fun! I got to indulge my fantasy as the kick-ass heavy metal drummer, and Dylan would play the guitar while little Scarlett danced around the room with her plastic karaoke microphone and sang along with us.

—

MUSIC CAN BE A GREAT WAY TO CONNECT WITH YOUR CHILDREN—UNTIL IT ISN'T. Because as anyone with children knows, the day comes when they're just done with it. I remember being caught off guard, kinda heartbroken, and regretful, recalling all the times that I was too busy when our jam sessions were all they wanted to do. Inevitably, there's the moment when that musical generation gap rears its ugly head and you realize that you and your kids no longer share the same musical taste. Suddenly it's goodbye, Stones, Aretha, B. B. King—and hello, Sir Mix-A-Lot!

One day, we were driving somewhere with a couple of neighbors' kids in tow, blasting my son's most recent mix CD, when some lyrically horrifying track came up. While I'm pretty sure they were clueless as to what the words actually meant, Scarlett and her little friends in the back, like innocent parakeets, started singing along word for word with some truly steep, adult lyrical content. So I reached over to shut the stereo off—only to be instantly chastised with a huge wave of protest.

"*Dad!* We're listening to that!"

Suddenly I found myself sucked into (and on the wrong side of) a philosophical argument about censorship with a group of children, the oldest being eleven.

"Look, this is just not a good message for the youth of America!" (Even *I* couldn't believe I said that!)

That's when my son, the master of irony, hit me with: "Yeah, Dad, because your band's record with a giant reefer on the cover—now there's a perfect message for the youth of America."

Snatching defeat from the jaws of . . . well . . . defeat, I just reached over and turned the music back up.

That's one of the most annoying skills that some kids master early on: the uncanny ability to leave their parents speechless. I remember another such occasion in the late '90s, when Napster was a thing and most kids, including my own, were downloading all their favorite music for free. I endeavored to explain to my son and his tween friends the need to "protect intellectual property" and how these digital downloads were "negatively affecting the revenues" of all these artists they so admired.

"That's their livelihood. Just like it's my livelihood," I explained to him. "That's how we have this car we're driving, the clothes you're wearing, the house we live in . . . When you just download it for free, the artists don't get paid. It's like you're stealing from them."

To which my son deftly replied, "Yeah, well, Dad, not to worry—'cause no one's downloading *your* music anyway."

This kid rarely missed a shot, and once again—I got nothin'.

To Dylan and Scarlett, the idea that their dad was, in some people's eyes, a "celebrity" always struck them as a bit silly—and sometimes even intrusive. Having said that, they also weren't beyond using their "connection" when it served their interest.

When Dylan was maybe six or seven, he came backstage after one of my shows and said, "Dad, there's two girls that want to meet you. I told them to wait and then you'll come out and sign something for them." Which I thought was kinda sweet.

So once I got changed and said my good nights to the band and crew, I walked out of the venue, and there, along with the usual contingent of nice people waiting for photo ops and autographs, I saw Dylan with these two "older" girls—all of maybe twelve—corralled over to the side. Not wanting the larger congregation to interfere with his plans, he started barking at them like a pint-size club bouncer.

"Folks, go on home—the man's tired! He's worked all night. Go on now, the show's over!"

Then, turning on a dime, he very suavely waved me over.

"Dad, say hello to Melissa and Jennifer."

For Dylan and Scarlett, those fifteen years in Nashville amounted to big chunks of their childhoods, and it was where they formed lifelong friendships.

Nashville was also where our family would face one of our biggest challenges, and I believe we were fortunate to be right where we were when it happened.

CHAPTER 27

TEARS TO COME

In 1996, when we had been enjoying our new life in Nashville for a little more than a year, Amy was tending to a new garden she had planted. We hadn't gotten around to landscaping yet, so there was no sprinkler system in place, and she had to literally go down the hill to fetch a pail of water. One day, as she was carrying the buckets from the pond back up to the garden, she felt something in her breast—a knot that didn't seem to ease up. Knowing enough to be concerned, she went and got a mammogram, and that's when they saw it: a tumor.

At first, I managed to not go to the darkest place, imagining the worst outcome. I somehow decided there was no need to go there till I needed to go there; I determined there must be a way to solve this, and we'd find it.

Still, there are moments when reality knocks at the door of hope with a message you don't want to hear.

I waited anxiously near the nurses' station outside of where Amy underwent surgery to remove the tumor to be biopsied. When I was informed that the surgery was over and Amy was in recovery, I approached the nurses' station to ask when the results might come through from the lab. I assumed it would fall to the surgeon to walk us through the results and the prognosis as soon as he was free, but the nurse on duty cut to the chase when she answered simply, "Yeah—it's cancer."

It felt like a gut punch. I broke down right there in front of this woman I didn't even know. I don't think I realized just how stressed and tense I was. I apologized to the nurse. "I'm sorry. It's just . . . you caught me by surprise."

I wanted so badly to hear that it was nothing, but that wasn't what I heard. However well I thought I had prepared myself for the worst, it obviously wasn't enough.

Based on just that tumor biopsy, the doctors weren't sure precisely how advanced the cancer was, but knowing it to be an aggressive form, they had removed fourteen lymph nodes from under her arm for testing during the surgery, and it would be a week or so before we got those results.

We kept busy in the meantime, but it seemed like an eternity. I remember I was doing some grading in the corrals next to the house when I saw Amy burst out the front door, running toward me holding both hands over her mouth, visibly upset. I jumped down off the tractor and ran to her. She collapsed in my arms and in a trembling voice told me that the doctor's office called; out of the fourteen lymph nodes they removed, eleven turned out to be positive. That alone sounded so ominous. They still refrained from making any certain judgment about what stage it was or giving any prognosis over the phone, but suggested we meet with the oncologist at our earliest convenience. We wasted no time making that appointment, hoping it would shed more light on our situation.

The kids were still quite young—Scarlett was four; Dylan, eight—so we didn't initially share the severity of the news with them, and we did our best to put on our bravest faces, but it wasn't easy. Going to see Scarlett in her school's spring recital that first week after the diagnosis, I remember Amy looking at our daughter onstage, and I just knew she must've been wondering if she would even be here for this come next year.

That period of uncertainty was one of the most torturous points of this journey for both of us, but it was also in that moment, I believe, that Amy decided whatever she had to do to be there next year and stay in her kids' lives, she was gonna do it. One of Amy's greatest assets in all this would be her stubbornness. We learned that when positive thinking wanes and gives way to fear or despair, plain old stubbornness comes in pretty handy. There were also the angels who came along at the right time to help us on this sojourn.

It was still the early stages of stem cell rescue treatment, and wanting to make sure we were getting the best medical advice, we flew up to New York to get a second opinion from a highly regarded expert, a Dr. Holland—which all by itself felt encouraging; when the doctor has the same last name as the patient, that's got to be a good omen (even if it was just Amy's stage name).

Dr. Holland, it turns out, was actually one of the pioneers in early chemotherapy research, so his word carried a lot of weight with us. When he told us that he personally knew of Dr. Greco, the oncologist we were seeing in Nashville, and assured us we couldn't be in better hands, we were greatly relieved.

There would be many touch-and-go points throughout this ordeal, not to mention a whole litany of residual side effects from the treatment that no one told us about. And because it was still in a clinical trial phase, there were consequences *they* may not have even known about yet. For instance, Amy would go through sudden and severe menopause, resulting in a chronic loss of bone density and bouts of lymphedema—enough to cause even the most determined person to despair. At times it seemed too much, but I've never known anyone more courageous than my wife as I've watched her get over each and every hurdle in her path to be here for the ones she loves.

During one of those intensely potent chemo sessions toward the end of the oncology regimen (which by this point was already making her pretty weak and sick), I remember sitting silently with Amy in a room full of other patients in other beds, all receiving chemotherapy. There was a moment when she looked at me with a sad, resigned smile as if to say, "I'm sorry to put you through this." Right then, in the middle of all she was enduring, while fighting for her life, she was mostly concerned about me. It was in that moment I realized that the real character of love can only be seen in moments like these, the desperate, scary, and uncertain times. When the measure of who you really are, your true character, is revealed in how much you care about someone else. At that moment, with just a scarf around her bald head, no eyebrows, no eyelashes even—just her blue eyes looking out at me from behind an ashen complexion—she was never more beautiful.

There's a level of selfless love you're not going to tap into under ordinary circumstances. You have to be walking through fire. That doesn't mean you won't wander off course or forget to be grateful in the future, but moments like these will forever change you and, like a beacon, point the way back when you need it most.

—

FEW EXPERIENCES CARRY THE TRAUMA AND REALIZATION OF YOUR MORTALITY MORE than cancer, and one of the consequences, not so uncommon, is how intensely you bond with the people on your support team: your nurses, doctors, therapists . . . You easily find yourself depending on them for emotional support maybe more than you realize. Then there comes that day when they say, "Okay . . . We've done everything we can do, you're on your own now, so . . . good luck." All of a sudden, you're left alone with this potentially great pall over the rest of your life, which is what cancer really is for so many of us. And how cancer manifests itself psychologically down the road is in that depression that can just blindside you. When you're left to ponder the possible consequences of this disease and their psychological impact, it can feel like there's somehow no place to go but down. It's not the same for everyone, I'm sure, but for many, this PTSD is a real consequence of having survived cancer.

Amy and I both experienced it, but Amy, naturally, more acutely. The cancer itself was hers alone. So on top of the disease, though she was on the other side of her treatment, she now found herself with another new nemesis: flat-out depression. "Am I ever gonna have another carefree moment in this life after all of this? Because it feels like the wolf will always be just outside the door." It can take you to places of fear in a very heightened, exaggerated way.

It was heartbreaking and frightening to witness my best friend, the woman I cherished, who'd survived so much, go through this additional emotional turmoil. But it was also a dangerously negative mindset for me to succumb to, given my history of codependency.

Pure, unconditional empathy is always appropriate and should always be the first step toward being helpful to someone else's emotional suffering. However, it began to feel like we were in a mudslide together, and I, at least, had to keep my head above it, so as to recognize any opportunity to seize a handhold for both of our sakes. There comes a point when, if only for your own survival, you may have to dig your heels in and say to someone you love, "I'm here, I'm with you, but I can't go *there* with you."

Of course that's just about the last thing a depressed person wants to hear. And with all the drugs they were pumping into Amy at the time, it wouldn't be hard to imagine that she was also suffering a bit of chemical depression. I had to be conscious of and sensitive to that possibility, but I also needed to be careful not to go down the rabbit hole of depression myself. While it seemed like the right thing to do was try to encourage her to keep a positive outlook no matter what, I don't want to give the impression that I did everything right in this situation; there were certainly times I did succumb to my own bouts of self-pity.

Ultimately, it would be Amy's courage and incredible strength that allowed her to keep the faith and find her way, and, in the end, be the example for me.

The whole experience, with its feelings of desolation and the complete deconstruction and rebuilding of our relationship, brought us to a more transcendent place of gratitude. I don't believe we'd have ever gotten there the easy way. Like these events tend to do, family tragedies can bring us face-to-face with our greatest weakness or potential for failure, but they also present a great silver lining: you find an appreciation of each other and the life you have, a connection and understanding on a much higher level that might have remained elusive but for that uninvited drama. It anchors and solidifies the precious history that you share. I don't think I would ever have known Amy as well or as deeply as I came to know her if we hadn't experienced those most trying times.

Fortunately, both our kids were still young enough to comprehend all this in only the simplest of terms: "Mom has to go to the doctor a lot." And they were resilient enough to get through the ordeal, trusting that we were gonna do our best in any way we could to bring about the most positive outcome. I drew strength once again from the memory of my dad driving me to get stitches that time. It helped me just stay the course and believe it was all gonna be all right in the end.

And it seems that's pretty much how it's turned out. It's been almost thirty years since that initial diagnosis and the radical treatment and emotional roller coaster that followed. We've since been given a clean bill of health. Amy is doing wonderfully and will more than likely outlive me.

That is certainly my sincere hope.

CHAPTER 28

AS LUCK WOULD HAVE IT

If my life had a motto, it would surely be: "As luck would have it." I mean, by this point, at the beginning of the new millennium, I had probably missed enough opportunities, burned enough bridges, and made enough dumb choices to kill any once promising career in the music business.

In my early years as a solo artist, I felt very fortunate to be managed by some very capable and powerful managers who handled some of the biggest artists of the time. The downside to that, however, is that if you're not one of their bigger revenue producers, you may *technically* still be on their roster, but you can slowly become the old dog on the porch whose time has apparently come but no one has the heart to shoot.

In mild desperation, and in keeping with my history of self-will run riot, I decided to be more proactive in my career's direction and took on some projects that, frankly, management really didn't approve of. For one thing, I started a small record label with a couple friends as partners: my old friend guitarist/producer/engineer Chris Pelonis and actor/musician Jeff Bridges, whom I had more recently become friends with when I coproduced a recording project of his with Chris. We all lived in Santa Barbara, and it was on a surfing trip just north of there that the three of us came up with the idea to start our own label. It wasn't like we thought it through in any great detail, but it seemed like an exciting prospect nonetheless.

The legendary struggle between artists and their record labels for a more equitable split (and delivery) of royalties—a battle to which

I'm no stranger—has been ongoing since the earliest days of monetizing recorded music, the record company's position traditionally being, "Well, ours is a large financial investment up front, and therefore, if the record sells, we should be able to recoup our costs off the top." Fair enough.

However, that seems to be the classic trapdoor built into most every recording contract. So, after the artist falls through, from that point on, the official company response concerning any monies down the pipe is "We're not recouped yet." Even if your album goes triple platinum, the follow-up explanation is almost sure to be: "Yeah, well, you still owe us from the two previous albums." Such is the ever-elusive recoupment.

There is always some pending debt that precludes the company from paying you an artist royalty, always some litany of bullshit items they point to as expenses: records returned by distributors, bloated manufacturing expenses, production costs of videos, trade ads . . . Once you are successful, it seems they ultimately incur little to none of the actual costs of doing business. It's all taken out of the artist's share.

This usually goes on until an expensive audit is initiated, obviously paid for by the artist, who, along with their small group of advocates, usually just a manager and an attorney, goes up against the extensive corporate legal arm of the label. If the artist is lucky, they may get a mere percentage of what is owed by way of a settlement, which they inevitably accept so as to not go broke from this whole procedure. And that, in essence, has always been the cat-and-mouse relationship of record labels with their artists.

Not to mention (but of course, I will): aside from the label having their hand in your pocket, there are the lesser offenders. I've heard tell of producers and studio managers who would jack up the price of two-inch tape on their invoices and split the overage, which over the course of a year could be a significant sum. And then there are stories of artist managers who would block out weeks of studio time for their artist, knowing full well the artist would be out on tour some of that time, which was an opportunity for said managers to bring in one of their fledgling acts to record some demos on the touring artist's dime.

So the idea that Jeff, Chris, and I had was maybe we could finally steer clear of all that. We thought by owning our own label, we could manage the financing of it ourselves and avoid the whole recouping mystery, a template for making sure the artists didn't get stiffed.

Also, it gave us some much-desired artistic freedom. At the time, I was increasingly being perceived at the label as "adult contemporary"—not the worst moniker in the world, but still a perception that had me feeling a little smothered and stifled. My belief was that all new releases should be promoted unilaterally—throw it against the wall and see where it sticks. It shouldn't be predetermined what is and isn't suitable for any radio format.

I had already moved to Nashville and recorded the album *Blue Obsession* there, and while I should note that Warner Bros. was nice enough to let me out of my contract and take the album with me, my decision to release that CD on our new label (along with Jeff Bridges's album) was the beginning of the derailment of my relationship with my management team.

But the handwriting was on the wall before that. Around the time of my last Warners release, *Blink of an Eye*, I was asked by one of the folks at my management office how my latest album project was coming along. To his total surprise, I informed him that it had been released the week before. But thanks for asking.

The simple truth was that as much respect as I had—and still have to this day—for that team and their abilities, I just had to acknowledge that I wasn't very much on their radar anymore.

Around that time, I'd been hearing good things about a Nashville-based company called Vector Management who had an impressive roster of artists I greatly admired, including John Hiatt, Lyle Lovett, and Emmylou Harris. That Americana/singer-songwriter world—

where the priority was creative freedom and artistic growth, and the expectation wasn't necessarily to sell millions of records—seemed to be a more natural fit for me. So I made the leap and went with Joel Hoffner and Ken Levitan at Vector, with whom I remain to this day.

—

SOMETIMES, THIS LUCK—OR UNFORTUNATE *LACK* OF IT—WAS JUST A CASE OF BAD TIMING.

In 1991, my band and I worked up a solid arrangement of the Percy Sledge classic "When a Man Loves a Woman." We even had it recorded and in the can, ready to be mixed—but not before Michael Bolton put out his version and had a huge hit with it (and deservedly so, as it was a remarkable record).

Then on our next album, after cutting a more guitar-driven, traditional blues arrangement of Stevie Wonder's "Higher Ground," I thought, "This just might be our next shot at some radio play!"—a moment of excitement soon followed by a feeling of utter deflation as I watched the Red Hot Chili Peppers' new video of the song on MTV. They had beat any hope of our releasing it by maybe a month.

So when it was suggested I do an album of classic R&B songs, I felt like that train had already left the station. It just didn't seem like the fresh, clever idea anymore. It had been done. So in my infinite wisdom—or, once again, lack thereof—I dismissed the idea.

But as luck would have it, that door opened again.

While playing a gig in London—two nights at the legendary Royal Albert Hall—among our post-show guests were three execs from Universal Music UK who presented me with the idea of doing an album of Motown covers.

Universal UK at this point owned the Motown catalog and masters, and one of their initial ideas was to have me put my voice *over* the original instrumental tracks, which begged two immediate questions. The first was: Could I in all good conscience be part of a plot to take Marvin Gaye's voice off one of his classic recordings and replace it with my own? The easy answer to that one for me was a resounding "Fuck no!" That would be sacrilege. Those recordings are seminal artistic moments. It would be like rewriting the history of the American Revolution and inserting my name in place of, say, George Washington's.

The second was a two-part question that only the execs could answer: With all the remarkable, younger vocalists out there, why me? And then there's this: Out of respect to the Motown legacy, shouldn't it be a Black artist? Someone like D'Angelo, Brian McKnight, or even Prince? (Who, by the way, were all selling a hell of a lot more records than I was.)

But at the same time, part of me was thinking, "Take a breath. Think about it. You've been singing these songs as far back as the Castaway Club in Ferguson with the Sheratons." They had been a deep and intrinsic part of my musical history for over forty years. So maybe I *could* bring something unique to this project, simply based on the fact that these songs were wired into my musical DNA.

The more I thought about it, the more intrigued I was by the whole idea. But if I was to take on a project this daunting, with such a potential upside, I would also have to avoid the myriad potential pitfalls. The execs at Universal UK, thankfully, understood my reluctance to replace anyone's voice on the original Motown masters. With that hurdle behind me, I endeavored to make clear that I also didn't want the project to turn into some unnecessarily uber-trendy urban contemporary production. I could hear Don Was in my head: "Nobody's gonna cross the street to hear Michael McDonald do a hip-hop record."

I wanted to be respectful of the Jobete catalog (Motown's publishing arm) and its organic soulfulness, and yet I had always been intrigued by the atmospheric mojo that British musicians and producers later brought to those classic songs—covers like the Beatles' "You Really Got a Hold on Me" and, much later, Simply Red's version of "If You Don't Know Me by Now" and Paul Young's "Wherever I Lay My

Hat (That's My Home)" and "What Becomes of the Brokenhearted." I felt that there might be some common ground between those two worlds that I could reach, and Simon Climie was, I believed, exactly the right guy to produce such a project.

—

I HAD BEEN GREATLY IMPRESSED WITH ERIC CLAPTON'S ALBUM *PILGRIM*, PRODUCED BY Simon. Besides his impressive skill in that arena, Simon was also a successful musician and composer whose songs had been recorded by Aretha Franklin and George Michael, Smokey Robinson, and Pat Benatar, among others.

On Clapton's album, Simon was able to bring his ethereal production value while remaining true to the spirit of some of Eric's most soulful recorded performances and penchant for classic blues. I was confident that in his capable hands we could easily reimagine these Motown songs. (I also suspected that Simon's recent successes would immediately garner the respect and confidence of the label's execs, whereas I might have been a little more vulnerable in my position as an artist whose major successes were . . . let's just say not so recent.)

So I approached Simon with the idea, and thankfully he was interested—and available. We met for some preproduction discussions in LA, and then, in case getting to record some of the best music ever with a brilliant producer wasn't already an embarrassment of riches, I learned we'd be recording the album in Simon's home studio in the South of France.

I'd be hard-pressed to imagine a more idyllic setting. Just outside of Nice, looking out over the Mediterranean, the view from Simon's state-of-the-art studio included an eleventh-century medieval village peeking over steep stone walls tucked into the cliffs above the Riviera and a quaint fishing village down below called Villefranche-sur-Mer.

Summer was in full swing down on the strand of beach near the harbor and in the small plaza lined with bistros, shops, and the quaint, centuries-old apartments above them. I stayed in a small hotel right on the water, where a couple of mornings, just before dawn, I'd sit on my balcony and watch the village wake up. Hours before other shopkeepers opened their businesses, a local chef-restaurateur stood outside smoking a cigarette while waiting for a local fisherman to row his small boat up to the stone steps that led to the street, whereupon he'd choose that afternoon's seafood specialty du jour. I spent many a morning sitting outside a small café, half reading the paper, half watching the world go by.

Oh, yeah . . . I also worked on the album.

Selecting the songs to record was a challenging but joyful process. With a catalog as deep and significant as Motown's, how do you pick your favorite twelve songs? Or twenty? Or fifty? There's just so much gold there.

My personal inclination was to go for the more obscure choices: songs that people would surely remember but possibly hadn't heard in years. I've always loved when I hear an artist's cover of a hidden gem, that moment of delight in the recognition—"Oh, man, I can't believe they did that song. What a great call."

The folks at Universal UK, not surprisingly, wanted the more obvious choices: all the chart-topping songs—the ones you hear every day on oldies radio—like "I Heard It Through the Grapevine." They brought that one up at our very first meeting back in London: "We gotta have 'Grapevine'!" And if memory serves, my initial response was something to the effect of "Please don't make me fucking sing 'Grapevine'!" A brilliant song for sure, but so many people had already covered it—and really well. On top of that, it had only recently been used in not one but two TV commercials, including Buddy Miles's version as "lead singer" of the California Raisins. Surely people had heard that song enough already.

But I saw this as a lesser battle. I understood their point; they felt they needed a surefire, radio-friendly hit to help market the record. So I negotiated. "Okay, I'll do 'Grapevine,' but just so you know, I'm also gonna be picking some more obscure things." And so began the process. (Worth noting: "Grapevine" was by far the biggest hit single from the record, the track that actually got the whole momentum started. So to their credit, these guys—Tony Swain, Max Hole, and Iain Snodgrass—sometimes know exactly what they're doing.)

—

ONE SONG THAT I WAS DETERMINED TO COVER WAS "SINCE I LOST MY BABY," A SONG I'VE loved ever since that day Chuck Sabatino played it for me in the record department of E. J. Korvette. And while we were all committed to remaining respectful of the material and the legacy of Motown, there were some songs with which we took a bit more creative license with the arrangements.

Sometimes it was as simple as slowing it down. I love to sit at the piano and revisit songs I've loved over the years, to "look under the hood," as it were: breaking a song down to its simplest rendering, reharmonizing the chords or taking it outside its original rhythmic cadence, sometimes both, just to see what happens when you give the song a new place to "live." Much like what Ray Charles did when he tackled some of his favorite country and western songs. It's a testament to his sheer genius that he saw the untapped potential of songs that might've been unfairly regarded as simplistic, and he took them deeper harmonically and melodically, adding orchestration and creating something new and magically thoughtful, yielding a much deeper emotional resonance.

Tony Bennett too. If you listen to his rendition of "Fly Me to the Moon," where he pulls the tempo way back, it becomes this whole other beautiful, shimmering interpretation of a song you might have heard many times, but somehow feel like you're now truly hearing for the first time. Lyrics that you've heard for years at a typically brighter tempo can become more poignant somehow when they pass a little slower and your ear sits with them a bit longer.

"Since I Lost My Baby" always struck me as one of those songs that might have more to reveal if the production was peeled back a bit. It certainly worked brilliantly in the Temptations' original upbeat version, with its lush strings and infectious, rock-solid groove. But at a slower tempo, suddenly lyrics like "Next time I'll be kinder / Won't you please help me find her" take on a whole new level of emotion. So that one we recorded at a slower tempo, a more intimate version—just myself on piano and Toby Baker on bass—recorded live in Simon's living room.*

One drawback to recording in someone's living room: Simon's house cleaner, who spoke no English, was there that day. And despite our best efforts, we were unsuccessful in explaining to her that we were actually trying to record; she thought I was just playing piano for my own amusement. And Toby was no help because the World Cup finals were on, and as a fanatical British football fan, his focus was pulled as he kept creeping closer to the muted television, ultimately playing bass on the couch across the room, while I stayed glued to the piano, trying to work around the remarkably dedicated housekeeper, who came up behind me in the middle of a take to clean the ashtray on the piano—that no one had used, by the way. In the spirit of still learning the nuances of the arrangement, undaunted, I kept playing till the end.

It wasn't till later that we would decide that was the best take overall, and that's the one on the album. So if you listen to that track

---

* The initial rhythm tracks for the Motown albums brilliantly sequenced by Toby, Nicky Shaw, and Pro Tools assistant Joel Everden were, frankly, strong enough to stand on their own, even before we brought in live musicians to overdub.

really carefully, you can actually hear the housekeeper setting the unnecessarily cleaned ashtray back down on the piano.

Though we spent most of our days in the studio, we never worked too hard; we didn't do any of that Big City, into-the-wee-wee-hours kind of thing. Our schedule was much more civilized: we worked every day for a solid nine, ten hours, after which we'd usually wind up back in Villefranche for dinner, always enjoying incredible food and great company. Friends of Simon's—artists, authors, actors, filmmakers, and musicians—who were, in a sense, "locals," even if only seasonally, would often join us, and it was on those evenings that I really felt like we were living *la belle vie*. Those few weeks were truly the experience of a lifetime.

—

UPON HEARING THE FINAL MIXES A FEW MONTHS LATER, I WAS BLOWN AWAY. SIMON AND engineer Mick Guzauski—and all the talented musicians, singers, and engineers involved—had, collectively, created something special, in my humble opinion. That moment for me felt like the culmination of an amazing adventure.

The album, simply called *Motown*, was released in the summer of 2003 to kind-enough reviews and sold moderately well; it wasn't taking the world by storm, but it seemed to be finding an audience. I remember thinking that if we could just get enough buzz going, this record, with these songs, could capture the public's imagination on a larger scale.

Then as luck would have it, an East Coast ad agency thought our version of "Ain't No Mountain High Enough" would be a good soundtrack for a TV ad it was putting together for a large telecom company. Truth be told, I never really understood the connection. But not being one to question such things, all that mattered to me was that it wanted to use our version of the song.

So the agency's people came down to the Birchmere, a great venue in the DC area where we were performing, and shot footage of us doing "Ain't No Mountain High Enough."

Uncharacteristically—as this was not the kind of spontaneous, out-of-the-box thinking I'm known for—I suggested that it might be helpful for us if they identified the name of the album with some text at the bottom of the screen, if only at the end of the commercial. It was later explained to me that it's called a "chyron" and that probably neither the ad agency nor the client was likely to agree to that, as this was, after all, not an advertisement for my album. All I knew was that it was just something I'd always seen at the end of most music videos. So even though we had very little reason to expect they'd grant us this freebie, as the saying goes, "If you don't ask . . ."

Well, lo and behold, we got it. With some much-appreciated push from client rep Patty Proferis, the commercial aired with a chyron at the end that said, "From the album: *Motown*. Artist: Michael McDonald." Boom! In the first week of the ad airing, our sales went from a few hundred copies a week to several thousand a week. The god of alternative promotion was smiling down on us!

From sputtering along on fumes, all of a sudden we had a full tank of gas and were picking up speed.

CHAPTER 29

TAKIN' MOTOWN TO THE STREETS

What a joy to be performing these tunes live. Not that I didn't enjoy playing my own songs or the Doobie Brothers hits—I absolutely did. But there was something about this music . . .

First of all, these songs were so much *easier* to sing than my own compositions. Easier on the voice. The melodies were more "logical"; they seemed to be written for singers, written in a way where you could easily wrap your voice around the melody and phonics of the lyrics. They weren't *angular*, like a lot of my own songs that just weren't always comfortable melodies to sing. Getting down and really living with these classics, I couldn't help but notice they were just so much less stressful on my voice, even if they were every bit as high.

When we initially approached these Motown songs, in our effort to retain the energy of the original recordings, I had set out to sing them in their original keys. I felt almost superstitious about it; I didn't want anybody to go out and buy this record and think these songs were in any way less intense than the originals. However . . . the originals were generally sung by vocalists in their early twenties, which for me, then rounding the corner and heading toward sixty, made some songs more of a challenge than others.

Like "I'm Gonna Make You Love Me." That one almost killed me. There are ten-year-old Bavarian choirboys who don't sing as high as Eddie Kendricks of the Temptations; that chorus is practically in the stratosphere.

Now, it's not uncommon for singers, as they age, to lower the keys of certain songs—unless they're Ray Charles.

"You know, I'm seventy-three years old," he proudly told me once, "and I've never lowered the key of any of my songs."

And I remember thinking, "Man, I'm gonna shoot for that!"

But I also really didn't like that constant anxiety of going out onstage thinking, "Uh-oh . . . here comes that part of the song I'm dreading . . . Am I gonna hit that fucking note? Am I gonna blow it again?"

And then I had a conversation with Jerome Anthony Gourdine—aka Little Anthony of Little Anthony and the Imperials. We were doing a gig together, and before the show he casually said to me, "So, you're lowering the keys on some of those Doobies songs from back in the day, aren't you?"

I said, "No, I probably should, but I'm reluctant to do that. Ray Charles once told me that he—"

"Are you crazy, man?" Anthony couldn't believe it. And to be fair, I couldn't help but notice that Anthony still sounded as great as ever.

I said to him, "You're still hitting all the high stuff like a teenager!"

To which he replied, "Yeah—'cause I lowered the damn key! Man, people don't care what key you're singing in as long as you bring it!"

He convinced me to give it a try, and, no disrespect to the Right Reverend Ray Charles, Anthony's advice worked—for me. I actually found it to be a rejuvenating experience. Beyond just saving your voice, what can happen is you start a new relationship with the song, one that you enjoy a lot more. And if the end result is the audience hears you singing with renewed confidence and conviction, it's a win all the way. A half or whole step is no big deal; no one seems to notice. After the first few times I sing it, I don't even notice the difference, but my voice thanks me every night from then on.

—

AND JUST AS THESE MOTOWN SONGS WERE EASIER TO SING (THAT MELODIC "LOGIC"), there was also something magical and intangible about *performing* them to a live audience. I especially remember two Ashford and Simpson songs we did as a medley that brought the audience to their feet every night. Maybe it's because these songs were already such an integral part of people's life experience, bona fide American music DNA, with such a deep well of familiarity and affection, that I somehow didn't have to push as hard to make the connection. These tunes almost sang themselves, along with the entire audience. I don't know; I never could quite put my finger on it. I only know that when I got to that part of the set, I could just feel my voice relax. It felt like I was home free.

As much as the band and I loved performing these songs live, though, there came a point where we felt that if we kept packing our sets with these classics, we ran the risk of becoming, in effect, a Motown cover band. So we started dropping them and putting back more and more of my original material, and I remember feeling kinda melancholy about that because I just loved doing those songs. Still do.

—

IN ADDITION TO THE EXTENSIVE TOURING I DID WITH THE BAND PROMOTING *MOTOWN* IN the States, I was asked by Universal to do a bit of a solo promotional tour through Europe and Japan, in the hope of parlaying some of our good fortune in the States into greater success in those overseas markets.

But the trip turned out to be a mixed bag of experiences: one wildly successful night at the sold-out Café Opera, a beautiful venue connected to the actual historic opera house in Stockholm, was followed—literally the next day—by a less than fortuitous experience in Milan, where a "friend of a friend" of the guy who was helping promote the record in Italy somehow arranged for me to perform at his friend's pastry/coffee shop. Not a renowned, legitimate venue with a quaint name, like the Café Opera, where I had just played the night before. No, this was an actual friggin' coffee shop and bakery—at four in the afternoon, no less—where the crowd numbered in the low single digits. And by that I mean *two*. That's right, there were two older women in attendance—and I use the term "attendance" loosely; I was as much a surprise to them as they were to me. These poor elderly women actually had to ask the waiter if he could have me stop playing so they could converse in peace and enjoy their macchiatos. (Once again: "That won't be necessary.")

Still, the most daunting performance of my entire career to date would come not too long after that, playing yet another solo gig—albeit in very different circumstances.

—

I HAD BEEN ASKED TO PERFORM AT A CHARITY EVENT AT THE HOME OF A RENOWNED music business attorney in Beverly Hills. I was happy to oblige and prepared a short set—four or five songs, which seems to be the appropriate length for gatherings like this, where the focus is generally not on the performer. Having just finished this album I was so proud of, I naturally built the set around some of my versions of these Motown classics I felt would go over well.

I couldn't tell you who for sure was there or if they enjoyed the performance. What I do know for a fact is that a couple of rows back, dead center, squarely in my line of vision, was none other than Berry Gordy. The man who created Motown! Like the tunnel vision that sets in when someone points a gun at your head and all you see is the end of that barrel, literally everything and everyone else in the room faded out of focus. All I could see was him. And while this may be just a representation of my paranoia at the time, he seemed to be giving me his undivided attention, leaning back in his chair with his arms crossed, looking at me blankly. I couldn't tell if the look was "Hey, man, nice job!" or "Oh no you didn't!" He had one of the greatest poker faces of all time. I'd have given anything to know what he thought, but I've learned over the years that sometimes it's best not to ask a question to which you may not want to hear the answer.

But it seems at least somebody must have liked what I was doing, though, because before too long, the album would go platinum and be nominated for a Grammy. I'd be lying if I said that didn't bring a certain sense of relief, like, "Wow, I'm still in the game." In between periodic successes in this business, you can tend to feel like you're frantically playing a one-armed bandit, wondering if you're putting more coins in than you're getting out. It's sure nice when the bells ring and the coins drop back into your bucket.

The *Motown* album even spawned two sequels, the last of which, *Soul Speak*, was a bit of a transition into a broader range of compositions. We moved beyond the Jobete catalog with songs like "Into the Mystic" and the classic "You Don't Know Me," which aren't R&B songs in the traditional sense, but earlier renditions by Van Morrison and Ray Charles were supreme examples of soulful expression. We even did a blues arrangement of Leonard Cohen's "Hallelujah," a far cry from the essence of Motown but, to my mind, one of the most honest love songs ever written.

Believe me: it wasn't for a lack of enticing Jobete options that we ventured into outside material; we probably could have made at least five more Motown retrospectives of nothing but chart-topping hit singles. That legacy of music is inexhaustible.

CHAPTER 30

THROUGH THE MANY WINTERS

It seems the longer two people are together, the more precious their shared history becomes, and Amy and I found ourselves reminiscing all the more often about California—the music and magic of the place we had both run away to as kids and where we first met. There was still enough wanderlust in both of us to want to return to that place, as if there were something there we might have left behind. So somewhere around 2010, with Dylan and Scarlett now grown and both living on their own, Amy and I decided it was time for us to say goodbye to Nashville and head back to Santa Barbara.

I have, for years, stuck religiously to my plan of having no plan and still managed to keep myself more than occupied, with nary a dull moment. While I can't say I've maintained the nonstop pace of those early Doobies tours, I have consistently hit the road with my own band, in all its many iterations. In fact, with the exception of the first few years after the birth of my son, I've never really been off the road, averaging about a hundred days a year.

But in these post-Doobie years, I've enjoyed the luxury of getting to say yes to some wonderful and varied opportunities that have presented themselves along the way.

I got to tour Japan with Christopher Cross.

After our initial "Ride Like the Wind" experience, Chris and I became good friends. (Our daughters have been "besties" for over twenty-five years.) Part of the reason I think Chris and I have remained friends all these years is our vastly different but ultimately compatible personalities: Chris likes to stick to the plan. I usually can't remember what the plan was in the first place. He's more of a type A personality, whereas I'm more the type *ehh, whatever* . . .

In Japan, we did a "co-bill" tour, performing with a combined band: Chris on guitar, myself on keys, along with the wonderfully talented keyboardist and vocalist Kiki Ebsen (daughter of actor Buddy Ebsen); drummer and vocalist Gigi Worth (daughter of early television comic and accomplished musician Gisele MacKenzie); and one of my favorite bassists, the great Charles Frichtel.

On our very first night, the difference in Chris's and my personalities was strikingly on display. We were performing in Fukuoka at the Blue Note, an intimate jazz / supper club venue, playing two shows back-to-back, with just a short dinner break in between. Things were already off to a questionable start when, after the early show, they sat us for dinner *in the showroom*, in full view of the early show's audience filing out and, on the other side of the room, the second audience already lining up against that wall, waiting to be seated.

As if this wasn't awkward enough, the club manager then approached us just as dinner was served and, pointing to the line of fans against the wall—their eight-by-ten photos, white autograph boards, Sharpies, and cameras in hand—asked if Christopher and I could take a few minutes to sign some autographs and take some pics with the nice paying customers.

Chris's instant and intractable position was "You must be kidding." And being much more confident (and far less codependent) than I, he explained to the gentleman very matter-of-factly that "no, we won't be doing that, as we only have a short break between shows, this is not part of our contractual obligations," etc.

In between Chris's increasingly emphatic protests, the manager deftly played the "not sure I understand" card, repeating, ever so politely, "Ah, could you, please?"—all the while persistently gesturing "right this way," as if our hesitation were merely a matter of us not knowing where to go.

Finally, with the guy clearly not taking no for an answer, Chris got up and left—just walked out!—going back to the hotel for a quiet meal before the next show.

So now the manager turned to me, slightly astonished, and asked, "He is coming back, right?" I responded, "Uh . . . probably not." And all the while, he's still gently trying to usher me to the line of eager fans (now several hundred people long), repeating, "Ah, please?" At this point, I figured it was easiest to forget dinner, just take some pictures, sign some autographs, and be done with it. So I motioned to the first person in line to step forward, and as the young woman approached, she inexplicably waved her hand over my midsection and asked, "May I?" Safe to say something was terribly lost in translation here, and I apparently shrugged and gave the very weakest, confused nod of consent.

Big mistake! I came to learn that in Japan it's considered good luck to rub the stomach of Buddha, and in the absence of an actual Buddha, apparently the nearest fat guy will do. So now this lady was giggling ecstatically while rubbing my stomach. The thrill she experienced was evident and obviously contagious, as everyone else in line was now clapping enthusiastically and making the same hand-rubbing gesture.

I spent the next forty minutes signing and posing for photos while each and every person in that line took their turn rubbing my stomach. All while Chris was back at the hotel enjoying a nice steak dinner.

I also got to tour with Donald Fagen and Walter Becker again as part of their New York Rock and Soul Revue, an informal and ever-changing ensemble of supremely talented players. It wasn't lost on me that I wouldn't have even been there in New York, in that moment, in the company of those wonderful friends and musicians, but for that random encounter at a wrap-party gig all those years ago, where I first met Jeff Porcaro. It was Jeff, after all, who opened that door to the world of Steely Dan for me.

Tragically, it was while rehearsing for that tour that we learned Jeff had died, a complete shock to all of us there. I couldn't help but reflect on how much my life had changed because of Jeff's kindness and on the close friendship we'd developed over the years. I will be forever indebted to Jeff.

A few years later, I was invited to join Donald and Boz Scaggs and a similarly assembled coalition of great musicians—this time dubbed the Dukes of September and still drawing heavily from the New York–based Steely Dan stable of players—for a very civilized (read: short) tour, playing a mix of Steely Dan, Scaggs, and McDonald originals, along with some obscure R&B, jazz, and Top Forty tunes—more or less indulging ourselves a bit by revisiting songs from our youth. I did a duet with Catherine Russell called "Don't Mess Up a Good Thing" (originally recorded by St. Louis native Fontella Bass and Bobby McClure). I hadn't performed that song since singing it with the Sheratons at the Castaway in Ferguson as a duet with Jodi Brumagin.

As much of a thrill as it is any time I get to play with Donald, I confess that still, after all these years, I tense up whenever he shoots me a sideways glance across the stage. We've been friends for fifty years, but no matter; if he looks over at me from the piano, I'm right back to being that twenty-year-old rookie who just joined Steely Dan, thinking, "I'm getting canned right after this gig! I know it!" Talk about your "Goodbye Look"!

A few years later, my band opened for Steely Dan at the New Orleans Jazz and Heritage Festival, and I got to join them on their set for a rendition of "Pretzel Logic." It was good to see Walter back onstage again; he had been on hiatus for about a year, recuperating from some health issues.

I never would have dreamed that would be the last time I'd see him, as he passed away shortly afterward. We had a brief but heartfelt conversation backstage before both bands went their separate ways. I was always taken by how in spite of his sardonic sense of humor and penchant for irreverence, he was truly a sweet and empathetic soul, and I look back on our friendship with great fondness.

There were also, over the years, those wonderful experiences of joining Quincy Jones in live performances, taking the stage with the great George Duke and Greg Phillinganes, and Patti Austin and James Ingram. One night, standing just offstage in the wings, I was literally brought to tears listening to James and Patti sing their iconic duets, "Baby, Come to Me" and "How Do You Keep the Music Playing?"

And then there was the magic of performing on the islands of Hawaii with my good friend, premier Hawaiian artist Henry Kapono. What a way to experience paradise.

My adventures in Hawaii led to conductor Matt Catingub, who had the idea to write some orchestrations of my music and have me perform with the Honolulu Symphony Orchestra. It was thrilling to hear these songs in a way I'd never heard them before, in that lush, harmonic atmosphere. It was such a wonderful experience, playing piano and singing in front of a full orchestra, and that led to subsequent performances with symphony orchestras around the country. (It was once again my assistant Lisa Patton Souther's extensive experience in dealing with conductors and symphony librarians that was so helpful in this new endeavor for me.)

—

I HAVE TO SAY: ONE OF THE UNFORESEEN BENEFITS OF HAVING BEEN AROUND AWHILE IS getting to work with artists who were not even born yet when I was first touring with Steely Dan and the Doobie Brothers. I've had my music sampled on several occasions by contemporary hip-hop artists like Warren G, who used our track of "I Keep Forgettin'" to underpin his 1994 release "Regulate" (featuring Nate Dogg), and by the electronic duo Chase & Status, who sampled "Yah Mo B There" for the track "Running." To be honest, I was at first a bit ambivalent about the idea, but these most inventive and now classic reimaginings went on to find their way to a whole new audience, and I certainly appreciated the rejuvenated interest they brought to our original record. (So much for the "Nobody's gonna cross the street to hear Michael McDonald do hip-hop" theory!)

I've been invited to perform and record with exciting new artists like Grizzly Bear, Holy Ghost!, Solange Knowles, and Jacob Collier, and, thanks to Kenny Loggins's initiative, we got to write and record with the amazing Stephen Bruner, aka Thundercat. Steve and I have written a couple songs together since then, and experiencing his genius took me in new directions as a writer. I was impressed at how—consciously or not—he seemed to draw from so many diverse musical traditions that manifested into something entirely original, and performing live with his band, a funky power trio, gave the songs yet another layer of muscle. The whole experience inspired a personal expansion of my overall perspective and reignited my desire to create.

—

WHILE I AM SURELY GRATEFUL TO STILL BE DOING WHAT I'VE LOVED DOING SINCE I WAS A teenager, I can't say *all* of it feels exactly the same.

In my more recent years, during a particularly busy performing schedule, I felt like I was perhaps punishing my voice a bit much and started to develop some problems, so I worked with a voice therapist (not a vocal coach), who gave me some therapeutic exercises to do before singing. Not the typical theatrical warm-up of scales and intervals, which I'm sure are great when your voice is in relatively good shape, but simple, more isolated lower-range exercises to do when the vocal cords are swollen or tight and my voice feels like it's waning. I found these to bring almost miraculous results.

One of the best exercises he taught me to do on just such occasions is to spend the afternoon before showtime finding the lowest note I can hold and pivoting back and forth from the half step above continuously until they become as clear as I can make them. It's meant to relax the vocal cords and give your voice a better physical foundation. What I used to do before that was start my warm-up (if I even did one) trying to see how *high* I could go, to "see what I've got for tonight"—which is actually the worst thing you can do, especially early in the day. I find it's much more helpful to not worry about the high notes at all and instead just go down to "the basement" and keep pivoting on those two lowest notes. I soon realized that by relaxing my voice in this way, it actually opened my upper range come showtime.

Another realization for me was when I was having the most consistent trouble with my voice; it turned out the culprit was actually acid reflux, which I came to learn wreaks havoc on the vocal cords. Who knew?

Even in putting together a set list for a show, I've learned to consider the demands on my voice; I try to take the songs that are easier for me to sing and fit them where I think I'm gonna need them, where I think I'll need a bit of a break. I may even try to start the show with a ballad or a song that allows me to ramp up a little slower; I don't want to hit anything too hard right up top and end up "limping" for the rest of the show. And though that adjustment was done to preserve my voice, the resulting song sequence surprisingly often made for an even better show aesthetically.

And while I've confessed to occasionally lowering the key on a song here and there and enjoying the reduced strain on my voice, what I hadn't anticipated was the terror of having to transpose to a new key on the piano. Having learned to play mostly by ear, transposing was uncharted territory for me. The difference between playing something in the key of C or G and then suddenly playing it in, say, A-flat, with all these new black keys in there and different finger spacings, is enough to produce a mild panic. It's a steep learning curve to get comfortable enough to play in a new key—while singing. (There is, however, an auto-transpose button on most electronic keyboards, a godsend in a pinch, if you're sitting in with a band and someone suddenly calls an audible "Hey, 'Knock on Wood' in F-sharp!" Especially if you're expected to play a solo, you might want to hit that button.)

But transposing songs to a different key also offers a bit of a growth opportunity: I know if I can get comfortable with it, my hands inevitably discover some new embellishments and riffs that are more natural to this new key.

That's an interesting part of the evolution of most musicians: over the years, highly developed physical agility and lightning-fast articulation often give way to more thoughtful invention. Think of Miles Davis. The trumpet is such a physical instrument; even if you're in good shape, your lips will likely not hold up forever. But as Miles got older, melodies that he might have embellished or elaborated on more in his younger years gave way to that less-is-more approach that was a hallmark of his later career. It becomes more about what you *don't* play.

Or Sinatra. When his voice was no longer as agile, he still retained that signature Sinatra phrasing, though in a more thoughtful application, improvising within a narrowing range, that was every bit as magical as what he produced in his earlier years.

Then there are iconic singers like Willie Nelson and Dean Martin, whose success had less to do with the tone and purity of their "instrument" and everything to do with their unique style; so casual and seemingly effortless, they often seemed to almost skate over what you think the melody is and manage to make it their own. That was one of Ray Charles's great gifts too: his melodic innovation and phrasing were so iconically imaginative and musical. Whatever he did more than made up for whatever he *didn't* do.

I think most vocalists develop their style around their limitations as much as their strengths. We all do the best we can with what we have to work with. For me, I've always been kind of short-winded. It's just a physical limitation I've learned to accept. (I'm sure that smoking in my youth didn't help.) I've had friends ask me to sing "Ave Maria" at a church service or family event, and I've always been a little uncomfortable explaining to them that I can't sing "Ave Maria." I don't have that kind of breath capacity. There are passages in the melody that don't sound right unless you sing them in one breath. Believe me, I've tried.

That limitation has also caused me to miss out on some potentially wonderful opportunities. I was asked to do the background vocals on "Dr. Wu" by Steely Dan. Donald Fagen had it in mind that the first two lines of the chorus—"Are you with me Dr. Wu / Are you really just a shadow of the man that I once knew"—should be sung in one breath. It didn't feel right to him to take the breath in the middle. To my disappointment, I was forced to admit the parameters of my ability. So the job went to someone healthier.

On occasion, for a TV appearance or a video, I've had to lip-synch to my original recording, and while I used to be pretty good at it, I've found that particular skill to be a thing of the past—because I no longer sing any song the same way twice. Therefore I have no idea how I sang it on the record or, for that matter, how I sang it last night.

That's another big piece of the puzzle: memory. In any given performance these days, I would say that easily two or three times a night I have that jolt of panic that I'm about to forget the words I'm supposed to sing in the next ten seconds. It's one thing if it happens in the middle of the show; you can kind of hide it there. But that first song? Especially when we ease into the show by opening with a ballad. It's harder to cover that up. Walking onstage, heading to the piano, turning to the band and stage-whispering in panic, "Psst! What's that first verse? Just gimme the first few words!"—those are not my favorite moments.

And while it's been pointed out to me that I generally have my eyes shut while singing, it's not because I'm praying to remember the lyrics. I suppose I do it for the same reason you close your eyes when you kiss someone. Singing is such an intimate act, and like kissing, it does no real good to see what the other person is doing. (Plus, I just know if I ever do open my eyes, the first thing I'm probably gonna see is that guy in the front row checking his phone, bored out of his mind. I'd just rather not know.) At any rate, it allows me to be more enmeshed with the song, more present in the moment. Before I start singing any tune, the exercise for me is to surrender to the feeling of a blank slate.

Of course one remedy for those aforementioned memory lapses is to simply use a teleprompter, but I've made it a point—at least so far—to not go there, because I've noticed that people who use one end up actually forgetting the words altogether. As long as they have the teleprompter, they're fine. But the minute you take it away or it malfunctions, whatever fragments of lyrics that might have been locked away in memory have now vanished completely. It can become a crutch that cripples.

I'm the same with charts. Once I make a chord chart, I'm done for, even if it's a song I've played a million times. It's as if the very introduction of a support system causes the brain to surrender authority completely. I find I'm much better off committing it to memory—as unreliable as it may sometimes be.

—

NOT TOO LONG AGO, I TOOK PART IN AN EVENT HONORING ELTON JOHN, WHERE I GOT TO sing "Take Me to the Pilot"—only the second time I ever performed the song, the first one being that demo I made for RCA back in 1970. Playing it this time with Elton's band, I was now, sweet irony, backed up by Davey Johnstone and Nigel Olsson, the very guys I heard originally playing on that cassette submitted by his publisher.

In the show that evening, a good portion of the performers were young millennials—bands and solo artists who sang with the house band of top-notch LA professionals. All the performances were respectable enough, though it was telling how some of the artists, even supported by the illustrious house band, seemed a bit out of their comfort zone without the enhanced audio production they were used to performing with.

Then Randy Newman came to bat, armed only with an acoustic piano and his "ten tiny assistants" (as he refers to his fingers), and he knocked it out of the park! He left the stage to a standing ovation from an enraptured audience.

There's something undeniably powerful about seeing an artist—and certainly someone of Randy's stature—perform solo. Over the years, I've witnessed other artists do the same—Karla Bonoff, Janis Ian, Jackson Browne, David Crosby, Joni Mitchell, and Bruce Springsteen—and I've been inspired not only by their incredible body of work but also by their amazing ability to perform their songs live, reinterpreting them unencumbered by any production value or extraneous instrumentation, and by their courage to trust the songs' ability to stand on their own merit.

It's a very bold act to perform solo. You can feel incredibly vulnerable out there alone, but at the same time, you enjoy an intimacy with the audience that can't be replicated any other way. You're giving them something special: a rare look into the essence of your songs, perhaps a glimpse of how the song was first conceived. Performing solo, you can surprise the audience here and there with an unexpected song choice or a new interpretation of a well-worn favorite.

Somewhere along the way, I made a promise to myself that I would someday take that plunge and take the stage alone, and I finally made good on that promise in 2019, booking a two-week stint at the Carlyle hotel in Manhattan, with its legendary café/lounge, Café Carlyle (opened in 1930 with Richard Rodgers), which has been home to Bobby Short, Eartha Kitt, and countless other iconic performers. It's a really intimate room with a maximum capacity of about eighty people. It felt like the uptown, dressed-up version of the saloons I saw my father sing in when I was a kid.

Perhaps hedging my bet just a bit, I asked jazz guitar great and New York bon vivant John Pizzarelli to join me for the gig. While that was, for sure, one body more than playing alone, I felt it was a big step closer to one day doing a totally legit solo performance.

—

WHEN YOU TAKE THE STAGE WITHOUT YOUR USUAL SUPPORT SYSTEM, THE AUDIENCE seems much more willing to take whatever journey you propose, with no real preexisting notion of what that will be. The setting allows you to explore a more sparse arrangement of the song. Reimagining the harmonic detail and rhythmic movement while accompanying yourself solo can be daunting at first; it has to be a bit more thoughtful. And what you're playing, in turn, can push you to change up what you're singing in a way that you probably wouldn't have thought of if you had other instruments in the mix.

On top of that, with a veteran like John there with me, I learned how to pace this kind of intimate engagement over the course of an evening. We made sure to include some of the staples that the audience might expect—"It Keeps You Runnin'" and "You Belong to Me"—and some more obscure tunes of mine, like "Matters of the Heart," albeit all of them pared down for the occasion. But the unique nature of the historic room also felt like the perfect invitation to dive into some songs I've loved since I was a kid but never had an opportunity to perform in public, like Nancy Wilson's "(You Don't Know) How Glad I Am," the hauntingly beautiful "Some Enchanted Evening" from Rodgers and Hammerstein's *South Pacific*, and another timeless song from the same musical, "This Nearly Was Mine"—which John played as an instrumental as a personal favor to me. I had heard John's dad, Bucky Pizzarelli, perform the song in that very room a couple years earlier, and John's mesmerizing solo performance was a beautiful tribute to his dad and a highlight of the evening.

Other highlights were having Amy, Dylan, and Peyton Parker join me to sing backup vocals on a few songs and Dylan's guest performance of the Kinks' "Sunny Afternoon" . . . Well, so much for taking the stage alone. But a great family week in New York.

Then, thanks to the pandemic, I finally did get to perform completely alone—albeit more out of necessity than anything else. During the lockdown of 2020, when there were no live gigs to be had, my daughter, Scarlett, recorded me at home doing a few random songs, which she put up on Instagram, and she also filmed my contribution to the *Tiny Desk* series on NPR (for which I'm proud to say I made the poster board backdrop myself with Magic Marker!).

We upped our game a bit as we continued to do a handful of live stream events. No audience. Just me at a keyboard or playing guitar (and even a bit of ukulele) in my buddy Dom Camardella's Santa Barbara Sound Design studio. Alone but for a camera/audio crew and Dom in the booth, we did our best to cope with the new norm. Not surprisingly, I really missed the presence of an actual audience. Live streaming, at least the way I experienced it, was really neither fish nor fowl; it's less gratifying than playing alone in a room for my own amusement, and certainly less fun than performing for people you can actually see and hear. I mean, I knew there were (reportedly) thousands of people watching in the comfort of their own homes, which was nice, but . . . when you can't feel the audience's enthusiasm, when you can't register what you're putting out and there's nothing bouncing back from them to you . . . it just ain't the same. Finishing a song—especially a normally rousing one like "Takin' It to the Streets" with a big finish—only to hear crickets . . . Well, it's just weird. I half expected some old landlord or neighbor to bang on the wall and yell at me to "knock it off!"

—

MY NORMAL ANNUAL TOURING SCHEDULE HAS ALSO BEEN PEPPERED WITH THE OCCAsional corporate gig, which are wonderfully lucrative but often memorable for the wrong reasons. Like the post–Super Bowl party where the team that hired us lost. So, like, six people showed up—and they were so depressed, they just came for the free booze, drank themselves into a stupor, and left.

Or the birthday party for a royal family member (of a country to *not* be named later). This was not your typical let's-have-a-cake-and-blow-out-some-candles birthday party. For starters, the swank hotel it was in was owned by the family, and the floral arrangements alone, I was told, cost over $2,000,000 (that's two *million*). James Ingram and I were part of the entertainment that evening, and after we did our set we started for the exit, only to be confronted at the door by a seriously buff security dude, more than likely armed, who politely instructed us to return to our table, as the birthday girl hadn't sung yet. It was her party, after all, and she and her personal band had a few tunes to share with everyone in attendance—and apparently that meant *everyone.* So we dutifully rejoined the festivities and sat there into the wee hours of the morning.

And lest you think it's only heat-packing security guards or all-but-empty Super Bowl parties that make for a memorable evening, let me share with you the occasion of Aunt Margaret's ninetieth birthday bash.

Margaret O'Brien wasn't technically my aunt, but she was one of my mom's best friends for fifty years and a dear part of our family, universally loved and admired. So for her ninetieth birthday, we loaded up a chartered bus and drove to a small Irish pub in downtown St. Louis for the big party.

Her son Jack had asked if I'd sing "Danny Boy" as a special treat for his mother, as she'd always loved hearing my dad sing it back when she, her late husband, Eugene, and my folks were all young. So after I did a quick bit of mingling and catching up with Margaret and some of her now grown kids, Jack let out an ear-piercing whistle and told everyone present to shut up. "Hey! Mike's come all this way to sing a special song for my mom!"

I wasted no time sitting at the piano and dedicating "Danny Boy" to Margaret, taking the opportunity to share with the packed crowd of friends and loved ones memories some of us shared of my dad singing the song, of our families' bond over the years, how grateful we were to be there to celebrate this wonderful occasion . . .

I started the song, and Margaret was already crying. Jack was standing by the piano, trying his best not to cry, feeling very proud of himself as he took in his mom's reaction; after all, it was *his* plan to surprise her with the song, and he was relishing this moment.

I barely sang the first couple lines before a woman at the bar started singing her heart out along with me—loudly, I might add. Not that it's unusual for the Irish to sing along on a song like "Danny Boy," but she kind of made it clear that she'd like to take it from there.

At which point Jack yelled across the room, "*Hey, Theresa—shut the fuck up!*"

As this was not my first time playing a bar when shit goes down, I did what one usually does in those situations: I just kept playing. Meanwhile, a vicious verbal brawl had now erupted between Jack and the other side of the room—Theresa and her cronies who'd come to her defense.

"Fuck you, Jack!"

"Yeah, ya prick! Let her sing!"

"It's none of your business!"

"Hey, the man's trying to sing to my mom, so just shut the fuck up for Chrissakes!"

All the while, me at the piano, doing my best to retain a tender rendering of "But come ye back when summer's in the meadow . . ."

CHAPTER 31

DOOBIE CONTINUED

Beyond the various one-off tours, random festivals, corporate gigs, and occasional family birthday parties that manage to continually fill my dance card, there are, of course, the frequent—and often unpredictable—welcomed reunions with my Brothers Doobie.

After that quickly abandoned attempt in '82 to see if there was still a viable way forward without Pat in the band, for all intents and purposes, the Doobies had called it quits, as far as I knew.

But in 1987, Doobies drummer Keith Knudsen, with the help of agents and Doobies management at the time, organized a reunion show of sorts at the Hollywood Bowl, a benefit for the National Veterans Foundation, an organization spearheaded by Keith's friend Shad Meshad, a veteran himself. The organization aimed to raise awareness of PTSD issues for Vietnam vets, establishing hotlines and discussion groups, as there weren't, at the time, many resources available for these vets, who were dealing with an epidemic of drug addiction and suicide. Keith jumped in to help, and the rest of us were happy to be a part of it. The Doobie Brothers seemed like a good fit for that event, as so many of the band's early hits were staples on Armed Forces Radio in the early '70s and were literally part of the soundtrack of these veterans' Vietnam experience.

It was that night and the warm sense of camaraderie—onstage and with the audience—that inspired the original guys to re-form, albeit with a new lineup. The Doobie Brothers were back, and they took off on a whole new trajectory that soon found them at the top of their game—with Tom back in the fold, Pat, Keith, John McFee,

Cornelius Bumpus, Tiran Porter, Bobby LaKind, and original drummer Michael Hossack—all performing, writing, and recording stronger than ever.

While I myself hadn't yet returned as a regular member of the band, I did join them for a number of special events after 1987, and I always looked forward to such gigs, if only to bring me back into the company of my old friends. Though I have to admit: with little or no rehearsal for those occasions, after a while I started to feel like some drunk who just wandered onstage, struggling to keep up with the newer revised and somewhat more complex live arrangements.

Over time, I've come to realize that my ties to the band go deeper on a personal level. I've always loved playing the Doobie Brothers songbook as a member of the band, Pat and Tom's songs every bit as much as my own. However, there was a realization that crystallized for me one day in what felt like a spiritual awakening of sorts.

We were performing at a beautiful outdoor venue in Oregon overlooking the Columbia River Gorge, right where it begins to flow into the Pacific Ocean. Majestic cliffs and mountains, magnificent expanses of towering green trees, stunning rapids, dazzling clear open sky as far as the eye could see.

And there, in the midst of this beauty, in the middle of our concert, I suddenly felt a deep sense of serenity and gratitude for every blessing in my life at that point: my kids, my beautiful wife . . . just getting the chance to make music my livelihood. Grateful to be back with these guys, this traveling brotherhood of musicians and technicians. After all we'd been through—the ups and downs of this incredible journey, the comings and goings, the separations and reunions, the endless days and nights of touring, the bloodbath recording sessions . . . all the bullshit—all of it felt, in that moment, entirely worth it. I thought, "If nothing else ever happens in my life that feels as good as this moment, this will be enough."

I was startled out of my reverie when I noticed our stage manager pointing and laughing. A bit rattled, I turned to see what he was pointing at: a beautiful and very large monarch butterfly had perched itself on my shoulder. With all of the great outdoors surrounding us and an infinite number of natural landing spots to choose from, this butterfly chose . . . me. And it seemed to be waiting for me to notice too, because no sooner had I seen it than it flew away.

As I watched it take flight against the breeze, lilting through the last rays of sunlight in surreal slow motion, it seemed to me to be a sign—some kind of otherworldly visitation—from someone who knew me well. Like . . . my father.

Which kinda made sense, because it had been only a few months since he had passed, so he had, naturally, been on my mind. And then there's the fact that he was with me for the very first gig I did with these guys, in that circular sports arena in Shreveport. So in that instant, it seemed perfectly reasonable that this butterfly was my father saying, "Hey, Mike—pay attention. This is one of those simple moments that will be important in the end. Take it all in."

I chose to overlook the fact that this didn't sound like him. My dad was not a be-here-now-in-the-moment kind of guy. He was the restless one-foot-out-the-door guy. So the idea that now, in the afterlife, he'd return with this sage wisdom—as a butterfly, no less—was a bit of a stretch. But still, in that moment, in the most wonderful way, it made perfect sense, and has stayed with me ever since.

The Doobie Brothers have become such a continuum in my life, now spanning the better part of five decades and overlapping every facet of my career. Not long ago, the band was inducted into the Rock & Roll Hall of Fame, and as I write this, we are in the third year of our Fiftieth Anniversary Tour—and I was grateful for the chance to have some concentrated rehearsal time and hopefully better integrate with the band. In many ways, this has been just as exciting as when they first invited me to fly down to New Orleans and join them all those years ago. And I have to admit, I'm as surprised as anyone at how smooth it's been. Like riding a bike. Other than a few newer songs I'd never played before, the drill and interaction were as if we'd picked right up where we left off, as though we'd never stopped.

In many ways our friendships have grown over the years, even in times when some of us were no longer active participants in the band. Our families are connected; our kids have known one another since they were little. Pat and I spent a lot of years on the island of Maui as neighbors and performed there together for a number of local events, raising funds for island schools and food banks. As for the band, it's not lost on any of us how fortunate we are to still be playing together—in arena-size venues!—to audiences who return faithfully year after year to hear the band play. We talk about it often. And if for some reason it all stopped tomorrow, I know these deeply rooted friendships would still remain.

CHAPTER 32

HOW DO WE LAND THIS THING?

And just as I couldn't have foreseen the beginning, middle, or, for that matter, any part of this journey to date, I certainly wouldn't hazard a guess as to how it ends.

Sometimes I wake up from naps on the road to a slight feeling of panic till I can figure out where the hell I am. I hardly thought that at seventy-two I'd still be in a bunk on a tour bus, bouncing down the road to the next musical whistle-stop.

Once in a while, I'll hear someone talk about retiring, and I'll think, "Well, that sounds pretty good. I could try that." But then I'll hear some music or see someone perform, living for that moment of creative pursuit, and it inspires me all over again.

Over the years, whenever my band played New Orleans, Chuck Sabatino and I would go down to Bourbon Street to a small club to hear the Gary Brown Band. Gary played tenor sax much in the style of Junior Walker, and the band was funky—they probably had one of the funkiest versions of the Stones' "Miss You" I've ever heard. These guys were joyous and grateful for this gig that lasted from eight o'clock at night till two a.m., six nights a week—despite the fact that they all had day jobs that started only hours later the next morning. They played every song like it might be the last chance they got.

One night we were invited to sit in with the band, and we got wonderfully lost in the moment. Just the ambience of the club—the sounds of lively conversation, laughter, and cash registers; the smells of perfume and beer-soaked carpets; the sight of folks embracing for all they're worth, those precious few hours of escape from the grind—it seemed to create a rush of nostalgia for the two of us, shooting us right back to our teenage years playing the clubs in St. Louis for the sheer joy of it.

—

BEING REMINDED OF THAT SIMPLE BLISS, I CAN EASILY FEEL GUILTY FOR MY OCCASIONAL complaints or whining about my career. Hopefully, somewhere in that wide swath between immense gratitude and vain complacency, supreme confidence and serious self-doubt, I'll find that middle ground and still encounter some good ol' manic creativity.

It's comforting to know, though, that people much more talented than I suffer from similar bouts of self-doubt. I remember sitting on the steps in front of Warner Bros. Records thirty years ago talking with Randy Newman about all the distractions that come with any success in the record business. Not the wine-and-women type of distractions, but the accountants, managers, taxes, and mortgages—that new level of grown-up responsibility. *That* type of distraction.

Our younger selves were focused entirely on making music and how to get better at it, which alone can take up a large part of anyone's concentration. So while we were blithely ignoring the world around us and the business of it all in those early days, what money we made was easy to keep track of because there wasn't much of it.

Randy's take on all that was: "Now we're just like sitting ducks! We don't know about that stuff, and what's worse, we still don't care about any of that! I have no idea how much money I have or make. And if my accountant turns out to be a crook, well . . ."

That's really how most musicians are: we're only concerned about the next gig.

However, it was another concern Randy shared in that conversation that has really stayed with me.

"I just don't wanna be that guy who should have quit ten years ago," he said. "I really don't want to be onstage with people in their seats watching me and thinking, 'Aw, jeez . . . this is unfortunate.'"

Certainly a fear many of us have felt. But for most of us, deciding on the time to let go of the very passion that somehow made your life go by in a flash, and a lifestyle that defined you for so many years, is much more easily said than done.

In recent years I wrote a song called "Hail Mary," which, though set in the context of a relationship between a man and a woman, for me personally has a more subliminal significance, dealing with the very thing Randy was talking about: When do you give it up? When is it time to walk away? Or is this in fact the very moment to make that last stab at it, that final Hail Mary?

—

THE TROUBLE WITH TIME IS THERE'S ONLY SO MUCH RENEGOTIATING YOU CAN DO. I FIND it entirely inconceivable that I'm actually this age, but here I am. There was a time I would have considered it extremely old. My dad, after all, passed away just shy of seventy, and my mom didn't quite make it to eighty.

There's no denying that at this juncture, there's more road behind me than still ahead of me, and I certainly do find myself looking back more often than I used to, trying to connect all the dots and make some sense of this wild ride I've had. But in all that contemplation, I'm at least relieved to realize that for the better part of my life, I've never really questioned the path I took, my choice of career.

For sure, I would've done well to pay more attention to the business side of things, and I could have made some better choices here and there . . . But hell—just to have beaten the odds that worried my dad so much and been given the chance to make a livelihood from playing music . . . I'd be a fool not to count my blessings.

Above all else, what I've come to view as my greatest success has been my kids, witnessing their growth into kindhearted, empathetic adults. Dylan has pursued his own musical path, having already released three albums of original compositions, and his music conveys that same character, courage, and honesty that I've admired in him since he was a little guy.

Scarlett has become a wonderful photographer and multi-talented artist and production coordinator, whose work consistently reflects her personality, viewing the world through that lens of compassion and love that has always been her essence. I take comfort in my true belief that both my children make the world a better place.

—

WHEN I LOOK BACK TODAY, SOMETIMES MY LIFE SEEMS TO BE THE RESULT OF A MILLION random events—good and bad. But I've come to see them all as pieces of the puzzle that ultimately is my story. Some pieces are smooth-edged moments of well-intentioned—if not always successful—efforts that are easy enough for me to claim, while other pieces are jagged and hard for me to even admit to myself, pieces that have taken me years to come to terms with—much less recognize how they also fit. Those dark secrets, some of which I'm still wrestling with, represent a person that I was, but hopefully not who I am today.

I've come to understand that those pieces all had to fall exactly as they did for me to be exactly where I am at this moment, and that I'd likely never have gotten here any other way. I've discovered that it's not necessarily life's biggest achievements that most directly impact who we become, but rather the smaller, seemingly insignificant—yet vivid—memories that often conceal their importance.

Not long ago, while walking in downtown San Francisco, I spotted a totally restored art deco period streetcar—exactly like the one my dad operated. With an overwhelming impulse, I grabbed my buddy and convinced him to run with me to catch it there at the bottom of Market Street.

We broke a pretty good sweat from that short sprint on that uncharacteristically muggy day for the Bay Area, and as we boarded, it was like stepping back in time. We found two seats in roughly the same part of the coach where I sat as a kid over sixty years ago on that Number 40 crosstown streetcar with my dad. Every detail of the interior was exactly the same, down to the small vintage electric fan oscillating over the driver's head. Observing the little fan's futile effort to give any relief from the stifling midday heat, my buddy asked, "Is that actually supposed to be doing something?"

I couldn't help but smile as my dad's words came back to me, as if they suddenly held some greater meaning. Perhaps all these years I'd misunderstood his need to be in perpetual motion. Maybe it *wasn't* about running away so much as anticipating what lies ahead. His personal secret to happiness.

And so it was in that moment, with total confidence, that I assured my friend, "Just wait till we get rolling. The breeze will feel really good."

MICHAEL McDONALD DISCOGRAPHY

Albums		
Title	**Performed by**	**Release Date**
Katy Lied	Steely Dan	1975
The Royal Scam	Steely Dan	1976
Takin' It to the Streets	Doobie Brothers	1976
Aja	Steely Dan	1977
Livin' on the Fault Line	Doobie Brothers	1977
Minute by Minute	Doobie Brothers	1978
One Step Closer	Doobie Brothers	1980
If That's What It Takes	Michael McDonald	1982
That Was Then, the Early Recordings of Michael McDonald	Michael McDonald	1982
No Lookin' Back	Michael McDonald	1985
Sweet Freedom	Michael McDonald	1986
Take It to Heart	Michael McDonald	1990
New York Rock and Soul Revue / *Live at the Beacon*	Michael McDonald	1991
Blink of an Eye	Michael McDonald	1993
Blue Obsession	Michael McDonald	1997
The Voice of Michael McDonald	Michael McDonald	2000
The Very Best of Michael McDonald	Michael McDonald	2001
In the Spirit: A Christmas Album	Michael McDonald	2001
A Gathering of Friends	Michael McDonald	2001
Motown	Michael McDonald	2003
Soundstage: A Tribute to Motown	Michael McDonald and Toni Braxton, Billy Preston, India.Arie, and Take 6	2003
Motown Two	Michael McDonald	2004
Soundstage Presents Michael McDonald Live in Concert	Michael McDonald	2004
The Best of Michael McDonald: The Christmas Collection	Michael McDonald	2005
The Ultimate Collection: Michael McDonald	Michael McDonald	2005
Through the Many Winters	Michael McDonald	2005

Soundstage: Michael McDonald and the Doobie Brothers	Michael McDonald and the Doobie Brothers	2008
Soul Speak	Michael McDonald	2008
This Christmas	Michael McDonald	2009
Southbound	Doobie Brothers	2014
Wide Open	Michael McDonald	2017
Live on Soundstage	Michael McDonald	2017
Season of Peace–The Christmas Collection	Michael McDonald	2018

Singles

Title	Performed by	Release Date
"(There's) Always Something There to Remind Me"	Delrays	1968
"God Knows"	Mike McDonald	1971
"Dear Me"	Mike McDonald	1972
"Where Do I Go from Here"	Mike McDonald	1972
"Bad Sneakers"	Steely Dan	1975
"Black Friday"	Steely Dan	1975
"Kid Charlemagne"	Steely Dan	1976
"Takin' It to the Streets"	Doobie Brothers	1976
"It Keeps You Runnin'"	Doobie Brothers	1976
"Peg"	Steely Dan	1977
"Little Darling (I Need You)"	Doobie Brothers	1977
"Nothin' but a Heartache"	Doobie Brothers	1977
"Minute by Minute"	Doobie Brothers	1978
"What a Fool Believes"	Doobie Brothers	1978
"Dependin' On You"	Doobie Brothers	1979
"Real Love"	Doobie Brothers	1980
"I Keep Forgettin' (Every Time You're Near)"	Michael McDonald	1982
"I Gotta Try"	Michael McDonald	1982
"Yah Mo B There"	Michael McDonald and James Ingram	1983
"No Lookin' Back"	Michael McDonald	1985
"Bad Times"	Michael McDonald	1985
"Lost in the Parade"	Michael McDonald	1985
"Sweet Freedom" (*Running Scared* soundtrack)	Michael McDonald	1985
"On My Own"	Patti LaBelle and Michael McDonald	1986

"Our Love" (*No Mercy* soundtrack)	Michael McDonald	1987
"Take It to Heart"	Michael McDonald	1990
"Tear It Up"	Michael McDonald	1990
"All We Got"	Michael McDonald	1990
"I Stand for You"	Michael McDonald	1993
"Hey Girl"	Michael McDonald	1993
"Matters of the Heart"	Michael McDonald	1994
"No Love to Be Found"	Michael McDonald and Wendy Moten	2000
"I Heard It Through the Grapevine"	Michael McDonald	2003
"Ain't No Mountain High Enough"	Michael McDonald	2004
"Reach Out, I'll Be There"	Michael McDonald	2005
"Baby, I Need Your Lovin'"	Michael McDonald	2005
"Stop, Look, Listen (To Your Heart)"	Michael McDonald	2005
"Deck the Halls" / "Jingle Bells"	Michael McDonald	2005
"Walk On By"	Michael McDonald	2008
"(Your Love Keeps Lifting Me) Higher and Higher"	Michael McDonald	2008
"Love TKO"	Michael McDonald	2008
"Enemy Within"	Michael McDonald	2008
"Have Yourself a Merry Little Christmas"	Michael McDonald	2009
"Dreams of the San Joaquin"	Michael McDonald and Willie Nelson	2021
"Until I Met You"	Michael McDonald	2021
"Tears to Come"	Michael McDonald	2022
"You Belong to Me"	Michael McDonald and Buika	2022
"Lahaina"	Doobie Brothers and friends: Mick Fleetwood, Jake Shimabukuro, and Henry Kapono	2023

Guest Appearances

Title	Performed by	Release Date
"One Love Stand"	Carly Simon, feat. Michael McDonald and Little Feat	1976
"It Keeps You Runnin'"	Carly Simon, feat. the Doobie Brothers	1976
"Red Streamliner"	Little Feat, feat. Michael McDonald and Patrick Simmons	1977
"Runaway"	Bonnie Raitt, feat. Michael McDonald	1977
"Sweet Forgiveness"	Bonnie Raitt, feat. Michael McDonald	1977
"It's the Falling in Love"	Carole Bayer Sager, feat. Michael McDonald	1978

"Fool for You"	Craig Fuller and Eric Kaz, feat. Michael McDonald	1978
"Minute by Minute"	Memphis Horns, feat. Michael McDonald	1978
"Pain of Love"	Rita Coolidge, feat. Michael McDonald	1979
"This Is It"	Kenny Loggins, feat. Michael McDonald	1979
"Ride Like the Wind"	Christopher Cross, feat. Michael McDonald	1979
"I've Got My Mind Made Up" (*Together?* soundtrack)	Michael McDonald, Jackie DeShannon, Burt Bacharach, and Jeremy Lubbock	1979
"Victim of Love"	Elton John, feat. Michael McDonald, Stephanie Spruill, Julia Waters, Patrick Simmons, and Maxine Waters	1979
"Coolsville"	Rickie Lee Jones, feat. Michael McDonald	1979
"You"	Max Gronenthal, feat. Michael McDonald	1979
"Pretty Girls"	Lisa Dal Bello, feat. Michael McDonald	1979
"Still in Love"	Lisa Dal Bello, feat. Michael McDonald	1979
"Lost Without Your Love"	Lisa Dal Bello, feat. Michael McDonald	1979
"Miracle Maker"	Lisa Dal Bello, feat. Michael McDonald	1979
"You're the One"	Randy Edelman, feat. Michael McDonald	1979
"Let Me Go, Love"	Nicolette Larson, feat. Michael McDonald	1979
"What's on Your Mind"	George Benson, feat. Michael McDonald	1980
"Send Me Somebody to Love"	Kathy Walker, feat. Michael McDonald	1980
"Heart to Heart"	Kenny Loggins, feat. Michael McDonald	1982
"Heart and Soul"	Bill Medley, feat. Michael McDonald	1982
"State of Independence"	Donna Summer, feat. Michael McDonald, Lionel Richie, Dionne Warwick, Dyan Cannon, Michael Jackson, Christopher Cross, Patti Austin, James Ingram, Kenny Loggins, Brenda Russell, Peggy Lipton, and Stevie Wonder	1982
"Old Wing Mouth"	Jimmy Webb and Kenny Loggins, feat. Michael McDonald	1982
"One of the Few"	Jimmy Webb and Kenny Loggins, feat. Michael McDonald	1982
"Why You Givin' Up"	Patrick Simmons, feat. Michael McDonald and Chris Thompson	1983
"Out in the Streets"	Patrick Simmons, feat. Michael McDonald	1983
"Have You Seen Her"	Patrick Simmons, feat. Michael McDonald and Chris Thompson	1983
"That's How You Start Over"	Diana Ross, feat. Michael McDonald	1983

"No Time for Talk"	Christopher Cross, feat. Michael McDonald	1983
"All Right"	Christopher Cross, feat. Michael McDonald	1983
"Good Friends"	Joni Mitchell and Michael McDonald	1985
"Endless Change"	Delta, feat. Michael McDonald	1985
"I Just Can't Let Go"	David Pack, feat. Michael McDonald and James Ingram	1985
"I'll Be Over You"	Toto, feat. Michael McDonald	1986
"Fool and His Money"	Wang Chung, feat. Michael McDonald	1986
"Love Has No Color"	The Winans, feat. Michael McDonald	1987
"Never Give Up"	Tim Weisberg, feat. Michael McDonald	1989
"You Break It"	John Tesh, feat. Michael McDonald	1989
"Next"	Tatsuhiko Yamamoto, feat. Michael McDonald	1990
"Same World"	Henry Kapono, feat. Michael McDonald	1991
"I'll Be Waiting for You"	Patti Austin, feat. Michael McDonald and James Ingram	1991
"Now or Never"	Kenny Loggins, feat. Michael McDonald	1991
"Ever Changing Times"	Aretha Franklin, feat. Michael McDonald	1991
"Time to Be Lovers"	Chaka Khan and Michael McDonald	1992
"Our Love"	Tia Carrere, feat. Michael McDonald, David Pack, and Robin Zander	1993
"Don't Walk Away"	Pointers Sisters, feat. Michael McDonald	1993
"All I Know"	Amy Holland, feat. Michael McDonald	1994
"If There's Anything I Can Do"	Vince Gill, feat. Michael McDonald	1994
"Wait and See"	Kiyomi Suzuki and Michael McDonald	1994
"Dive into the Pool of Love"	Stephen Bishop, feat. Michael McDonald	1994
"Maria"	James Ingram, Michael McDonald, and David Pack	1996
"The Only Way I Know"	Kenny Rogers, feat. Michael McDonald and Kim Carnes	1997
"Holy City"	Edwin McCain, feat. Michael McDonald	1997
"Let's Stay Together"	David Garfield, feat. Michael McDonald, Paulette Brown, and David Pack	1997
"The Back Porch"	Kirk Whalum, feat. Michael McDonald	1997
"Seven Shades of Blue"	Beth Nielsen Chapman, feat. Michael McDonald	1997

"Love Travels"	Kathy Mattea, feat. Michael McDonald	1997
"The Bridge"	Kathy Mattea, feat. Michael McDonald	1997
"The Kind of Fool Love Makes"	Wynonna Judd, feat. Michael McDonald	1997
"Better Man"	Warren Brothers, feat. Michael McDonald	1998
"Go Tell It on the Mountain"	Rob Mathes, feat. Michael McDonald	1998
"Silent Night"	Rob Mathes, feat. Michael McDonald	1998
"One Heart at a Time"	Michael McDonald, Garth Brooks, Billy Dean, Faith Hill, Olivia Newton-John, Neal McCoy, Victoria Shaw, and Bryan White	1998
"Right to the End"	Phoebe Snow, feat. Michael McDonald	1998
"Water for the Wicked"	Robben Ford, feat. Michael McDonald	1999
"Nothing to Nobody"	Robben Ford, feat. Michael McDonald	1999
"Among the Missing"	Kathy Mattea, feat. Michael McDonald	1999
"Eyes of a Child" (*South Park: Bigger, Longer & Uncut* soundtrack)	Michael McDonald	1999
"Deal with It"	Sonya Isaacs, feat. Michael McDonald	2000
"Till I Hurt You"	Larry Carlton, feat. Michael McDonald	2000
"Everyday"	Darwin Hobbs, feat. Michael McDonald	2000
"Circle Dance"	Jeff Bridges, feat. Michael McDonald	2000
"September Brings"	Jeff Bridges, feat. Michael McDonald	2000
"She Lay Her Whip Down"	Jeff Bridges, feat. Michael McDonald	2000
"Movin'"	Jeff Bridges, feat. Michael McDonald	2000
"Every Little Thing She Does Is Magic"	Lee Ritenour, feat. Michael McDonald	2002
"If I Ever Lose This Heaven"	Above the Clouds, feat. Michael McDonald	2002
"You Alone"	Bernie Chiaravalle, feat. Michael McDonald	2002
"Where You Runnin'"	Bernie Chiaravalle, feat. Michael McDonald	2002
"Act of Faith"	Olivia Newton-John, feat. Michael McDonald	2002
"It's About Time"	Kenny Loggins, feat. Michael McDonald	2003
"Heart of America"	Wynonna Judd, Eric Benét, Terry Dexter, and Michael McDonald	2005
"My Love's Leavin'"	Fourplay, feat. Michael McDonald	2006

"Thankful"	Jonny Lang, feat. Michael McDonald	2006
"All Through the Christmas Night"	Brian Culbertson, feat. Michael McDonald	2006
"Smilin' Song"	Vince Gill, feat. Michael McDonald	2006
"Baby, Don't Look Down"	Tony Joe White and Michael McDonald	2006
"Danny Boy"	Natalie MacMaster and Michael McDonald	2006
"When You Get Right Down to It"	Petula Clark, feat. Michael McDonald	2007
"You Belong to Me"	Chaka Khan, feat. Michael McDonald	2007
"Backdown"	Amy Holland and Michael McDonald	2008
"While You Wait for the Others"	Grizzly Bear, feat. Michael McDonald	2009
"The Storm Before the Calm"	Michael McDonald and the West Angeles Church of God in Christ	2009
"Where Worlds End"	Jimmy Webb, feat. Michael McDonald	2010
"I've Got News for You"	Jools Holland and his Rhythm & Blues Orchestra, feat. Michael McDonald	2010
"When You're High"	Dylan McDonald and the Avians, feat. Michael McDonald	2010
"Some Children"	Holy Ghost, feat. Michael McDonald	2011
"Easy"	Drew Zingg, feat. Michael McDonald	2012
"La Marea Humana"	Michael McDonald and Robben Ford	2013
"Walk a Fine Line"	Paul Anka, Michael McDonald, and George Benson	2013
"So Very Hard to Go"	Dave Koz and Michael McDonald, feat. Gerald Albright, Mindi Abair, and Richard Elliot	2013
"What a Fool Believes"	Michael McDonald and Sara Evans	2014
"Takin' It to the Streets"	Michael McDonald and Love and Theft	2014
"You Belong to Me"	Michael McDonald and Amanda Sudano Ramirez	2014
"Peace"	Michael W. Smith, feat. Michael McDonald	2014
"Moondance"	Nathan East, feat. Michael McDonald	2014
"Miracle River"	Judy Collins and Michael McDonald	2015
"Johnny B. Goode"	Mesey & Scorfina, feat. Michael McDonald, Johnnie Johnson, and David Sanborn	2015
"Coming Up"	John Pizzarelli and Michael McDonald	2015
"Merry Christmas Baby"	India.Arie, Joe Sample, and Michael McDonald	2015

"Lovely Day"	Gerald Albright, feat. Michael McDonald	2016
"Swing Street"	Steve Porcaro, feat. Michael McDonald	2016
"Night of Our Own"	Steve Porcaro, feat. Michael McDonald	2016
"Prove That by Me"	Amy Holland, feat. Michael McDonald	2016
"Freedom Highway"	Mavis Staples, feat. Michael McDonald	2017
"Better Change" (A Tribute to Dan Fogelberg)	Michael McDonald	2017
"Show You the Way"	Thundercat and Kenny Loggins, feat. Michael McDonald	2017
"Cry Like a Rainy Day"	Michael McDonald	2018
"What the World Needs Now"	Barbra Streisand, feat. Michael McDonald	2018
"Stone Tree Fairy"	Dylan McDonald and the Avians, feat. Michael McDonald	2018
"Empty World"	Bonerama, feat. Michael McDonald	2019
"Jingle Bell Rock"	Dionne Warwick, feat. Michael McDonald	2019
"The Last Time"	Johnnyswim, feat. Michael McDonald	2019
"Someday We'll Be Together"	Grace Potter and Michael McDonald	2020
"O Come, O Come Emmanuel"	Karla Bonoff, feat. Michael McDonald	2020
"A Change Is Gonna Come"	Brian Owens, feat. Michael McDonald and David Sanborn	2020
"River Rise"	David Crosby, feat. Michael McDonald	2021
"The Best of Me"	Toad the Wet Sprocket, feat. Michael McDonald	2021
"Go Now"	Jake Shimabukuro, feat. Michael McDonald	2021
"Hot and Cold"	Dylan McDonald and the Avians, feat. Michael McDonald	2021
"Lost Weekend"	Dylan McDonald and the Avians, feat. Michael McDonald	2021
"Stranger"	Edgar Winter, feat. Michael McDonald	2022
"My Place in the Sun"	Skunk Baxter, feat. Michael McDonald	2022
"Hey All Together"	Ivan Neville, feat. Michael McDonald, Bonnie Raitt, Trombone Shorty, David Shaw, and Aaron Neville	2023
"Someone Like You"	Tommy Emmanuel and Michael McDonald	2023
"Wherever I Go"	Jacob Collier, feat. Michael McDonald and Lawrence	2023
"Bittersweet"	Dolly Parton, feat. Michael McDonald	2023

ACKNOWLEDGMENTS

MMcD

I want to acknowledge all those who made my journey possible, starting with my parents, Robert J. McDonald and Mary Jane (Hanley) McDonald, who gave me life itself and their example of how to take a stab at it.

My sisters, Kathy (who's been looking after me since birth), for her tireless efforts in collecting the photos for this project, and Maureen, for fact-checking me every step along the way.

My grandparents, aunts, and cousins, for all being a part of my story since childhood.

Much thanks to the folks in the trenches who made this project possible: our friend Rob Weisbach, for his energy and expertise; Stuart Roberts and the team at Dey Street / HarperCollins, for their enthusiasm and editorial guidance—Carrie Thornton's oversight, Nancy Tan's keen copyediting skills, and the wonderfully energetic promotion and publicity team (Martin Wilson, Heidi Richter, Allison Carney, and Kasey Feather), for their creative insight and support. David Wienir, of the legal department, for his enthusiasm and astute overview.

A big thanks to Jeff Finkelstein for his legal counsel.

Thank you to Joel Hoffner of Vector Management and his excellent assistant, Skye Overstreet, for their help throughout this endeavor, and the team at Sacks & Co. publicity—Carla Sacks, Samantha Tillman, and Joe Cohen.

And last but certainly not least, my coauthor of this memoir and possibly the one most responsible for its existence, Paul Reiser.

—Mike McDonald

PR

First of all, I want to thank my good friend, literary genius and tireless enthusiast Rob Weisbach, for bringing this to the attention of Dey Street / HarperCollins—even though he's busy with a million other things and in no way needed to have gotten himself all sullied up with us, so hats off to you.

Sincere gratitude and thanks to all the great folks at Dey Street / HarperCollins who took the ball and ran with it: Stuart Roberts, for his immediate embrace of and enthusiasm for the book and for giving us a home—and his most valuable and insightful editorial guidance; Carrie Thornton, for overseeing the whole shebang; copy-editor extraordinaire Nancy Tan, who doesn't miss a thing and who (rightfully) removed two to three thousand commas we had in there, which if left to stand would have extended the page count to an unmanageable length; tireless production editor Jeanie Lee; the crackerjack promotion and publicity team, including Martin Wilson, Heidi Richter, Allison Carney, and Kasey Feather, for their creative and spirited support; and David Wienir, for keeping us out of all those potential legal snafus along the way.

Very grateful, also, for my longtime consigliere Jeff Finkelstein, of the supergroup Del Shaw Moonves Tanaka Finkelstein Lezcano Bobb & Dang, for his most expert legal counsel and friendship; Michael's manager, Joel Hoffner, for keeping the trains running; Skye Overstreet, for keeping Joel Hoffner running; and the team at Sacks & Co. publicity.

On the home front, I most wholeheartedly want to thank my lovely wife, Paula, and spectacular sons, Ezzie and Leon, for their understanding and patience as I was continually getting/staying up at all hours of the day to work on this. (And a special thanks to Leon Reiser for helping out with the transcribing of Mike's and my original Zoom conversations—and along the way inadvertently filling in some gaping holes in his knowledge of rock and roll history.)

Above all, I am beyond grateful to Mr. McDonald for taking this ride with me. To be honest, this whole thing started as an only half-serious lark of an idea ("You should really write a book someday") but in short order became a really joyful collaboration and—I hope you'll agree—a really great book. I had been an ardent fan of Mike's for years but somehow never quite had a handle on who he was as a person, or how his seemingly circuitous journey unfolded. I get it now, having learned the whole story, and remain deeply honored that he trusted me to help tell it. More than anything, I'm grateful for the friendship that developed. It's been a great hang. Can't wait to see what he does in the *next* seventy years.

—***Paul Reiser***

ABOUT THE AUTHORS

Rock & Roll Hall of Famer **Michael McDonald**'s career encompasses five Grammys and countless platinum hits and chart-topping successes. After years of recording and touring with Steely Dan, he was invited to join the Doobie Brothers as the band redefined their sound, with McDonald serving as singer, keyboardist, and songwriter on numerous Top Forty singles. Throughout the '80s and '90s, McDonald's solo career took off with a string of hits, including "I Keep Forgettin'," "Sweet Freedom," "On My Own" (with Patti LaBelle), and the Grammy-winning James Ingram duet "Yah Mo B There." McDonald has performed with a who's who of critically acclaimed artists, including Ray Charles, Aretha Franklin, Elton John, Joni Mitchell, Willie Nelson, Jackson Browne, Vince Gill, Thundercat, Solange Knowles, and Grizzly Bear.

Paul Reiser is a comedian, Emmy Award–nominated actor, and #1 *New York Times* bestselling author. He has recently appeared in Netflix's *Stranger Things* and *The Kominsky Method*, as well as in Hulu's critically acclaimed comedy *Reboot* and Amazon's *The Boys*. Reiser created and starred in (along with Helen Hunt) the long-running hit '90s comedy *Mad About You* and has appeared in classic films including *Diner*, *Aliens*, the *Beverly Hills Cop* franchise, and *Whiplash*. Reiser is the author of the bestselling books *Couplehood*, *Babyhood*, and *Familyhood*.